TOP DOG
SALES SECRETS

50 TOP EXPERTS SHOW YOU
PROVEN WAYS TO SKYROCKET YOUR SALES

D0822466

Edited by Michael Dalton Johnson

Presented by SalesDog.com

Published by
PENNY UNION CORPORATION

CARLSBAD, CALIFORNIA

Published by
Penny Union Corporation
2701 Loker Avenue West, Suite 148, Carlsbad, California 92010
www.salesdog.com

ISBN: 978-1-934346-14-3

Printed in the United States of America

Publisher's Cataloging-In-Publication Data
(Prepared by The Donohue Group, Inc.)

Top dog sales secrets : 50 top experts show you proven ways to skyrocket
your sales / edited by Michael Dalton Johnson.

p. : ill. ; cm.

ISBN: 978-1-934346-14-3

1. Selling. 2. Sales personnel--Training of. 3. Sales management. I.
Johnson, Michael Dalton.

HF5438.25 .T67 2007
658.85

This publication is designed to provide accurate and authoritative information with regard to the subject matter covered. It is sold with the
understanding that the publisher is not engaged in rendering legal,
accounting, or other professional advice. If legal advice or other expert
assistance is required, the services of a competent professional person
should be sought.

This book is available at quantity discounts.
For information, call 760-476-3700.

CONTENTS

ACKNOWLEDGMENTS vii

INTRODUCTION ix

PROSPECTING:
Referrals: The Easy Way to Prospect.............Jim Domanski 13
Making the Most of Internet Inquiries ....Tina LoSasso............................83
Avoiding Internet Flameout.......................Mark Shonka
                                                and Dan Kosch......................120
Jumpstart Your Prospecting ....Dave Kahle 169
Selling Is *Not* a Numbers Game...................Tim Connor 239

COLD CALLING:
Creating a Successful
Cold-Calling Script ....Wendy Weiss............................26
Cold Calling Do's and Don'ts ....Art Sobczak.............................80
Are You Getting the Cold Shoulder? ....Jim Meisenheimer....................133
Fear of Phoning ....Art Sobczak.............................241

PHONE SKILLS:
The Top 10 Phone
Mistakes of All Time ....Art Sobczak.............................42
Would *You* Return This Call?......................Jon Brooks............................113
Your Voice Is Your Instrument....................Wendy Weiss............................171
Follow-up Calls That Work ....Art Sobczak............................192

SALES CALLS:
Naked Sales Calls Pay Off ....Jill Konrath.............................18
Do You Have a Sales Call Checklist? ....Bill Brooks..............................58
Stop Your Sales Pitch,
Start Your Conversation!..............................Ari Galper..............................116
Passing the
"Tell Me More" Test ....Jill Konrath............................153
Collateral Damage ....Jill Konrath............................194

QUESTIONS:
The Anxiety Question:
Your Ace in the Hole....................................Julie Thomas 37

Your Most Powerful Sales Tool ....Dave Kahle 74
Scenario Selling...Jim Domanski 123
Who Is Your Greatest Competitor? ....Joe Heller............................ 173

STALLS AND OBJECTIONS:
The Dreaded Price Objection ....Brian Jeffrey.......................31
Terminating the Sales Stall ....James Maduk.......................77
Transforming Customer
Complacency into Urgency..........................Mike Schultz......................144
Sometimes the Best Defense
is a Good Offense ....Jill Konrath 214
"Let Me Think About It" ....Jim Domanski 244

PRESENTATIONS:
A Hands-On Approach ....John Boe.............................34
Ten Tips for Persuasive Presentations...........Dianna Booher 89
Power Pitching for the Personal Edge ....Patricia Fripp 127
Going Beyond Show and Tell......................Kevin Davis 188
Make Your Proposal Sell.............................Steve Waterhouse..................220

SALES SKILLS:
Don't Lose Another Minute ....Art Sobczak...........................1
All the (Sales) World's a Stage ....Joel N. Sussman 16
The Fine Art of the Handshake ....Michael D. Johnson.............52
Laugh All the Way to the Bank ....Michelle Nichols.................66
Listen Like a Homicide Detective................Art Sobczak.......................104
Does the Opposite Sex
Drive You Crazy?..Will Turner 118
The Four Biggest Time Wasters ....Dave Kahle 129
Power Tips..Michael D. Johnson.............136
A Picture is Worth a Thousand Sales...........Tom Richard 151
Means, Motive, Opportunity......................Bill Stinnett 166
Success Is An Inside Job..............................Bill Caskey 177
Commitment is a Two-Way Street...............Craig James........................184
Seven Essential Selling Skills ....Shamus Brown....................228
Listen Your Way to More Sales ....Rick Phillips 232
Read Your Prospect Like a Book!................John Boe............................247
If You're Not Selling...................................Michael D. Johnson.............262

STRATEGIES:

It's All About the Risk! ....Dave Kahle 23
How to Sell to Techies...............................Mark S.A. Smith 49
Dump the Feature Dumping.......................Anita Sirianni..........................63
Why Sales 101 No Longer Works ....Tom Freese 86
Getting Past Purchasing............................Steve Waterhouse....................106
What to Do When Your
Regular Buyer Leaves ....Art Sobczak.............................141
Help—I'm Talking and
I Can't Shut Up!.....................................Michelle Nichols...................148
Cash In On Every Contact
with Add-On Selling ....Jim Domanski 163
Asking Customers About
the Competition ....Linda Richardson...................197
Is High-Tech Selling
Really That Difficult? ....Jacques Werth.......................203
What to Do When
You Don't Get the Sale ....Garrison Wynn....................236
How to Avoid RFPs
and Price Quoting ....Dave Stein 250
Recession-Proof Business Strategies ....Bob Bly 256

VALUE:

Before You Cut That Rate, Read This ....Joe Guertin 40
Value is in the Eye of the Beholder...............Jill Konrath 94
Gotta Have It ....Julie Thomas 157
When You Can't Compete on Price ....Tom Reilly..............................186

CLOSING:

Rewriting the ABCs of Selling ....Dave Stein 9
Closing with Confidence ....Linda Richardson...................55
Do You Believe in Magic?..........................Ron Karr...............................97
The Lost Art of Closing..............................Joe Guertin 206
Are You Suffering From
Premature Assumption? ....Art Sobczak.............................217

NEGOTIATING:

To Discount or Not to Discount.................Ed Brodow.............................20

Winning the Negotiating Game ....Colleen Francis 69
Negotiating Win-Win Deals ....Tony Alessandra 109
Don't Give Away $100
When $67.50 Will Do.................................Roger Dawson 224

CUSTOMER RELATIONSHIPS:

Steer Clear of Persuasion Pitfalls...................Al Uszynski..................................5
The Power of the Handwritten Note............Tom Richard 61
Are You a Yesaholic? ....Keith Rosen 101
The Salesperson's Guide
to Gift-Giving ....Tina LoSasso...........................159
Are You Teaching Your
Customers to Mistreat You?........................Colleen Francis 180
It's a Jungle Out There................................Michael D. Johnson................200
Juggling After-Sale Customer Care ....Tony Alessandra 210

ABOUT THE AUTHORS

ABOUT THE AUTHORS 264

ACKNOWLEDGMENTS

I wish to thank my friends, colleagues, and the many nationally renowned sales trainers who have contributed to this book. This project was fueled by their advice, encouragement and enthusiasm. Each sales expert has made a unique contribution to this book by giving us their "best-of-the-best" advice. Thanks to all.

Managing Editor and friend Tina LoSasso made a deep contribution to this work. She handled much of the crucial business details, kept things flying smoothly and guided the project in for a smooth landing. Thank you, Tina.

Special appreciation is offered to Editors Doug Matthews and Karen Lawrence for their unflagging energy and editorial professionalism. Graphic designers Dave Tucker and Becky Bacoka captured the exact look we wanted. Thanks to Ted Nguyen for his programming excellence and priceless advice. We appreciate all your work.

I want to acknowledge my deep debt to the sales community and the thousands of people it has been my privilege to come into contact with during a lifetime spent in sales and marketing.

Lastly, I want to thank Kathryn, the wonderful spirit I married, for her patience, encouragement and loving support, not only during this project, but for the past 27 years. ∎

"Everyone lives by selling something."
Robert Louis Stevenson

INTRODUCTION

On the way to the office today I stopped for my morning fix at the local coffee shop. When I placed my order, the barista smiled and said, "Would you like a poppy seed muffin with that? They're still warm...just took 'em out of the oven." I was on the final push to get this book to the printers and had left the house early without having breakfast. "Sure," I said without hesitation. Sold! Unfortunately, as anyone in sales will tell you, most sales are far more complicated and time consuming than selling a warm muffin to a hungry man.

With increasing competition and the growing influence of the Internet, selling is getting a lot tougher. Even the most seasoned sales pros can no longer afford to simply maintain the status quo. Instead, they must continue to educate themselves to stay productive and successful.

As the founder of SalesDog.com, a sales training publishing site, I have had the good fortune and privilege of working with America's leading sales experts over the past six years. I have come to appreciate their passion for excellence in sales and their generosity in sharing their knowledge and ideas with the sales community at large.

Collectively the Top Dogs, who have contributed to this book, have trained and inspired tens of thousands of sales professionals and literally changed the fortunes of untold companies.

These experts understand that effective salesmanship is an art, a science, *and* a profession. They know that the people who achieve the highest level of success in sales are those who understand the dynamics of selling and master the skills needed to succeed.

This book contains real-world advice to help you unlock the secrets of successful selling and accelerate your career. If you want to gain the knowledge, skills, and confidence to succeed in today's fast-paced and ever changing selling environment, this book is for you. ■

Michael Dalton Johnson

Editor's Note: I still have ten-year-old copies of Art Sobczak's Telephone Prospecting and Selling Report *on my bookshelf, from the days when I had a large telemarketing division in one of my publishing companies. It was good stuff then, and it still rings true today. Art doesn't just tell you what to do. He clearly outlines how to do what you need to—in this case, find more time for selling. Powerful tips for optimizing your time!*

Don't Lose Another Minute
by Art Sobczak

Have you ever felt like you could use a few more hours in the day? Welcome to the club! I think most of us would agree we could sell more if we only had more time—or more realistically, better control of our time. After all, we can't manage time any more than we can manage the weather. We can only control what we do with our time, to squeeze more productivity from every day. For salespeople, good time management starts with two fundamental strategies to prevent you from spinning your wheels, and allow you to spend more time doing what you do best: selling.

- **Do the important stuff first.** Do the stuff you get paid to do! Make the critical calls and work on the larger proposals first. Tackle the more difficult projects early, before the inevitable little annoyances begin chipping away at you.
- **Police interruptions.** Don't let the constant arrival of email messages, voicemail messages or postal mail interrupt you. Instead, discipline yourself to manage these interruptions at predetermined times of the day. When reviewing email and voice messages, identify the items needing immediate attention and add them to your master "To Do" list. The others can be left for later, or trashed.

On a tactical level, Dan Wallace wrote an article called "Do Twice as Much in Half the Time" in *Home Office Computing* magazine. I've excerpted and adapted the ideas that apply to sales.

- **Ask for the first appointment of the day.** On the phone or in person, the first appointment of the day is the least likely to start late.
- **Update your contact management program and keep it current.** Place a printout of your accounts/prospects by the phone. When mail comes back marked "Return to Sender" or you find someone has moved on, make manual corrections to the printout. Then, when you are on terminal hold with someone, update the list on your computer.
- **Rearrange your workspace.** Use the "near-far" rule. Keep things you use frequently at arm's length, and things you don't use often out of the way. If piles clutter your desk, invest in some shelves. If you're right-handed, place the phone on your left, and keep a pad and pencil nearby. If you're a lefty, do the opposite.
- **Police your voice mail.** When you accumulate a voicemail backlog, write or type the messages, then delete them. This eliminates scrolling through previously-heard messages the next time you check your system.
- **Return calls.** Use the lunch hour to return calls requiring only a short answer, or those in which you're asking a simple question. Many people will be away from their desks, and you'll reach voicemail.
- **Discourage interruptions.** If you have an office, stick a sign on the door that says, "Important sales call in progress." Or hang one on your cubicle that reads, "Door closed."

Finally, here are some personal tips I've accumulated over the years to help squeeze more productivity out of every day:

- **Flush your account files.** I am astounded by the amount of rubbish residing in many reps' follow-up files. Read the skimpy account notes, and you see a long list of comments like, "Not ready now, check back in six weeks." Simple math tells you the time spent trying to push a two-ton rock uphill would be better invested looking for someone with whom you have a chance. Set an objective for a decision of any type on your next contact with these people. Ask, "When do you feel you'll move forward with a purchase?" You'll save time on your calls, and the results will be more pleasing.

- **Know when and how to say "no."** Far too many sales reps feel obligated to jump through hoops for prospects who merely want to pick their brains, or obtain obscure product information. They comply without even knowing if they'll get something in return! Before investing inordinate amounts of time with prospects, be certain there is a potential payoff. Don't be afraid to say, "I'll be happy to do this for you. I assume you want it because this is something you're interested in, and we'll be working together on a purchase?"
- **Help people get to the point.** Those who just want to chitchat with you are pickpockets. You would not let them snatch a $20 bill off your desk; why let them do this with your time? Whether they're customers, peers or vendors, politely help them explain the reason they are calling by asking, "So how may I assist you?" or, "What can I do for you?" Use the past tense; signify the end of a call by saying, "It's really been great speaking with you." or, "I'm glad we had the chance to talk."
- **Reschedule personal interruptions.** When friends call to chat, let them know you're busy, but want to speak with them. "Mike, great to hear from you! I want to hear all about your vacation in North Dakota. I've got some business calls I need to make, so what's the best time for me to call you back tonight?"
- **Use "Power Blocking."** Set aside blocks of time (45 minutes) for specific activities, and do nothing else during those times. For example, you might have two blocks of prospecting, and three blocks for follow-up calls during the day. This keeps you from scattering your attention in too many unproductive directions.
- **Take the "Why am I doing this?" test.** When engaged in a questionable activity—such as stuffing envelopes, or writing a proposal to a marginal prospect—ask yourself why you are doing it. If you can't honestly say it is making (or saving) you or the company money, delegate it to someone else.

- **Analyze and adjust your work hours.** You might be physically present for eight hours, but how much do you get done during that time? Perhaps by coming in a half-hour earlier, you could accomplish in that time what would normally take two hours later in the day. You'd be squeezing out another ten hours of production each week!

- **Never write memos or email again.** Got something important to say to someone internally? Say it as you walk by their desk. Or call them, for goodness sakes! I realize some situations require covering your behind with a written record, but most memos simply waste your precious time.

- **Go public with your intentions.** If you must do something for someone else, commit to completing it by a specific time. For example, "I'll have that price quote to you by two o'clock." This forces you to complete the task on time and avoid procrastination.

- **Turn wait time into productive time.** Think of all the places you wait: airports, doctors' offices, the mechanic's shop. Carry a file of reading or light paperwork you can get done during those down times. This will ease the frustration of waiting, make the time productive, and free up your work time for more important tasks.

If you think it's stupid to waste money, it's even more foolish to waste time. You can always make more money, but not even Bill Gates can buy more time. The bottom line is: if you want to get more done, you will. From that desire will flow plans for monthly, weekly, daily, and hourly plans for accomplishment. There's no magic in time management; it's all about getting back to basics. If you have that burning desire, give these ideas a try. You'll find yourself getting more done in less time, and selling more both in person and by phone. ■

Art Sobczak is president of Business By Phone Inc. For biographical and business information, see page 274.

Editor's Note: Al Uszynski is a sales trainer and speaker with over 17 years' experience as a sales professional. From sales rep to national sales manager, Al has sold for small companies and big companies alike. As national sales manager for a division of a $1.6 billion company, he achieved double-digit percentage growth in each of his three years on the job. Today he provides customized training programs for clients like Bloomberg, Philadelphia Weekly, *and Hunter Douglas.*

Steer Clear of Persuasion Pitfalls
by Al Uszynski

Sometimes we fall into the habit of saying things the same way we've said them for years. By doing so, we often miss opportunities to be more persuasive. Without realizing it, we may even put another person on the defensive, or create a negative image of our business and ourselves. As a sales professional, you can enhance your success by improving your persuasive communication skills. Here are six common phrases and habits to avoid or alter in order to become more persuasive.

- **"To be honest with you..."** Why do people feel the need to announce their honesty? Does this mean that they're lying otherwise? Generally, people use this phrase to set up a statement that might be inconsistent with the goals they are trying to achieve, for example, "To be honest with you, our competitor's system is somewhat faster."

The alternative is to omit the "be honest" phrase altogether and get to the point. If you feel compelled to announce that you are being upfront, do what Mel Kass of Bear Stearns in New York City does. He replaces the phrase with one word: *candidly.* It's simple, and it focuses more on spontaneity than honesty. It goes without saying that we should always be honest—and when we are, it's much easier to remember what we've said!

- **"What I want to talk about is..."** People don't care about what you want, especially if you're trying to persuade them about something. They only care about what *they* want. When it's time to introduce a new topic in a conversation, tie it to the other person's benefit.

For example, you might say, "So that we can find out how to best (save you money, increase your productivity, give you another benefit), let's discuss… ." Do this, and you'll be appealing to your customers' concerns, rather than forcing your agenda upon them.

- **Negative language.** The well-known optical illusion below is a good example of how context affects perception. Which horizontal line is longer? They're both the same length, but the top one looks longer. The arrowheads at each end of the lines have a significant impact on the viewer's perception. Similarly, different words packaged around the same information in persuasive speech can have a huge impact on the listener's perception.

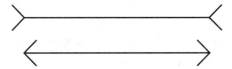

Persuasive speakers communicate by using positive language. Instead of saying, "We can't ship the products until next Tuesday," say, "We can ship the products as early as next Tuesday." What a difference! Put yourself in your listener's shoes; which version is more appealing?

The habit of using positive speech has helped me to achieve more results than I ever thought possible. You can practice this skill all the time, too. Try it with coworkers, family, and friends. You'll begin to see things in a whole new light!

- **"So what you're saying is…"** I hate it when someone pulls this one on me. Half the time his interpretation of my words is off base; I have to correct him and reiterate my ideas. Since he's summarizing me and I'm correcting him, this dangerous phrase puts both of us on the defensive. Often his summary is not necessarily wrong, but incomplete and missing major points. That causes me to restate my points while he clings to his "brilliant" summary. This also sends the message that he perceives my points as long-winded and vague, forcing him to rescue my message from obscurity. Obviously, this doesn't put me at ease, or give me a sense of confidence in him. The same may be true for the people you deal with.

Here's a better way to ensure that you and your customer are on the same page. Turn the confirming statement into a question seeking confirmation. Instead of, "So what you're saying is... ," try, "Am I correct in understanding your (points, ideas, reasons, etc.) to be... ?" This demonstrates that you are listening and trying to synchronize with him, rather than forcing your own interpretation down his throat.

- **"What you have to do is..."** Barking orders is not conducive to persuasion. When someone says the above phrase to me I immediately think, "Who the heck are you to tell me what I have to do?" This phrase usually precedes how-to information. For example, while the following statement gets the message across, it's not persuasive: "What you have to do is buy an inexpensive interface in order for our hardware to be compatible with your system." You'll appear much friendlier and less bossy when you say, "Our hardware is compatible with your system by using an inexpensive interface, purchased separately." Customers don't like being told that they have to buy or do something.
- **"I don't know how much you know about (topic), but..."** I just love this one. The person openly admits to not knowing the listener's level of knowledge, then babbles on hoping that his points will stick. One of three things happens in this situation:
  1. The speaker talks over your head and wastes your time. He comes off as a know-it-all who can't relate to you.
  2. He tells you stuff you already know, and wastes your time. He possibly insults your intelligence, and appears condescending.
  3. By some random happenstance, he appeals to your level of knowledge, and drives home his point.

  Choose this route, and your odds for a negative outcome are two out of three. Persuasive communicators don't take those kinds of chances.

Here's an easy alternative. Ask, "How much do you know about (topic)?" Be quiet and listen. Then speak to the client's appropriate level of expertise. When speaking to a larger group, ask for a show of hands with, "How many of you know a lot about (topic)? Something? Nothing?" Then speak to the consensus level, or slightly below it.

Your journey to more persuasive communication begins now. Employ these ideas, and keep your antennae up for other ways you can become more persuasive. Like any new skill, this will feel awkward at first, and will take a lot of practice. But when you begin to win over and persuade more people, you'll likely agree that it is well worth the effort! ∎

Al Uszynski is founder of Results Resources. For biographical and business information, see page 276.

Editor's Note: Dave Stein has held a variety of technical, sales and executive positions: programmer, sales representative, vice president of strategic alliances. He worked in the technology sector for Fortune Systems Corporation, Datalogix International, and Marcam Corporation. In 1996, he founded his sales consultancy, serving clients like AT&T, Honeywell, McGraw-Hill, and Unisys. Most recently Dave co-founded a sales training evaluation company, ES Research.

Rewriting the ABCs of Selling
by Dave Stein

Are the ABCs (Always Be Closing) of selling still working for you? I doubt it, because they quit working for me a long time ago. Like it or not, the New Economy is forcing us to change the way we sell. Today's buyers are savvier, tougher, and more willing to play us against our competition. They've also become more reluctant to divulge their decision-making processes. Moreover, today's executives do *not* like to be hard-closed. They can see a close coming a mile away. Once they sense a hard close, they'll have their defensive shields up faster than you can say, "Set phasers on stun." If your credo is, "I close hard, fast and often," your next close may well be your last.

What does this mean for today's sales professionals? The answer to that question is complex. Closing is a critical component of every sales process, and the salesperson must meet certain dependencies, milestones and conditions in order to effectively execute the close. Many companies believe that closing deals is their main sales problem. Yet after analyzing their situations, I often find the root of the problem goes back to ineffective qualification, or lack of process.

If an opportunity is not effectively qualified, the sales rep will proceed with the mistaken impression that the deal is his to win. That's like assuming you've won the lottery just because you correctly picked the first number. Why? Because any number of conditions could still be wrong. The competition may already have set the ground rules. The product or service may not fit the prospect's requirements. Or the prospect hasn't budgeted enough money to fund the investment.

Attempting to close under any of those circumstances is worse than a waste of time: it's an embarrassment to the sales profession, and will ruin the reputation of the salesperson's employer. Even when the opportunity has been properly qualified, the lack of a logical selling process will inevitably lead to failure. When the close is not integrated with other critical components of the sale, the buyer will be caught off guard, and may become angry or resentful. In that situation, the salesperson will not be able to consummate the sale.

A Logical Selling Process

In today's new economy, a logical selling process must include the following steps:

- **Name the pain.** For starters, the prospect needs to agree that his company has an important business issue (i.e., pain, problem, or challenge) that is not being addressed. For example, the prospect might say, "You're right. We don't have the appropriate level of internal expertise to comply with certain requirements of the Sarbanes-Oxley Act." Ideally, you are in a position to uncover the prospect's pain before the competition does.

- **Identify the expected results.** Next, the prospect must agree on the business results he expects to receive from investing in a product or service such as yours. You might ask, "Do you agree that once you have clear, concise and compelling messages, and your salespeople have been trained on how to employ them, they will be better equipped to prospect more effectively?" The prospect needs to respond with something like, "Yes, I can see that."

- **Identify the time frame for achieving the desired results.** The prospect also needs to agree on the time frame in which he will make a decision, based upon appropriate lead times for achieving the expected business result. Suppose the prospect says, "We need to have this capability by August 15, or our most important customer will transfer 50% of their business to another supplier." Your response would be, "We can do that."

- **Quantify the value.** The prospect must also agree on the value this new capability will provide. For example, you might ask, "From my business assessment, can you see that you can expect a 10%-15% reduction in customer attrition, resulting in approximately $3 million in additional revenues next year?" And the prospect replies, "Yes."

- **Acknowledge the benefits.** The prospect must acknowledge how the benefits will be delivered or realized, making a direct connection between your product or service and the highest-level business value he expects to receive. For example, your prospect might say, "I understand the installation of your RFID equipment and implementation of the related software will take three months. At that point, we will be fully compliant with Wal-Mart's requirements."

- **Clarify your unique value.** The prospect needs to recognize that you, your company and your solution provide unique and measurable value. To emphasize this point, you might say, "Do you agree we are the only potential supplier whose balance sheet is strong enough for you to undertake the risk of this investment?" The prospect should respond, "Yes, I understand."

- **Check for lingering objections.** At this point, the prospect will have acknowledged that your proposal went into sufficient depth on all the items above, and provided an ROI within his departmental, agency, or corporate guidelines. Now is the time to say, "We've gone through each section of my proposal in considerable detail. Is there anything you feel is missing or has not been explained fully?" The reply should be, "Your proposal is fine."

If you have done your job properly, the prospect will acknowledge that all his questions and concerns have been addressed, potential risks have been mitigated, and pricing and terms have been agreed upon. *Now* you are ready for the close!

More importantly, your client is expecting and even anticipating your close, because early on you explained what to expect at each step. You integrated your selling process into his buying process, and collaborated with him every step of the way. As a result, you can now transform him smoothly and gracefully from a prospect into a customer. ∎

Dave Stein is CEO of ES Research Group. For biographical and business information, see page 274.

Editor's Note: Jim Domanski spent 10 years selling phone systems for Bell Canada, before starting a consulting business showing companies how to strategically use those systems. A pioneer in business-to-business outbound telephone sales, Jim has found that top reps take personal responsibility for their results. If they don't like the leads, they don't waste time complaining: they make things happen, as you will find out here.

Referrals: The Easy Way to Prospect
by Jim Domanski

I have a client who hates cold calls—in fact, he despises them. He ranks as one of the top sales reps in his company, yet he absolutely refuses to make cold calls. He will only make warm calls, and he closes over 50% of those! His secret? Referrals, and lots of them. In fact, he consistently gets referrals from existing clients whenever and wherever he can. To uncover the secret of his selling success, let's look at how he gets those referrals.

What's the Big Deal?
Referrals close faster and easier than any other single approach in the selling world. This is fact, not fiction. In business-to-business selling, referrals will close at 40%, 50%, even 100%. When a customer supplies you with a referral, your job is made easier in two ways. First, when you call the referral, you have a common connection: the source of the referral. You also have a pretext for calling, and typically, the referral listens closely to what you have to say. Because it's not a cold call, you've already won half the battle. Second, perhaps more importantly, there is the explicit or implied endorsement of you, your company, and your product/service by the source. This endorsement creates an element of trust almost immediately. And the referral, if he wants to, can check up on you with the source.

Why Reps Avoid Referral Selling
Unfortunately, many sales reps avoid this veritable gold mine of leads for two reasons: they fear that asking for a referral is pushy or aggressive, and

they don't know how to ask. Some reps think customers won't like them if they ask for a referral. However, when you do a good job of selling the product, and your client derives positive benefits from it, you create an element of trust and satisfaction in the relationship. This is powerful equity—so use it! Never be afraid to leverage your equity, and use the goodwill you have created. If this feels too pushy, get over it! When you ask for a referral, the worst thing that can happen is that the client does not cough up a name.

Not knowing how to ask is a different story. My client, who relies heavily on referrals, employs this simple, two-step approach:

> **Step 1: The Request.** After he has taken care of any business issues, and ensured that the client is completely satisfied with the program, he says, "Dr. Maynard, I've got my manager on my back about getting sales in…you know how they are…and I was wondering if you had a name or two of any doctors who could benefit from the program like you have?" Then he shuts up and waits. My client's approach is candid, nothing fancy, straight and to the point. He explains exactly what he is asking for, and why. His approach is also clever because he references the "benefits" of the program, and uses that to remind his client that the request is not just beneficial to him, but to others. In other words, it is a win-win situation. Clients like that.

> **Step 2: The Reward.** After he has been given a referral or two he says, "Thanks, Dr. Maynard. I really appreciate that. Listen, if I convert any of these, I'll be sure to send you a cap or golf shirt. Which would you prefer?" Interestingly, the reward is held back until a name is given. In other words, he does not use it as a bribe to solicit a referral up front, because that would come across as cheesy. Instead, he uses the reward afterward to say thank you: a much classier approach.

There's nothing particularly difficult or complex about my client's approach to referral selling. He has created an effective technique, but more importantly, he *uses* it. That's why he is one of the top sales reps in his company. In all the times I've monitored his calls, not once has he failed to receive a referral. What does that tell you? If you're not using referral selling, you need to get over your fear, devise an approach, and start asking! You'll soon be closing more easily, and at a higher rate. ∎

Jim Domanski is president of Teleconcepts Consulting. For biographical and business information, see page 267.

Editor's Note: Joel Sussman is a business writer and Internet marketer with over 23 years' experience in journalism, public relations, and marketing communications. He is the creator of Marketing Survival Kit.com, an online resource for small business owners. Joel delivers sound advice on using a sales script.

All the (Sales) World's a Stage
by Joel N. Sussman

Selling is a lot like acting in a play, in that both an actor and a sales-person need a well-written script in order to communicate most effectively with the audience. However, in the sales world, a script is often a double-edged sword. On the one hand, it can help you present your selling points and sales rebuttals in an organized, strategic way. Used incorrectly, though, it can undermine your sales effectiveness, and actually cause you to lose sales.

Good sales scripts contain proven tactics for converting prospects into customers. But regurgitating memorized lines or sounding like you're reading from a script will quickly drive a wedge between you and prospective clients. Bridging the gap between salesperson and sales prospect requires a conversational, informal delivery that can't be achieved by reciting a script. Here are some tips for delivering your sales lines without sounding like an actor in a high-school play.

- **Lighten up!** In the business world (and in the business of life) we sometimes take ourselves too seriously. Being serious and rigid not only impairs your likeability factor, it can cancel out much of the enjoyment you derive from your business or career. Injecting your presentations with a dose of humor and spontaneity helps avoid sounding rehearsed and pushy. You may need to experiment to find what works best for you, but that's all part of the process.

- **Get on the same wavelength.** Flexibility is vitally important when developing rapport with prospects, and winning their confidence. When you adhere rigidly to a script, you can't respond very well to the prospect's needs, concerns, and questions. Granted, listening and being empathetic is more of a challenge for some people than others. But if your success hinges on your ability to persuade and influence, then it is a skill worth cultivating. The most fascinating, likeable, and persuasive people are those who have perfected the art of active listening.

- **Focus on bullet points.** Rather than memorizing a sales script word for word, consider writing up an outline or set of bullet points to guide your conversation. You may need to review the original script every couple of weeks to make sure you're ad-libbing effectively and accurately. But don't lose sight of how you communicate nonverbally, because that is what your prospects notice most.

- **Put the brakes on.** Communications experts know it's not so much what you say as how you say it. A lot of sales and marketing people talk too fast, either because they're so excited about what they're selling, or they've had one cup of coffee too many. Some feel the need to speak quickly if they have a lot of information to impart in a short period of time. In most cases, talking fast is a major tactical error. First, rapid speech makes it difficult for prospects to absorb all the information coming at them; if they are confused, they will not commit. Second—well, you know what they say about "fast-talking salespeople."

To get a reality check, videotape and critique mock sales presentations with a few of your associates. Getting their feedback and seeing yourself as others see you are effective ways to iron out some of the wrinkles that may be thwarting your sales performance, and limiting your income. ■

Joel N. Sussman is president of Optimal Marketing Communications. For biographical and business information, see page 275.

Editor's Note: Jill Konrath was destined to be a sales trainer. A top performer at Xerox, she helped her colleagues with their sales problems for no additional money, title or perks. When she realized this was her favorite thing to do, she launched her consulting firm, Selling to Big Companies. Jill's clients include such well-known corporate giants as 3M, General Mills, Hilton, and Imation. A bestselling author, speaker and trainer, Jill is frequently featured in top business publications, including The New York Times, Business Journal, *and* Selling Power.

Naked Sales Calls Pay Off
by Jill Konrath

My daughter went to a small Midwestern college that is famous for two things: an excellent music program, and (drum roll)—Coed Naked Soccer. Every year, some students manage to sneak in a game or two, despite the administration's threat of dire consequences if they get caught.

What does this have to do with sales? Recently, I spoke with two sales professionals who are enjoying extraordinary success. Their business is skyrocketing. Pricing is virtually a non-issue. And their closing ratios have climbed to all-time highs. All this happened because they started going into sales calls stark, raving naked.

At least, that's how they felt when they stopped bringing brochures into meetings with prospective buyers. You see, armed with only notebooks and pens, they had nothing to hide behind. They couldn't direct the prospect's attention to the marketing collateral. They couldn't point out hot new features. They couldn't show the exciting new technologies. They couldn't even display their incredible portfolio of work. Instead, they sat there naked, totally vulnerable, with the prospect staring at them. Watching. Waiting.

Without the brochure, these reps had no choice but to focus on the prospect's business. They asked how it was going. They explored the challenges and issues the prospect was concerned about. They discussed the prospect's goals, ideas and expectations. And because they were naked, with no brochures to fall back on, they had totally client-focused conversations.

Not surprisingly, the prospects loved it. They felt listened to. They felt valued and understood. They felt like the reps cared, and were concerned. They asked for the reps' advice, and even wanted specific recommendations. Despite this ultimate temptation to pull out a brochure, these reps suggested a second meeting as the next step. They got it, and shortly thereafter landed bigger contracts than even they could have imagined at the outset.

If you rely too heavily on your marketing collateral or samples, try shedding them for a while. Go naked into your sales calls, and try having a real discussion with your prospects, instead of a pitch meeting. It won't be long before you start seeing a difference! ■

Jill Konrath is Chief Sales Officer of Selling to Big Companies. For biographical and business information, see page 270.

Editor's Note: "I am the only negotiation expert who's made love to Jessica Lange - on screen, that is!" Ed Brodow jokingly confides. After 12 years as an actor, Ed left the movie studio for the training stage. Drawing on his experience as an actor, salesman, manager, and corporate negotiator, Ed teaches negotiation techniques to big-name clients like Microsoft, Goldman Sachs, Cisco Systems, and the Pentagon. Brooklyn-born Ed shoots from the hip. When asked what advice he'd give sales-people, he replied, "Keep your big mouth shut."

To Discount or Not to Discount
by Ed Brodow

To be, or not to be: *that* is the question! Had he worked in sales, Shakespeare might have written, "To lower the price, or not to lower the price: *that* is the salesperson's dilemma!" Indeed, for most salespeople the issue of how to deal with customer price objections represents perhaps their greatest ongoing challenge. On the one hand you want the sale, and the customer is giving you an easy way to close it (offer a discount). On the other hand, you're convinced that your product or service is worth the asking price.

In my experience, there are two essential reasons for resisting the objections and sticking to your price. First, closing the sale means nothing if it is not profitable. Many fine companies have gone out of business by offering major discounts. Profitability always represents a more realistic measure of success than sales volume. Second, the most satisfied customers in a sales negotiation are the ones who pay top dollar. Why? *Because they appreciate the value of their investment.* Invariably, buyers perceive higher-priced items to be more valuable (think Mercedes-Benz, Rolex, and Giorgio Armani). In my selling career, the happiest customers have always been the ones who have paid full price, while the unhappiest have been the buyers who received a discount.

What Would You Do?
Shortly after I started my speaking and training business, I received a call from Susan, a manager at a Fortune 500 company. "We want you to train

a large group of our key employees in negotiating skills," she said. "I've seen your work and I think you're the best." I was very excited, as this account would be worth about $50,000. I was about to ask Susan where to fax the contract, when she dropped a bomb. "You should know," she went on, "my boss likes another company which is less expensive than you are. If you lower your fee, I think we can get you hired."

There I was: a professional negotiator faced with the classic sales negotiation dilemma. Only this time, is was personal! Obviously I wanted the deal—but was I willing to drop my fee in order to get it? As I wondered what was really going on, I envisioned the following scenarios:

- The buyer was telling the truth. If I lowered my fee, I might have a better chance of beating out the competition.
- There was no competitor. The buyer was using the "squeeze tactic" ("We can get a better deal elsewhere") as a negotiating ruse to move my fee downward.
- This was a test of my own negotiating skills. The potential client wanted to find out whether I practiced what I preached, and how I would respond when challenged on price.
- The company had already decided to go with my competitor. They wanted a lower number from me to give them leverage in negotiating the competitor's fee.

What would *you* do in this scenario? Would you hold fast on your price, or cave in and lower your fee? The fact that I didn't know all the specifics of the situation only clouded my thinking. Fortunately, I had enough prospects and clients in the pipeline to justify the decision I made.

Stick to Your Guns

I decided that lowering my fee would almost certainly lower the client's perception of my services. Conversely, if I held to the price I had offered I would at least send a positive message, and have some chance to do business with Susan's company in the future. When I called back, I politely refused to play ball. "I'm really sorry, Susan," I told her. "I'd love to work with you, but I can't destroy the credibility of my fee structure. My other clients will be upset if they find out that I gave you a discount." (This was certainly true.) Susan said she understood, and would get back to me. A week later, Susan informed me they had selected my competitor. "That's too bad," I said. "Please call me if I can help in any way." Two weeks later, Susan called back and said management had experienced a change of heart, and the job was mine.

After the first seminar, I sat down with Susan and queried her about the decision-making process. "Was there really another company that your boss liked?" I asked. "Oh yes," she said. "In fact, they wanted to do business with our company so badly, they offered to put on the first seminar for nothing." "For nothing!" I repeated. "That's quite an offer. If you were so concerned about the fee, why didn't you accept?" "For the best of reasons," Susan replied. "When they offered to do the seminar for nothing, we figured the value of their seminar was worth the price—namely, nothing."

Thanks to my confident negotiating posture, the client perceived my seminar as having more value. The lesson is clear: if you present your price with confidence and are willing to walk away, often the prospect will conclude that you must be worth it. Like everything in sales, this approach won't work all the time. But it will work often enough, if you negotiate from a position of strength. To do that, of course, you must make prospecting and new business development a part of your daily routine.

Brodow's Law states, "Always be willing to walk away from a negotiation." In other words, never negotiate without options. For salespeople, this means having enough legitimate prospects in the pipeline so they can comfortably say the magic word: "Next!" ■

Ed Brodow is CEO of Ed Brodow Seminars. For biographical and business information, see page 265.

Editor's Note: Number one salesperson in the country for two different companies in two different industries? That's Dave Kahle. General manager of a start-up who pushed growth from $10,000 monthly to over $200,000 in only 38 months? Dave again. Known as The Growth Coach, Dave has been training sales professionals since 1988. Dave shares his advice on the best ways to minimize risk in your customer's mind.

It's All About the Risk!
by Dave Kahle

Sometimes it is so frustrating. You *know* you have a better product than what your prospect is currently using. Your price is attractive, your service outstanding. If the prospect would switch to your solution, it would save him money, streamline his processes, reduce his inventory, and generally make his life simpler.

So why doesn't he switch? Are people really that stupid, or is it something you did to put him off? Don't worry. In most cases, a prospect's refusal to switch to your product or service is not due to his IQ, or your deodorant. It's the risk! Risk is the combination of financial, social, emotional and time costs that the company and the individual decision-maker will bear as a result of making a mistake. Risk is often the number one issue in the mind of the customer, particularly when the account has no history with your company. This makes it the number one issue to address in the sales process.

In addition, risk is what the customer perceives it to be. Risk can't be quantified, like the price or delivery of your offer. It is not objective or tangible. Instead, it is much more insidious, lurking beneath almost every conversation between you and your customer. Because risk arises out of fear, it often goes unmentioned. To acknowledge risk is to admit fear. In many people's minds, to admit fear is to expose weaknesses—and no one wants to look weak. Risk is the answer to both these questions: What happens to the company if he makes the wrong decision? And what happens to the decision-maker himself if he makes the wrong decision?

Measuring the Risk

Let's look at two very different examples of risk. Let's say that on your way home tonight, your spouse calls and explains that some friends are coming over for the evening. You need to stop at the grocery store and pick up some disposable cups to serve drinks in. So you stop at the grocery store, rush in, and find brand A and brand B disposable cups. You select brand B, scoot through the express lane, and get home a few moments before your guests are to arrive. Your spouse has mixed a pitcher of margaritas, and you pour yourself one in the disposable cup you just bought. Raising it to your lips, you discover it's leaking. Quickly grabbing another cup, you pour the contents of the defective cup into it and raise it to your mouth. Oops! A leak in that one, too. One after another, you discover that every one of the cups you bought is defective.

What price are you paying for your mistake? I don't know about you, but in my house, there would be a social and emotional price to pay. In addition to some very vocal and negative feedback from my wife, I would also have to invest additional time running back to the store to fix the problem with another bag of disposable cups. I'd have to pay for them, too, so there would be some financial costs: all because of a simple purchasing mistake.

When you compare the risk of this decision with all possible decisions in your life, there is relatively little risk. On a scale of 0 to 25, with zero being low risk and 25 high risk, most people would put the risk of buying a package of disposable cups at close to zero. But what if the risk is high? For many years, I had an international adoption agency as a client. For a young woman with a crisis pregnancy, the risk involved in releasing her unborn child for adoption is exponentially higher. Her decision will have lifelong consequences for at least four people. On our 0 to 25 scale, most people would rate her decision a 25.

The point is that different decisions carry different degrees of risk. To understand what prospects and customers go through, put yourself in the shoes of the person making the decision to buy your products. What happens to that person if he makes a mistake? You may think there is no risk because your company will always make it right, but that is your perspective, not the customer's. He has no proof that you will make things right. Even if you say your company always makes things right, he doesn't necessarily believe it. Ask yourself, "On a scale of 0 to 25, how would this customer rate the risk of saying 'yes' to our product offering?" To calculate the answer, ask yourself what happens to that individual if you or your company make a mistake. If the risk to that person is too high, the only way to make the sale is to reduce the risk. Here are three strategies for reducing risk.

- **Develop a closer personal relationship.** The greater the relationship, the less the risk. The lesser the relationship, the greater the risk. That is why prospects prefer to buy a less effective product at a higher price from the salesperson who has been calling on them for years. *Focus not on reducing the price, but rather on increasing the relationship.*

- **Make the deal tangible.** The more intangible the purchase, the riskier it seems. To reduce the risk, take all the imagination out of the buy. Bring in the prospect so he can see you really do have an office/production facility. Take him to a location where the machine is being used. Hand him certificates of warranty, instead of just describing them. Show him pictures of the product being used. *Look at every aspect of your offer and decide how you can make each piece more tangible and objective.*

- **Use proof.** What is proof? Someone other than you saying something about your product, company, or service. Proof is letters of recommendation from other customers; photographs of other customers using your product or service; testimonials; case studies; lists of clients; third-party studies; or copies of articles from trade journals. *Anything you can find that adds substance, even if it is only distantly connected to your offer, will go a long way toward reducing the risk.*

The concept of risk and its role in the buyer's mind is one of the most powerful concepts in the world of business-to-business sales. Planning to reduce the risk in every buying decision will be one of your most powerful sales strategies. ■

Dave Kahle is president of The DaCo Corporation. For biographical and business information, see page 269.

Editor's Note: Wendy Weiss is a former ballet dancer who set appointments for clients as her day job. She was so effective, one of her clients dubbed her the "Queen of Cold Calling." The title stuck. When injuries sidelined her dance career, Wendy transformed her day job into a full-time career as a sales trainer, coach and author. Her clients include ADP, Avon, and Sprint.

Creating a Successful Cold-Calling Script
by Wendy Weiss

Imagine sitting through a play where the actors and actresses walk onto the stage and make up their lines, hemming and hawing as they go along. Now picture yourself being on the receiving end of a phone call when a salesperson does the same. Doesn't sound like much fun, does it?

As the Girl Scouts say, be prepared. Nowhere is that more applicable than in the world of cold calling. A good script—a well-thought-out presentation that says exactly what you want to say while still leaving room to maneuver—is essential to a successful pitch. Why? Because cold calling is all about communication, and being prepared. You're crafting a message, and focusing that message on your prospect. You're also sending the subliminal message that you took the time to prepare, which will help you achieve the main goal of getting the prospect "hooked" on what you have to say.

Here are three steps for writing a cold-calling script that will position you as a well-prepared salesperson who has something of value to say.

Step 1: Have a Great Opening

A great script starts with a strong opening that grabs the prospect's attention, and sets you apart from every other salesperson who calls. To create this opening:

- **Get real.** Written language and spoken language are very different. A script in written language sounds stilted and phony. So, write the way you talk. Real people do not speak in complete sentences. Instead, we speak in phrases or fragments, sometimes using improper grammar, with pauses and the occasional "er" or "um."

You must sound real; if you have a hard time writing this way, try talking into a tape recorder, playing it back, and writing down what you say.

- **Get to the point.** Don't bother asking the prospect, "How are you today?" or "May I have a moment of your time?" Instead, ask for your prospect by name, then greet her by name. Next, introduce yourself. "My name is Alice Brown, my company is ABC Hardware." Or, "My name is Alice Brown, and I'm with ABC Hardware."

- **Get different.** Next, use a sound bite—one sentence that succinctly expresses what you do, or what your product or service is—to further introduce yourself. Example: "Wendy Weiss teaches people to get what they want over the telephone." Your sound bite should position you as the expert, someone (company, product or service) who stands out from the pack. A good sound bite will preempt the objection "I can't meet with every salesperson who calls."

- **Get creative.** If you say the same things everyone else is saying, you will sound exactly like every salesperson who calls. To stand out from the crowd, get creative. When I started my business, there was no shortage of competitors making phone calls and setting appointments for sales representatives. These people worked in-house, were not particularly well-paid, and were called telemarketers. To differentiate my business, I introduced myself as a marketing consultant specializing in new business development. That put me in a different category, and positioned me as an expert: the outside consultant hired to help develop new business.

There are many ways to position yourself as the expert. Use phrases like, "We specialize in…" or "We are known for… ." Name-drop credentials by mentioning clients or customers in similar businesses as your prospects. This lets them know you're familiar with their industry, and makes them feel safer if they haven't heard of you before. If someone has referred you, always use that person's name during your introduction.

Step 2: Focus on the Benefits

Next comes the heart of the script, where you describe your product or service while focusing on relevant benefits. Remember, prospects are above all interested in benefits and buy for their reasons, not yours. That's why it's so important to do your research, and have a sense of what your prospect may need. Focus your message on your prospect and speak in her language. If your industry has a particular jargon, use it. You can't be the expert if you don't know the language. If the prospect doesn't know or use that jargon, speak plainly. Your goal is to communicate and be understood.

This part of your script should not be long and unwieldy; a few salient points will do. Look for a way to bolster this section with a success story regarding something you, your company or product did for a customer. For example, describe how you saved the client time or money, or rescued him from a tight spot. By inference, this means you will do the same for the prospect. Stories provide a terrific way of pointing out customer benefits without actually having to say, "…and the benefit to you, Ms. Prospect, is… ."

A good script is fluid. The manner in which your conversation with the prospect proceeds will determine what parts of your script you use. Build some maneuvering room into the script, so you can easily change tactics (i.e., tell a different success story) when the situation calls for it. To create this maneuvering room, be prepared, know your customer benefits, and know which benefits may interest a particular prospect. Have several success stories available, depending on the point you're trying to make. And don't be afraid to say the unexpected, or use humor.

Step 3: Ask for What You Want

At last comes the close, when you finally ask for what you want! Don't expect your prospect to know what you want, guess what you want, or offer what you want. It is *your* job to ask, clearly and precisely. What *do* you want? Obviously, you want to turn your prospect into a customer, so he buys your product or service. But that comes later. For now, the primary goal is simply to get your foot in the door: to introduce yourself, your product and/or your company so the prospect can be induced later to buy.

All you want now is an appointment. At this moment you're not selling a product or your service, you're selling an appointment—and only an appointment. You want the prospect to give you 10 to 15 minutes of his time, so you can introduce yourself, your company, and your product or service. You're not asking him to buy anything, or change anything he does; only to meet with you.

Ask for an appointment or a meeting. (I prefer the word "meeting" because it has more weight and substance.) Say, "I would like to meet with you," or "I would like to introduce myself, my company, my product," or "I need 10 minutes of your time." Be clear, bold, and to the point. Give your prospect some choices of times. For example, "Is this Thursday good, or would next Thursday be better?" It is easier for your prospect to choose between options like different dates, than to decide whether or not to schedule.

Once you have scheduled the meeting, confirm the prospect's name, title, and address. Make sure he has your name, company, and telephone number. Repeat the date and time of the meeting at least twice. Speaking s-l-o-w-l-y and distinctly, let your voice direct your prospect to write everything down. This way he, too, will have the meeting in his calendar, and there should be no mix-ups.

The Script Formula

You don't have to be a polished writer in order to put together an effective cold-calling script. Stick to the following formula, and your script will put you way ahead of salespeople who don't take time to prepare.

1. Ask for the prospect by name.
2. Say hello. "Hi, Ms. Prospect!", or "Hi, Jane!"
3. Identify yourself and your company. "My name is Alice Brown. My company is ABC Hardware."
4. Say what you do (sound bite) and position yourself as the expert. Use phrases like, "We specialize in...", "Our reputation is...", "We are known for..." When appropriate, name-drop your credentials with similar or well-known clients.
5. Articulate the benefits of your product or service, using success stories to illustrate them.

6. Ask for what you want: an introductory meeting. Try saying, "I would like to meet with you...", "I would like to introduce myself, my company, my product...", "I need 10 minutes of your time", "Is this Thursday good, or would next Thursday be better?"

Remember, all great scripts include three basic steps: a great opening, a focus on benefits, and asking for what you want. To maximize your cold-calling success, get organized, follow these three steps, and keep asking for what you want. ■

Wendy Weiss is known as the Queen of Cold Calling. For biographical and business information, see page 276.

Editor's Note: An electronics technician, Brian Jeffrey was left in charge of the sales department for a few months. Sales shot up so dramatically his bosses had him take over permanently, and his sales career was born. Over 35 years, Brian has sold everything from electronic instruments to computers, satellite communications equipment, state-of-the-art test instruments, consulting services, training, tangibles and intangibles. A noted sales trainer and writer, Brian recently founded a new company, Salesforce Assessments Ltd., to help sales managers with the hiring process.

The Dreaded Price Objection
by Brian Jeffrey

What's the number one sales objection in today's economy? The price objection, of course. We get it so often you'd think we would have developed an answer to it by now. Unfortunately, most salespeople don't take the time to prepare a proper response to this challenge.

Where does the price objection come from, and how can you counter it? For starters, your product or service may actually be priced too high compared to what else is available. Or perhaps the prospect can't afford it. Primarily, the price objection arises because the prospect does not *want* to afford it. In fact, any price will be too high if your prospect does not feel he wants or needs your product or service.

Price will always be a factor in every sale, but rarely is it the deciding factor. In fact, in a recent survey, only 14% of respondents put price first. Other factors, such as confidence in the salesperson or product, quality, selection, and service, all came before price.

We can't eliminate the price objection, but we can minimize the possibility of it arising by practicing value-added selling techniques. This means showing the prospect beyond a shadow of doubt that he will receive good value for his investment. Even then, price-sensitive prospects may challenge your price, so it pays to be prepared to meet that challenge.

Though all of us want to hold onto our hard-earned money, we still buy things. Your job is to get people to buy from *you*. Here are ten strategies for dealing with the dreaded price objection.

1. **Focus on the price *difference*, not the price.** Your price is high in comparison to what—someone else's price? Instead of arguing price, find out what the other price is, and focus on the difference. You may be 10% more expensive than your competitor, but if that 10% buys your prospect 30% greater benefit, you are adding value. The key is to avoid using the larger number in your discussions. Use phrases like, "For an investment of only $50 more, you'll be getting…" or "Let's see what that extra $75 gives you." This focuses the prospect's attention on the relatively small dollar difference, not the greater dollar value of the sale.

2. **Make the price seem smaller.** If the product is something your prospect will use for a long time, amortize its cost over the life of the product. Break down the price into cost per day, week, month or some other suitable duration. Again, focus on price difference rather than total price. This way, the comparison seems even smaller. "For only $2 a week, you'll have all the additional benefits we talked about."

3. **Make it an investment, not an expense.** Show, don't just tell, your prospect how much he is saving and benefiting. Contrast this with the small additional amount your product or service actually costs. By focusing on the benefits, you help the prospect see the added value of dealing with you.

4. **Compare results, not price.** This is often called the "spotlight" method of handling objections. Focus on the parts of your offering the prospect really likes, then remind him that what really matters are the results your product or service delivers, not just what he pays for it.

5. **Explain the potential drawbacks.** Discuss the drawbacks of purchasing cheaper goods or services. Point to limitations in use, expandability, lower resale value, lower quality, fewer features, and so on. You really have to know your competition to use this technique well. And while it is appropriate to contrast yourself with a competitor, never knock your competition.

6. **You get what you pay for.** Ask your prospect to recall a time he regretted making a purchase based on a low price.

7. **Compare with more expensive products.** Show how your product has features found only in much more expensive products. This will make your price seem lower, and build perceived value.

8. **Use easy payment terms.** Make the terms as easy as possible by using low down payments, installments, leasing, extended terms, or some other payment option.

9. **Extra benefits.** Smart salespeople always keep a few benefits up their sleeves for just this occasion. Point out to the prospect previously unmentioned benefits your product offers.

10. **Hidden benefits.** Call your prospect's attention to the hidden benefits of dealing with you and your company. Explain that the price you quoted is a reflection of the total value received, including other benefits like dependable service.

Experienced salespeople also know the value of "under-promise and over-deliver." I promised you only ten techniques, but here are two more good ones:

11. **Know why your product is worth its price.** If you don't know why the prospect should pay your price, don't expect him to know.

12. **Challenge your prospect.** Ask your prospect to make sure he is comparing exact specifications. Mention features and benefits that may be different. Ask him to compare quality and workmanship. Many products which look alike and seem equal are in reality quite different, and one may be inferior.

The bottom line is simple: practice these techniques in advance, and be prepared for the dreaded price objection. That way, when—not if—it comes up, you can handle it like a pro. ■

Brian Jeffrey is president of Salesforce Assessments Ltd. For biographical and business information, see page 269.

Editor's Note: John Boe flew helicopters in the Army. Perhaps that's where he developed the courage to tell our editor at SalesDog.com, after just a brief phone conversation, that she's an introverted germophobe with neurotic tendencies. You see, after two minutes John can't help but tell you your temperament style, and how best to establish rapport with your type. John so charmed our editor that she didn't hang up on him, and later admitted his analysis was right on. John has an uncanny ability to analyze an individual based on a picture, brief phone conversation, or face-to-face meeting. He teaches his techniques to trial lawyers, poker players and salespeople.

A Hands-On Approach
by John Boe

Do you look for ways to keep your customers actively involved during your presentation, or do you just babble on, hoping you might say something that will generate a sale? Regrettably, far too many salespeople display poor listening skills, and are inclined to talk more than they listen. These people also have a tendency to use a "show and tell" presentation style that fails to promote customer participation—which means they're closing far fewer sales than they could. The show and tell approach quickly turns customers off, and causes them to shut down mentally. On the other hand, by developing your listening skills and finding ways to keep your customers engaged during your presentation, you'll dramatically increase your effectiveness and closing ratio.

One of the most overlooked principles in the selling process is the value of self-discovery. When you show or tell customers about your product or service, they have a tendency to doubt the information. But when you guide them to discover a feature or benefit on their own, they believe it! Auto dealers have long known and practiced the power of self-discovery and prospect participation. They will be the first to tell you that it's the hands-on experience of the test drive, not the colorful brochure full of features and options, which sells the car.

Though not every product or service lends itself to a hands-on demonstration, you can always find ways to increase involvement. Any time there's a choice between you or your prospect doing something, let the prospect do it! For example, if you have numbers to crunch, hand your prospect the calculator, and let him do it. When it's time to demonstrate benefits and features of your product, don't just show clients; let them experience the benefits and features for themselves.

A Striking Example

Several years ago, I heard an interesting story about a successful glass salesman named Bill Johnson. Far and away the top producer in his company, Bill consistently outsold other salespeople by a significant margin. After setting a new company quarterly sales record, Bill received a congratulatory call from the president. Curious about his methods, the president asked Bill to divulge the secret of his success. Bill replied he was still selling the way he'd been trained, but recently had made a minor change to his sales presentation that was creating a major difference in his results.

During his presentation, Bill now used a hammer to strike the safety glass several times, demonstrating its strength and durability. Excitedly, the president asked Bill if he would be willing to teach this hammer technique to his colleagues at the next training meeting. Bill readily agreed, and several months later, after demonstrating his technique to the entire sales team, the company shattered all its previous records for safety glass sales.

The president was delighted with the overall results, and noticed that Bill's sales had also increased dramatically. Surprised that Bill continued to outsell the rest of the sales force by a wide margin, he asked Bill if he'd discovered any new techniques. Bill replied that he'd made another subtle change in his presentation. "I still use the hammer technique," he explained. "Only now when I get to the part where I demonstrate the strength of the safety glass, I hand the hammer to my customer, and let him hit the glass."

By handing the hammer to his customer, Bill discovered the secret of successful selling: letting his prospects personally experience the benefits of his product. He took his sales career to the next level by finding a way to get his customers actively involved during his presentation. If you're not keeping your customers actively involved, take a lesson from Bill, and find a way to put the hammer in your customer's hand! ■

John Boe is president of John Boe International. For biographical and business information, see page 264.

Editor's Note: Julie Thomas is a noted speaker, author and consultant. She spent over 16 years successfully selling in the technology field, rising from sales rep to vice president of worldwide sales development at Gartner Inc. In the fast-declining minicomputer industry, she not only met her quota, she exceeded it. Julie credits her success to the Value Selling training she received. She liked it so much, she ended up buying the company!

The Anxiety Question: Your Ace in the Hole
by Julie Thomas

A sales rep was trying to get a meeting with a CEO. When he called for an appointment, the administrator said the CEO was not taking any appointments unless the meeting directly pertained to the company's IPO, scheduled for two months out. Instead of moving on to another opportunity, however, this determined sales rep called his stockbroker and asked for an analysis of the pending IPO. The broker suggested that the offering was sure to rise dramatically in the first few days of trading. However, the company had not yet demonstrated the ability to penetrate other market segments, and analysts expected the stock price to fall by the end of the year if this issue went unresolved.

The next day, the sales rep waited in the company's lobby, hoping to catch the CEO as he headed out the door to lunch. Sure enough, the CEO came walking through the lobby. The sales rep said hello, and asked for a meeting. Without breaking stride, the CEO instructed the rep to call his administrator to set up an appointment. Knowing where this would end, the rep blurted out, "OK, but I was wondering what will be the impact on your stock price if you don't penetrate some other market segments?" The CEO stopped in his tracks, looked at the sales rep, and asked, "Is that something you can help us with?" The sales rep nodded, and asked if they could talk. The CEO agreed, and immediately sat down in the lobby for a 25-minute meeting.

That is the power of an anxiety question!

Use it Wisely

Anxiety provides a powerful tool in many selling situations. Generally, it can be applied any time a prospect will not engage with you, whether during your prospecting attempts, trying to get a return phone call, or most importantly, closing the opportunity. The idea is to get prospects to consider the impact of *not* taking action. In the two seconds it takes prospects to consider your anxiety question, they journey to a place where they recognize their personal motivation for taking action.

For example, suppose you're trying to close a deal this month in order to make your quota. The prospect has gone through all the motions with you, confirmed that you have the best solution, and agreed that you can impact both his business and his personal agenda. He even has buy-in from the right people in his organization, and has seen all the proof he needs to make an informed decision. Yet he finds a reason to stall. *The holidays are distracting. It makes more sense to use next year's budget. I'm going out of town.* The list goes on and on, and you've heard it all before.

Now is the time to use a compelling anxiety question, created by using what you know the prospect cares about personally. For example:

- What's the cost of not taking action now?
- What happens if you don't start reducing costs this year?
- What's the impact on you if the cost management initiative is delayed?
- Are you confident you'll be able to support management's 35% annual growth plan without impacting costs?
- Do you feel there's any connection between your current capabilities and your lower profits?

Put yourself in your prospect's shoes. If someone were to ask you one of these questions, what would run through your mind? Maybe part of his compensation plan is tied to this initiative. Perhaps he has a presentation to make on this subject at the next executive staff meeting. Or maybe he realizes how much effort he's put into the initiative so far, and does not want to lose it now. Ideally, the prospect will review all of the potential impacts in that two-second time period. Inevitably, some nagging concern will rise to the surface, and cause him to reconsider the delay.

Anxiety questions are designed to rattle a person and prod him into action, but be careful not to overuse this tactic. Consider it your ace in the hole—something to use when you need it, but not in every situation. ∎

Julie Thomas is president and CEO of ValueVision Associates. For biographical and business information, see page 275.

Editor's Note: Joe Guertin has 25 years of outside sales experience, specializing in new business and customer relationship development. As a speaker and consultant, Joe has worked with thousands of salespeople, managers, and business principals. His firm, The Guertin Group, conducts customized corporate sales training, both in person and online.

Before You Cut That Rate, Read This
by Joe Guertin

Do you give away your best "stuff" for nothing? Almost every company I work with has incredible value that their customers never see. These "hidden assets" include traits, habits, and resources that can be powerful selling points to help differentiate you and your company from the competition, and win you more business. These assets never show up on the invoice, and you would never think of charging the customer for them. But when you leave customers in the dark, they may never perceive the full value of your product or service offering.

What are your hidden assets? First—especially if you are an entrepreneur—there is your drive, motivation, experience, and desire to help. While I might tell a customer, "If you need anything, just give me a call," I could really sell the point by saying, "Here are my home and cell numbers. If you need help, call me—I don't care if it's 2:00 a.m.!" How about the time you spend learning new skills, techniques or technologies? If I am one of your customers, that time has "pre-sell value" as well. Next, look at your support team. Have you ever told a customer, "I want to take this to our team's brainstorming session" to show the scope of your solution power? Do you have a sales assistant or technical engineer who can accompany you on calls? Then there is the aggregate knowledge of management and ownership. There's an old and very true saying that "nothing sells better than bringing in the boss." A boss's experience and connections can be of immense value to your customer.

Even before presenting your value, you can start positioning your price. For example, very few customers think of themselves as low-price leaders, and often despise cut-rate competitors. This gives you a chance to create a special connection. Suggest that, "Every industry has businesses that sell value for more money, down to the low-price discounters. Where are you on that scale?" Most will say they are in the middle, or even near the top. That is when you make your first connection with them by saying, "That's us, too." Now, price alone can't be an issue because they said it themselves. Not only that, people like to know they are dealing with someone of quality, and that they will get what they pay for.

A wise mentor once told me, "You've got to stand out and get noticed." If a customer is comparing your price to another, one of two things is happening. Either he doesn't see any real difference, or he is somewhat sold, but not enough to justify the dollars you are asking. Sometimes a customer just wants to feel he has negotiated the best deal possible, or needs to use "I can get it cheaper from XYZ" as leverage with you.

The best closers rarely have to deal with price objections, because they sell their value first and get the whole pricing issue out of the way early. But if customers don't know about your hidden assets, they may not fully understand your value. If you want to stand out and get noticed, stop giving away your stuff for nothing, and start making customers aware of all the things you can do for them. ■

Joe Guertin is president of The Guertin Group. For biographical and business information, see page 268.

Editor's Note: In the 22 years he's been running his telesales training business, Art Sobczak's heard it all. He shares with us a summary of the biggest phone mistakes he's seen during his career. Make sure you highlight Art's recommended "Action Steps."

The Top 10 Phone Mistakes of All Time
by Art Sobczak

If you would like to make another call, please hang up and try again.

This frequently-heard phone message wasn't created with salespeople in mind—but it could have been! The fact is, based on the results they get when contacting prospects and customers by phone, most salespeople *would* be better off hanging up and trying again. In my career, I have listened to, received and placed thousands of sales calls. Based on that experience, I've put together a list of the top 10 mistakes salespeople make when using the phone. This list details the most heinous, avoidable errors sales reps commit every day, miscues that sabotage their sales efforts, and inhibit their ability to produce the results they want.

You won't see this list on Letterman anytime soon. But if you follow the advice given in the action steps, you'll eliminate some serious errors, learn to use the phone more productively, and take important steps toward improving your overall effectiveness as a professional salesperson.

Mistake #10: Sending Unnecessary Literature

One of the best stalling techniques used by prospects (usually *non-prospects*) is, "Send me some information on that." Every day, this phrase sends sales reps scrambling for the literature rack, in the mistaken conviction that they've got a hot one on the line. Never confuse, "Send me literature" with legitimate signs of interest. Printed materials make a fine complement to your sales efforts, but don't get fooled into thinking that literature does your selling. If you can't generate interest to the point where the prospect deserves literature, you're wasting valuable selling time.

Action Step: When a prospect requests literature, make sure he is a legitimate buyer, and not someone trying to get rid of you. It's better to get the "no" now rather than later, after investing a few dollars' worth of paper and postage and lots of your precious time. If you hear the request early in the call, respond with, "I'll be happy to send something that summarizes what we discussed. Let me ask you, though: if you like what you see, can I assume we'll be able to do business together?"

Mistake #9: Poor Telephone Image

It's astonishing how many people give more thought to what color socks they wear than to how they sound to another person. On your next 10 telephone calls, try an experiment. Divide a piece of paper into two columns: *Desirable* and *Undesirable.* For each call, put a checkmark in the column that describes the image you project based on what the other person says and how he says it. At the end of the calls, tally the checkmarks to see what they reveal about the impression you make.

Action Step: The best way to improve the way you sound is to listen to yourself on tape. Athletes, actors, singers, dancers and professional speakers all review their performances on tape. Professional salespeople should do the same.

Mistake #8: No Post-Call Review

Do you (like most salespeople) grind out call after call, putting your fingers into speed dial mode and pounding the keypad immediately after disconnecting the previous call? If so, you're wasting valuable learning opportunities. Learning does not take place during an activity; it takes place afterward, when you dwell on it. Like reading a book, you always retain more when you pause to reflect on and react to what you just experienced.

Action Step: At the end of every call, ask yourself two questions:

1. What did I like about this call?
2. What would I have done differently on this call?

If you think you don't have time to perform this activity, think again. You can't afford not to!

Mistake #7: Lousy Listening

For some reason, getting on the phone prompts salespeople to turn on the verbal waterfall. But success on the phone does not mean dominating the conversation. In fact, the other person's desire to listen to you is inversely proportional to the amount of speaking you do. Talking too much reduces the prospect's interest and desire to participate in the conversation. It can also raise points that lead to objections.

Action Step: Everyone knows how to listen; the key is making sure you do it. The next time you find yourself taking a mental vacation during calls, ask yourself, "Why do I need to listen to this person?" Your answer— "Because what this person says will tell me exactly what I need to say in order to help them buy, therefore putting more money in my pocket"— will snap you back into the proper perspective.

Mistake #6: Screener Misuse and Abuse

Basic psychology says the more you push someone, the harder he resists. Yet I've heard sales reps refer to screeners as The Bulldog, The Iron Gate Maiden, The Rejectionist, and other equally unflattering monikers. Worse, they use strong-arm tactics trying to go through, around, above or under the screener. Consequently, they experience exactly what they expect: resistance, frustrating, penetrating questions, and downright humiliation.

Action Step: To get through to your buyers, help the screener do her job, which is to protect the buyer's time, so that only callers with something of value get to spend time with the boss. How? Prepare a "justification statement" to answer the screener's most important question: "What's this in reference to?" Just as you qualify prospects in the sales process, the screener is qualifying you. Be ready to explain the results and benefits you bring to the table. For example, "My ideas have helped other retailers in your industry cut down on their advertising expenses while generating more store traffic. I'd like to ask Mr. Bigg a few questions, to see if it would make sense for him to take a look at them."

And whenever prospecting, ask questions before you get to the decision-maker, so you are better prepared when you ultimately reach him. Switchboard operators, screeners, worker bees, and others in the decision-maker's department (people who actually use what you sell) all can provide valuable insight and information that gains instant respect, and creates interest in the mind of the buyer. You could say, "You probably work closely with Mr. Bigg, is that right?" Then begin your questioning: "So I'll be better prepared when I speak with him, there's some information you could help me with first ..."

Mistake #5: Nonexistent or Inadequate Questioning

When you ramble on without trying to uncover whether the listener might actually be interested in buying, you destroy your credibility, and turn off the listener. The prospect channels energy into thinking of reasons why he should get you off the phone, instead of participating in a meaningful conversation. Ultimately, prospects and customers bring up objections as a result of poor questioning (see Mistake #3) and lousy listening (see Mistake #7).

Action Step: Map out your questioning strategy before you call. Write all your benefits on the left-hand side of a piece of paper. Then draw two columns to the right. Label the first one *Needs Filled/Problems Solved*. For each benefit, identify the need or problem the benefit satisfies or solves. Label the second column *Questions to Ask*. For each need or problem, write a question that would determine whether that situation exists for the prospect. Use these questions during your call.

During the call, never present what you think is a benefit until you've confirmed it by asking the corresponding questions. For example, if you assume better delivery would be a benefit for the prospect, ask questions like these:

- How quickly do you normally need delivery?
- Do you ever require next-day delivery on orders you need to place later in the day?
- What do you do in situations like that?
- What happens when you need something the next day, but have to wait for two days?
- What kind of inconvenience does that cause?"

How the prospect answers these questions will determine whether a need/problem truly exists, and whether the benefit would be of real value.

Mistake #4: Poor Preparation

Poor preparation ensures a sloppy, rambling call that is like a kite without a tail, whipping in the wind, wildly changing directions. The best salespeople choreograph their calls before placing them. Jean-Claude Killy once said about ski racing, "The outcome is determined by the time the racer is in the gate." Similarly, the result of your call is determined *before* you pick up the phone.

Action Step: The most important step in a successful call is the first one: setting your primary objective. This involves evaluating where you are and where you want to be at the end of the call. Ask yourself, "What do I want to do at the end of the call, and what should the prospect do at the end of the call?" After you have set your objective, simply fill in the blanks with what needs to happen for you to travel from point A to point B. You'll realize what information you need, and the information you want to present based on those needs.

Mistake #3:
Misunderstanding Objections

Believe it or not, more objections are caused by sales reps than any other factor. People object when reps do not question effectively, when they talk too much, and when they present features that do not excite the prospect. Worse, when objections are voiced, reps often respond with a slick, prepared rebuttal, rather than trying to identify the real concern behind the objection.

Action Step: The best way to deal with objections is to prevent them from arising in the first place. However, when objections do arise, the way to professionally address them is to dig for the underlying reasons. Only then can you begin to understand, and respond appropriately. Keep in mind that real objections don't always have an answer—despite what some sales evangelists preach. That's why my favorite response to an objection is, "I see. Well, let's talk about that." This lets the person know I will not pounce on him for his beliefs, but sincerely intend to discuss the issue.

Mistake #2:
Reluctance to Get Commitment

Asking for the sale (or a commitment to take action) requires the least amount of skill, but is the hardest task for many salespeople to perform.

Even if prospects are leaning in your favor, they might not volunteer the action you want, unless you make it easy by inviting them to do business with you. I've seen a lot of money left on the table and hours wasted on unproductive follow-up calls simply because the salesperson did not ask for the business—or at least, some commitment from the prospect.

Action Step: Build the habit of asking. There's no secret here, no magic phrase that will guarantee they say "yes" to your offer. Very simply: if you want different results, change your routine! If you don't ask for the sale as often as you should, analyze why, then change your behavior accordingly.

Okay, drum roll please. The biggest mistake sales reps make on the phone is...

Mistake #1:
Opening Statements that Build Resistance, Not Interest

Within the first 15 seconds of a call, you create one of two emotions within the person you are speaking to: resistance, or interest. Unfortunately, most callers create resistance. This results in (what they perceive as) a morale-killing rejection, and an early end to the phone call. A caller starts with an uninspiring line like, "We sell product X, Y and Z and I'd like to talk to you about them." The listener justifiably thinks, "So what? Why should I listen?" Or the caller begins with, "I sent you a letter, and was wondering if you got it?" Even if he did, what are the chances the prospect even read it? Not very good.

Action Step: To evoke interest rather than resistance, try this simple three-step formula.

1. First, introduce yourself and organization.
2. Next, mention an interest-stimulating, curiosity-piquing benefit that appeals to the prospect's desire to gain or avoid loss.
3. Finally, get him involved in a conversation. Keep in mind that you want to do more listening than talking. Tell him that in order to deliver the potential benefit you alluded to, you need to get information.

For example, "I'm Dan Fleming with Graphics Industries. We specialize in working with retailers to lower overall advertising expenses while generating more store traffic. I've got a few ideas I'd like to discuss, to see if this would be of any value to you and your company…"

Or, "This is Karen Hamilton with Canton Supply. The reason I'm calling is there's a possibility we might be able to help you reduce your expenses for the very same cleaning items you're now buying. To determine this, I'd like to find out what you're using… ."

If you asked questions of the screener (as mentioned earlier) and received good information, you can use it to personalize your opener even more. For example, "Ms. Davis, I'm Paul Cooper with Public Engineering. I understand your division is now looking at upgrading your finishing process on ultramagnetic components. We have a process that has worked well for other manufacturers, and depending on your requirements, might be something that would fit in nicely with your system… ."

Finally, every call must have a value-added point: something that allows customers to feel they have gained by simply talking to you. It can be good news, useful information, notice of a sale, ideas you have: anything they will perceive as useful. For example, "Sandra, it's Linda with Dino Services. I was studying what you've been buying from us over the past two years, and I've got an idea here for a program that might make your job a little easier. I heard some interesting information, and you came to mind as someone who could really profit from it… ."

The real test of a winning opener is to put yourself in the position of the person hearing it. Ask yourself, "If I were the buyer, would I want to hear more? Would I set aside whatever I'm doing to willingly participate in the call?" If not, head back to the drawing board, before you fail the quiz with a real prospect.

Make sure your opener says as much as possible using as few words as possible. Only by appealing to your prospect's desire to gain—or fear of losing—something, will you cause him to spend productive time with you, and eventually buy from you. ∎

Art Sobczak is president of Business By Phone Inc. For biographical and business information, see page 274.

Editor's Note: Mark Smith knows how to talk to techies because he is one. And his understanding of sales professionals comes from 20 years spent in high-tech sales, marketing and development. Mark draws on his unique combination of skills—electrical engineer, computer programmer, hardware salesman, software marketer—to teach companies like AT&T, IBM, Oracle, and Raytheon how to get more out of their distribution channels. If selling to techies frustrates you, let Mark show you how to get inside their minds—so you get the sale.

How to Sell to Techies
by Mark S.A. Smith

For many salespeople, selling to technical types like IT professionals and engineers is harder than passing advanced calculus. But the difficulty doesn't lie in the analytical nature of these prospects. The problem is that most salespeople overlook certain needs these professionals have. As a result, salespeople inadvertently do things that can kill the sale, and the relationship, forever.

As a trained engineer with many years of experience selling to engineers, I know how my colleagues think and make decisions. In addition to my own observations, two accepted psychographic sales models, the "Mind Map" by Dr. Bill Gallagher, and the VALS study by the Stanford Research Institute, can be useful in providing real insight into how these people communicate, how they are persuaded, and how they make decisions. While people can operate out of more than one style and behavior mode, and not all technical professionals operate in these modes, these models help identify the key buying mode for IT professionals and engineers.

Understanding Techies

According to the Mind Map model, the majority of technical professionals fall into a single set of psychographic categories. Techies are primarily in the "Authority" mode. Authority types operate by the rules, and feel duty-bound to do things the right way. (I personally believe this is due to innate personality traits, as well as their training.) Their cognitive priority is to control the situation, though they will relinquish control to those they respect. They tend to be more comfortable with data, numbers, and observable facts than they are with people, and will sometimes argue just for the fun of it.

Authority types tend to dislike and distrust salespeople, and are judgmental of them. They sometimes suffer from paralysis by analysis, requiring incredible amounts of data before making a decision. Authority types actually prefer to have detailed literature that they can use to support their position rather than relying on a salesperson, over whom they have little perceived control. Their voiced and unspoken question is always, "What are the *facts?*" Although they may not be using standards such as ASTM or IEEE, they prefer to have standards available, and will have very good and highly-detailed reasons if they are not using them.

In the VALS study, engineers fall into the Societally Conscious (SC) category. SCs want and will go to great lengths to do the right thing—in some cases, doing things that appear ridiculous to others. Their greatest fear is of being manipulated, and they will reject forever anyone they perceive as manipulating them. Once a salesperson is perceived as manipulative, the relationship is over. SCs do not particularly care what other people think about them, as long as they have their rules and standards to back them up.

What's the best way to sell to technical types? Here are some essential guidelines.

- **Play by their rules.** In general, Techies prefer to have an authority set the rules, so then they can do the right thing. They prefer to use standards whenever possible. To support this need, show prospects how facts and industry experts identify your product as being the logical choice. Give them statistics to back it up.

- **Understand their centers of influence.** Purchase decisions often come from consulting with others, for example, experienced designers suggesting solutions. A suggestion may come from a magazine article outlining the success of others, or from a salesperson showing that his device is the logical solution.

- **Establish and prove that what you sell is an industry standard.** Do this with proof statements from satisfied customers, industry leaders who have standardized on the product, and key influencers who embrace your concept.
- **Position yourself as an expert.** Write and publish articles that illustrate your product being used in target market segments. Establish the standard in the techie's mind with regular mailings that show what you sell as an emerging or established standard. Keep in mind that standards are in the mind of the buyer, not necessarily in the industry.
- **Address their comfort level.** Show them how what you are offering fits into what they are doing now. Unless they are calling with an emergency, they are comfortable with their current procedures. Show them how they will be comfortable with the new procedure being offered.
- **Avoid manipulation at all costs.** If anything at all smacks of manipulation, eliminate it from the discussion. Techies prefer to draw their own conclusions, thank you.
- **Give them all the data they need to make a decision.** Create detailed data sheets, operating notes, and application sheets. Offer a buyer's guide, identifying the steps one should take to make a decision. Offer a decision tree structure. For maximum market impact, the data sheets must reflect the communications style of the reader, not of the marketing department.

Above all, let the techie calculate the payback for making the decision. Everyone wants to save money and time, but techies need to determine for themselves just what the payoff will be. Follow these guidelines, and selling to technical experts will be no different than selling to any other type of buyer—and may be easier than advanced calculus! ∎

Mark S.A. Smith is founder and president of Outsource Channel Executives Inc. For biographical and business information, see page 274.

The Fine Art of the Handshake
by Michael Dalton Johnson

Your handshake says a lot about you. It can convey confidence, warmth, and honesty, or it can signal weakness, uncertainty, and disinterest. Either way, it sends a subtle yet powerful message about who you are, that is not lost on prospective buyers. Use these pointers to make sure your handshake sends the right signals, and creates a good impression with prospects and customers.

- **Avoid the power grip.** A handshake should be firm, but not overly forceful. Beware of the unconscious tendency to pull the other person toward you as you shake. This can be interpreted as aggressive, and the prospect's resistance to you will go up a notch or two.

- **Nothing wimpy.** It may seem painfully obvious, but it's amazing how many salespeople offer weak, perfunctory handshakes. This is a major turnoff to many customers. Firm and friendly always wins the day.

- **Look 'em in the eye.** As you extend your hand, establish eye contact and smile. Show some teeth! A warm and sincere greeting can make you an instant friend—and all things being equal, people prefer to buy from friends.

- **Get a grip.** Never grasp the other person's fingers. Take their entire hand completely in yours, and gently pump it two or three times.

- **Turn on the charm.** You've been talking with a customer on the phone for several months, and meet them in person for the first time at a trade show. To express your pleasure at finally meeting face to face, you may want to cover his extended hand with your left hand briefly during the handshake. This increases the familiarity and warmth of the handshake. Do not attempt this with someone you don't know. However, it is often a pleasant gesture when you are shaking hands with someone you've met previously. It simply says, "I'm very glad to see you again."

- **What to say?** No handshake is complete without a spoken greeting. You can't go wrong with, "It's a pleasure to meet you." When meeting someone of high rank, such as the chairman of the board or founder of a company, you may want to up the ante with, "It's a great pleasure to meet you." After the initial greeting, your conversation should begin while you are still shaking hands, for example, "John tells me you've made some significant additions to your product line." Your hand should be slowly and somewhat reluctantly withdrawn as the person begins to speak. This slow withdrawal indicates your keen interest in the person and what he is saying.

- **What's your body language saying?** Posture is important, so stand erect, about three feet (one pace) away from the client, with your hands out of your pockets. Face the client squarely; never approach from an angle, or when the subject is engaged in conversation or otherwise distracted. Wait until you have his full attention before extending your hand.

- **Saying goodbye.** When the meeting is over, it's time to shake hands again. You now have the opportunity to leave a lasting impression. If you've established rapport with the buyer, it's a good idea to gently grasp his right forearm with your left hand during the handshake, and restate any promises you may have made during the meeting, for example, "I'll put the technical report you requested in the mail to you today, and give you a call next Wednesday. I enjoyed meeting you." This two-handed shake signals your interest and commitment to your customer.

- **Practice makes perfect.** Much like dancing, the fine art of the handshake takes practice. Stand before a mirror and extend your hand. Check to see if you're projecting an image of confidence, warmth, and enthusiasm. Keep in mind that your handshake reflects your personality, and should be a spontaneous gesture of friendly greeting that comes naturally from within. With a little rehearsal, you will develop the ability to tailor your handshake to every situation you face, and each individual you meet.

Your handshake is a powerful business asset that can help you close more sales, and build lasting and profitable relationships. The time you spend working on it will be time well spent. ■

Michael Dalton Johnson is founder and president of SalesDog.com. For biographical and business information, see page 269.

Editor's Note: Linda Richardson is a recognized leader in the sales training industry. An educational psychologist and consultant, Linda has over 28 years' experience in sales consulting and training. She's authored nine books on selling and sales management, and teaches sales and management courses at the Wharton Graduate School of the University of Pennsylvania, and the Wharton Executive Development Center. Her advice will help you become a confident closer.

Closing with Confidence
by Linda Richardson

Think back to your last attempt to close a sale. Did you crisply and confidently launch into your close, knowing that it was the appropriate time to ask for the business? Or did you hesitantly offer some vague action step, and hope the prospect might close the deal for you? To effectively close a sale, it's essential to either ask for the business or specifically confirm the next action step. Yet far too often, salespeople attempt to wrap up sales calls with a comfortable closing statement such as, "I'll write up... ," "I'll send you... ," or "I'll call you... ." Or, they end a call without having a next step in place. Why does this happen? For the following three reasons:

Fear of Rejection

Perhaps the biggest reason salespeople are hesitant to close is that they are anxious about facing rejection, or shutting down communications. This typically happens when they haven't elicited enough feedback or signals from the client to know if it's safe to close. Most often, they haven't received these closing signals because they haven't asked for them during the call.

Checking is the process of asking for feedback throughout the call. For example, after positioning your message, responding to an objection, or answering a question, ask, "How does that sound?" or "How would that work?" or "What do you think about... ?" Asking for feedback on what you've just said provides critical information, and increases your confidence either to ask for the business, or proceed to the next step. When you fail to check for feedback, asking at the end of the call becomes an all-or-nothing situation. Hence, many salespeople are reluctant to ask.

Fear of Looking Bad

Another reason salespeople don't close is because they don't want to seem inappropriate. They see closing only as asking for the business, so they worry about being too pushy and risking the client's disapproval. By setting a reasonable, appropriate and measurable action step objective before each call, and getting feedback throughout the call, you'll know where you stand.

Lack of a Process

The third reason salespeople fail to close is that they do not have a closing process. To close more effectively, treat the closing process as distinct phases each with specific goals. In the beginning stage, set specific measurable objectives before each call, so that you have a clear picture of the action step you want. During the middle stage, check for feedback throughout the call to gauge where you are. In the latter stage, ask confidently for the next action step, or ask for the business. Finally, be religious in your follow-up.

Today's selling environment demands disciplined management of every sales call, requiring the ability to close at the right time, with full confidence that it is the right action to take. Follow the adage, "One step at a time!" Get feedback throughout the call, and even if you are not at the point of asking for the business, never stop taking small steps.

End each call on an action step, so that you move to your close more quickly. Make sure that your next step is very specific, and moves the process forward. The difference between "I'll follow up with you next week," and a specific close like "Can we have the go-ahead to begin?" is the difference between marking time and closing business.

When the time comes to ask for the business, based on the feedback you've gotten from checking, confidently ask, "Will you give us the go-ahead?" If you're not comfortable closing, practice by asking for small next steps at the end of each call. Create the habit of relentlessly moving forward. Practice looking in the mirror and asking for the business. Practice is the key to getting comfortable and becoming a confident closer. ■

Linda Richardson is president and founder of Richardson. For biographical and business information, see page 272.

Editor's Note: Bill Brooks is founder and CEO of The Brooks Group, a leading sales training and consulting firm. During a 25-year career, Bill has been the top producer in an 8,000-person sales force, the CEO of a $300 million corporation, and a winning college football coach for 14 seasons. Bill is the author of 17 books, including the bestseller High-Impact Selling. *Clients include Bank One, General Motors, Hewlett-Packard, and MetLife.*

Do You Have a Sales Call Checklist?
by Bill Brooks

In the aviation world, pilots prepare for flights by going through a very thorough and extensive checklist. Without question, this process reduces the chances of an accident, mistake or crash. How do you prepare for your sales calls? Do you engage in a similar exercise to maximize your readiness? Or do you plunge right into the call, and hope that you won't crash and burn?

Every salesperson, regardless of what he sells or to whom, can benefit from using a daily sales call checklist. Here's what the list should cover:

- Be sure you are making your presentation to a qualified prospect.
- Confirm your appointment, to ensure you will have a receptive welcome.
- Make sure you understand the formal and informal structure of the prospect's organization, as well as the competitive environment.
- Do your best to understand the dynamics behind buying decisions, business drivers, and events that could influence timing and resistance.
- Prepare all necessary sales aids and tools. Organize these according to what you must have, and what you will use only if you have an opportunity.
- Ensure you have proper directions to the meeting site, including driving times.
- Understand the business culture, dress code, and style of the environment, and act and dress appropriately.

- Leave for your appointment early enough to guarantee arriving no less than 15 minutes prior to your meeting.
- Confirm with internal advocates any last-minute dynamics that may have affected the purpose of your sales call.
- Check your briefcase, materials, and sales aids one final time before leaving your office for the sales call.
- Organize your materials so you know exactly where everything is. Brochures, business cards, sales aids, and other materials should not only be easily retrievable, but neat, clean and fresh.
- Gather as much final data as necessary. Review the prospect's website, news releases, reports, brochures, and other pertinent information so that you are on top of who they are, what they do, and the latest developments within the company and its industry.
- Prepare a list of essential questions you will be ready to ask the prospect regarding problems, challenges, difficulties, needs, and potential growth opportunities where you might be able to help.
- Visualize your success. See yourself achieving whatever end result you are trying to achieve with your sales call. Remember, every sales call is not meant to make a sale. However, each and every call should move the sales process closer to that objective.
- Expect a positive, receptive, and open hearing, no matter how difficult a situation you might be entering with the sales call.
- Mentally prepare yourself for the first few minutes of your sales presentation. Remember not to dominate the conversation, or conduct a monologue.
- Approach all prospects in "neutral." Do not be too aggressive, or too passive. Instead, let the prospect dictate the pace, tone, and tempo of the sale. But always remember that you are in control if you know precisely where you are going next in the sale.

Successful sales calls don't happen by accident. Knowing precisely what the prospect expects, then exceeding those expectations, requires proper planning and preparation. I realize many salespeople prefer to "wing it" or "fly by the seat of their pants." But sooner or later, their radar lets them down. Don't expect to achieve your sales goals by relying on luck, instinct or pure spontaneity. Instead, rely on this checklist, or one like it. It may help you make a few more sales—and maybe even more money. ■

Bill Brooks is CEO of The Brooks Group. For biographical and business information, see page 265.

Editor's Note: Tom Richard is a syndicated weekly business columnist. His heroes are people like Earl Nightingale, Dale Carnegie, and Norman Vincent Peale. When I say he's a young man with an old-fashioned philosophy, he takes it as a compliment, which is how I mean it. Tom firmly believes that the old ways—establishing a personal relationship, having a conversation, and visiting a client—are just what sales folk need to succeed in an increasingly depersonalized business environment. Here's advice from Tom on how to forge a personal connection with customers.

The Power of the Handwritten Note
by Tom Richard

The hardest part of courting a new customer is getting your message heard. Most salespeople make this task even harder by delivering their message in an impersonal, forgettable way. In doing so, they abandon the personal touch that separates them from all the "Buy Me!" messages whizzing past their customers every day. With automation and emails, technology makes it highly convenient for salespeople to become an inconvenience to their customers. Email and voicemail accounts are overflowing with masses of annoying, impersonal sales messages. Using this method ensures that your message will be ignored and deleted as fast as your customer receives it.

The good news is that there are some things you can do to improve sales: things that are just too effective to ignore. For example, picking up that old, blue pen of yours to write a note is one of the simplest, most powerful ways to grab your customer's attention. Unlike emails, telephone calls and unannounced visits, handwritten notes are always well-received. Handwritten notes are rare and intriguing; they spark curiosity and thought. They are opened and read because they don't look or sound like junk mail. People actually *want* to read them.

The true power of the handwritten note is that it is personal. Think of the people who send you handwritten notes. Mostly family and friends, right? Receiving a handwritten note from you is as comforting and pleasant for your customer as hearing from an old friend. It does more than just say "thank you" for the meeting, lunch, phone call or referral. It sends an important message about you, and how you like to conduct business.

When it comes to customers, my friend Rebecca Booth follows the philosophy that you should try to "make their day." Sending them something personal will brighten their day, if even for just a moment. Creating that feeling in your customers makes you unforgettable, because they will associate their positive reaction with you. Your note will remind the prospective customer that you are the personal choice, and that you care about him as a person. You understand he has choices when it comes to buying products, and you fully appreciate the opportunity to earn his business.

Of course, it's not like a customer's wallet will jump out of his pocket and into your hands the moment he receives your handwritten note. Customers will buy when they're good and ready. However, you certainly want them to think of you first when that need arises. By sending handwritten notes on a regular basis, you remind customers of how great you are without being pushy or annoying. Think of the note as a gentle tap on the shoulder, just to say hello.

There are plenty of other ways to show customers that you are thinking of them, and that you understand their needs. Try sending an article you think they would want to read, letting them know you thought of them while reading it. Give them a heads-up about a networking function they could benefit from; invite them to lunch; mention a new product you'd love to show them. Don't ask for the sale directly, or use methods that will be perceived as pushy or purely sales-driven. Your customers know why you're sending them cards; you don't need to spell it out for them.

If you think sending handwritten cards is a lot of work, you're right. That's why your competitors aren't doing it. In today's selling world, success depends on separating yourself from the competition every chance you get. The only thing keeping you from that sale might be three minutes and a stamp! ∎

Tom Richard is an author and sales trainer. For biographical and business information, see page 272.

Editor's Note: For over two decades, Anita Sirianni dominated the sales charts, reaching the top 5% for every company she represented. As The Professional Sales Coach, she's been sharing her secrets of selling success with her clients for the past 10 years. Here she weighs in on the feature-benefits debate.

Dump the Feature Dumping
by Anita Sirianni

Harry S. Truman once said, "If you can't convince them, confuse them." While this philosophy may sustain a political career, it has no place in the world of selling. Nevertheless, many salespeople regularly confuse their prospects and customers by engaging in "feature dumping," a common—and often fatal—selling strategy. Feature dumping involves enumerating a variety of qualities about a product or service without connecting them to the buyer's situation. Rather than clarifying how the product or service meets the customer's needs, wants and expectations, the salesperson tosses out a laundry list of product features, in hopes that the prospect will hear enough to decide to buy.

With prospects and buyers, feature dumping is about as welcome as an IRS audit. Despite this, feature dumping remains popular among salespeople for three reasons:

1. It's logical. From a purely rational standpoint, it makes sense to think that the more features or reasons the prospect has to compare with the product he is using, the more likely it is he will buy.
2. It's easier to memorize a list of product qualities, and recite them in the short period of time available, than it is to bridge the gap from need to product capabilities.
3. It's ego-boosting. As salespeople, we love to show off how much we know, and feature dumping gives us a great chance to showcase our product knowledge.

Despite the good reasons we may have for bombarding prospects with features and benefits, it is not the most effective way of selling. Feature dumping forces the prospect to figure out what features and benefits apply to her, a task for which she is not well-qualified. In addition, bombarding prospects with features and benefits opens the call to performance misinterpretations, and failure to demonstrate just how well-suited your offering is to the prospect. This poor connection, coupled with the prospect's limited ability to connect her needs with your products, is precisely why feature dumping is ineffective.

Fortunately, there's a better approach that will give you more control over the selling process, and improve your closing ratio. Begin with the end in mind. In every selling situation, buyers ask themselves two key questions before making a buying decision: "What's so special?" and "Why should I care?" Answering these questions in your sales presentation, positions your offering as a solution—not simply a product or service sold. What is so special about your product or service that would compel a prospect to buy it? Why should a customer care about these qualities? Since your answers get to the bottom line of what every customer wants to know, we call them *bottom line benefits:* product features and benefits expressed to encourage a positive buying decision. This approach is more powerful than conventional feature dumping, because each benefit is tied specifically to the prospect's needs, wants, and expectations.

Determine what the customer is looking for by asking effective questions. Then, based on the answers to those questions, create clear, concise bottom line benefits and memorize them until they roll off your tongue. You will be amazed at how well prospects respond to this simple, yet powerful approach. Bottom line benefits reduce the prospect's fears, and allow her to make an educated decision to buy your product. They give you a great opportunity to outdistance and outpace your competitors— who are, in all likelihood, still feature dumping. By matching prospect needs to unique features in your product, you gain a significant selling advantage. When you demonstrate how the capabilities and advantages of your product address prospect problems, they will get excited and enthusiastic about buying.

Educating prospects into the sale starts with excellent product knowledge. You must know the unique and important advantages of your product, and why they are important to the buyer. Prescription before diagnosis is malpractice, so make sure you do a good job of understanding prospect needs up front. Then use your products as powerful solutions, not only to meet, but exceed, their expectations. When you educate rather than confuse, customers will know exactly why your products are the best choice for them. ■

Anita Sirianni is president of ANSIR International. For biographical and business information, see page 273.

Editor's Note: For over ten years, Michelle Nichols was a top-rated salesperson for various companies, including NCR Corporation. She sold technical equipment and services before she started and sold two of her own companies. Today she is a popular sales speaker and columnist for BusinessWeek Online. *Have some fun playing with Michelle's ideas for injecting humor into your sales process. (A warning to the humor-challenged: these are just suggestions. If it doesn't feel right, hey—don't do it! Remember: with humor, a little goes a long way.)*

Laugh All the Way to the Bank
by Michelle Nichols

In the sales world, one of the most common stumbling blocks is price objection. A potential deal may be moving ahead smoothly until numbers enter the conversation, when eager customers suddenly turn and flee. But I've found that humor can be an effective tool for moving the sale along at almost every stage of the process. Using humor doesn't mean going overboard and acting like a goofball. Adding *appropriate* levity to a situation can increase your likeableness, and help establish that critical connection with customers. As a result, customers will listen more closely, and if trouble erupts, they're more likely to cut you some slack.

Thankfully for the joke-telling-impaired among us, humor does not mean just delivering one-liners. It includes all sorts of things, including funny quotations, cartoons, lists, analogies, definitions, and amusing stories. Keep in mind that in a business setting, your goal is simply to lighten the mood, not leave them rolling in the aisles. And make sure your humor is not offensive in any way. Joking that is racist, sexist, ethnic, religious, risqué, or demeaning is obviously a no-no. Here are a few methods I've found effective.

- **Get personal.** One of the most powerful sources of humor is stories from your own life. Personal stories are easier to remember, which makes it easier to tell them smoothly. A little self-deprecation never hurts. For example, if my prospects are parents, I might tell them about my daughter. When her junior high was having

Career Day, I asked if she wanted me to speak, since not everyone's mom is a columnist and speaker. "Oh great, how exciting," she moaned. "Why can't you be a pharmacist, or something that doesn't sound so boring?"

- **Go prospecting.** I am always on the lookout for funny stories in books and magazines. After all, the truth is often funnier than any joke. I also keep a file of sales cartoons, which I can refer to or show the prospect. And I frequently browse large card stores or joke shops for postcards, greeting cards, bumper stickers, posters, or other products that can help make my point in a funny way.

Keep an eye out for wacky news stories that might help you spark a conversation. "Did you see this in the newspaper?" can be an effective opener. For instance, this true story made me laugh. In February, 2005, President Bush spoke in Great Falls, Montana (population 56,000). The president of the local Republican Club attended, accompanied by his wife and their children, except for the youngest, Tim. "He has a dental appointment," the father explained, adding how hard it is to reschedule a dental visit.

- **Find some props.** A few choice items make for a more engaging sales presentation. I bought a $10 Tag Team Championship wrestling belt, about 10 inches wide, in a toy store. Sometimes I enter a meeting wearing it under my conservative grey suit, and make a point about teamwork or winning. I also have a rubber chicken named Larry, a huge eraser that says "For BIG mistakes," and a kit titled, "Grow a Brain." And I'm guaranteed at least a smile with my Hillbilly Calculator, a pair of wooden feet with the toes numbered 1-10.

- **Talk about price.** I have an old Mr. Boffo cartoon subtitled "The further adventures of the Bargain Hunter," depicting a guy displaying "Ed's Tattoo Parlor" tattooed on his chest in giant letters, saying, "Guess who got a free tattoo?" My point is, what is the real value of "free?" When I quote prices, the biggest potential sticking point, I like to say, "Your total is a mere $43,837.46." That always gets a laugh, and helps prospects over the price shock—at least for a moment.

- **Spin your weaknesses.** Suppose you work for the IRS, and someone is mad about the complexity of the tax code. Author Malcolm Kushner suggests you might start out quipping, "The tax code is really very simple—if you don't earn any income." The customer will probably laugh or groan, and you can go on to make some constructive points. If you spell a word incorrectly, volunteer that clear handwriting can sometimes be a handicap. If you lose your train of thought, say something like "My mind not only wanders, sometimes it walks right out the door."

- **Finish strong.** À la David Letterman, an original Top Ten list of funny reasons the customer should buy from you, or buy right now, is an unusual approach—and could seal a deal.

Rib-tickling gags, self-deprecating humor, and even corny props put your customers at ease, and help make the sale. If you don't have a funny bone in your body, try reading humor books or the daily comics as often as you can. Keep putting more humor in your head, and sooner or later, some of it is bound to seep into your selling. Remember: funny is money. Happy selling! ∎

Michelle Nichols is principal of Savvy Selling International. For biographical and business information, see page 271.

Editor's Note: For 15 years, Colleen Francis was a top performer in the technology and life insurance industries before founding her sales training company, Engage Selling Solutions. She has studied the business habits of the top 20% of sales performers in organizations of all sizes, creating a winning formula she uses in her acclaimed sales training program with clients like Corel, Merrill Lynch, Radisson Hotels and Resorts, and United Online/NetZero.

Winning the Negotiating Game
by Colleen Francis

Most salespeople believe the easiest way to make a customer happy is to lower the price. My experience says the opposite is true. In fact, by lowering price, you may be lowering your customer's perception of the value of the deal. I first became aware of this fundamental negotiating principle while watching my husband shop for running shoes. You see, my husband loves to negotiate—so much so that whenever I need to buy new running shoes, he always buys a pair too, hoping he can swing a deal by buying two pairs at once. Of course, he never gets a discount. What I find fascinating is the number of times he asks for a discount, doesn't get it, and buys the item at full price anyway.

I started thinking about this from the seller's perspective by analyzing my own negotiation techniques and those of my clients. I wanted to answer two important questions: one, what makes a successful negotiator, and two, what do the best negotiators do differently from the rest of us to get the price they want, while leaving their customers feeling like they got a good deal?

Eventually, I came up with a five-step format that top negotiators use to get the best deal every time they negotiate. It works wonders at every stage of the sales process, from negotiating price to discussing delivery, added product features, or any other terms on which your prospect is looking for a break. When used on a consistent basis, it ensures the best possible outcome for you and your customer.

Step 1: Get into the Right Frame of Mind

The first thing to do when negotiating is to make sure you're in the right frame of mind. Do you really believe your products or services are worth your asking price? If not, you will not be able to negotiate successfully—period! If you truly believe your products are worth the price you charge, the next four steps of this process will guarantee that you walk away with more full-price deals. On the other hand, if you think your products are too expensive, you will continue to sell at a discount.

Step 2: Hold Firm

Sales experts suggest that the top 20% of salespeople never cave in on the first round. So never give in right away to what your prospect is asking for. For those who love it, negotiating is a game; it is the "art of the deal." To make those people happy, you must be willing to play. Nothing frustrates negotiators more than a salesperson who drops his price on the first round. If a client asks for a 20% discount and you immediately say yes, he walks away feeling two things: that your price must have been inflated to start with, and that he should have asked for a bigger discount. And next time, he will! Neither of these outcomes is good for you. Instead of giving in when your prospect asks for a reduction in price, try one of these responses:

> "I can appreciate that you're looking for the best deal, but I can tell you we've already given you our best price."
>
> "You're smart to be looking for the best deal, but our pricing is always competitive, and I just can't go any lower."
>
> "A *discount?*" (in a surprised tone).

This stage of the negotiating process can and will challenge your belief system. In order to succeed, you *must* believe that you are already giving your prospect a great price.

While selling for London Life many years ago, I was approached by a client who wanted a 10% discount on his group health benefit plan. His request shocked me, because nobody had ever asked for a discount before.

I knew we had the least expensive plan he was looking at, and all I could say was, "Huh?" Not very eloquent, I admit. But he responded, "Well, I just had to ask," then paid full price for the plan.

Nearly half of all customers will respond the same way, saying, "I had to ask" or "I just thought I'd try." Unfortunately, more than half of all salespeople cave in on the first round and give the client the discount they're asking for—which is lose-lose for everyone. Your company reduces its profit, you reduce your commission, and your customer walks away dissatisfied because you refused to play the game. To avoid this situation, learn how to hold firm, and practice your responses in advance.

Step 3: Repeat

Some clients will press ahead with their request for a discount even after you have given them one of the above responses. The vast majority, however, are just looking for assurance that you really did quote your best possible price and have no wiggle room. In other words, they want to make it a little uncomfortable for you, make sure you sweat a bit. Again, my advice is to hold firm. Reassure your customer that he is getting the best price, and remind him of all the hard work you've both put into the deal. Try something like the following:

> "We've been putting this project together for six months.
> I would hate to see it not go ahead because we can't settle
> on price."

> "I knew you'd be tough, so we provided aggressive pricing
> up front. I would hate to see this not go ahead because we
> haven't been able to meet your budget."

When salespeople hold firm, an additional 20% of all business gets closed at this stage, which means that 60% of all business gets closed without ever having to reduce the price. Unfortunately, by this point 80% of salespeople have already caved in. You do the math.

Step 4: Take His Mind off the Bottom Line

If your prospect continues to push for a discount (4 out of 10 will), find something else to give him that does not reduce your price. For example, throw in free shipping, extra manuals and training, or a client profile on your website. What you concede will be specific to your business, your markets, and your client base. The key is to prepare in advance a list of things you are willing to offer, so you can draw on it during the negotiation. It's hard to think creatively in the heat of a negotiation; planning ahead gives you a ready-made solution that leaves both you and the client feeling satisfied with the transaction.

Step 5: The Last Line of Defense

After all this, if your client *still* asks for a discount, you may have to give it to them in order to close the sale. Before doing so, always ask one of these two questions: "What is important to you about a 15% discount?" or, "Why is a 15% discount important to you?" These questions will flush out any final details that might help you find a different way to structure terms and pricing, allowing you to keep your price while letting the customer walk away with his needs met. If, however, you ultimately choose to reduce your price, be sure to follow these two rules:

1. **Never reduce your price without getting something in return.** Getting something in exchange for a pricing concession is essential to managing customer expectations that future discounts will readily be dished out. As with the "no money" concessions above, what you get in return for a price reduction will be unique to your business and markets, but might include references or case studies, a bigger order, introductions to senior level executives, or cash up front. Again, whatever you ask for, prepare the list in advance so you can respond quickly and smoothly.

2. **Get a firm verbal agreement from the customer that this discount is all he needs to get the deal done.** For example, ask the customer "I'm not sure if I can get you this price, but if I can, is it fair to say we can go ahead?" or, "I'm not sure I can get this

discount for you. If I can, are you willing to sign the agreement this week?" Nothing is worse than coming to an agreement on price—especially a reduced price—only to discover that your prospect is still looking for other concessions. By asking this last question, you get all the issues on the table first, giving you the chance to deal with them fairly, once and for all.

This five-step process is not necessarily easy; it may take some discipline to implement. But if you put in the effort, it will make your negotiations easier, more natural and more rewarding. Most important, it will dramatically reduce the number of times you lower price to prevent losing a deal. ■

Colleen Francis is president of Engage Selling Solutions. For biographical and business information, see page 267.

Editor's Note: Dave Kahle is unique in the sales training field: he's been highly successful in the real world of sales. In addition, Dave's MA in Education makes him uniquely qualified to teach. Here he demonstrates how to wield "your most powerful sales tool."

Your Most Powerful Sales Tool
by Dave Kahle

Did you enjoy what you had for dinner last night? You're probably wondering what that question has to do with sales. Bear with me a moment, and answer the question. Now pause for a second, and think about what happened when you read that question. You probably flashed back to yesterday evening, and saw a picture of what you had for dinner. Then you recalled your response to the dinner, and made a judgment about whether you enjoyed it.

The point is: *I was able to direct your thinking simply by asking you a question.* You thought about what I wanted you to think about, and you thought about it in the way I wanted. This illustrates the remarkable power of a question to direct an individual's thinking, which is what makes asking a good question the single most effective action you can take with a customer. In other words, a well-phrased, appropriately-timed question is easily your most powerful sales tool. Here's what good questions will do for you.

Direct Your Customer's Thinking

When you use a good question, or a series of good questions, you penetrate your prospect's mind and direct his thinking. When we're asked a question, something in us makes it almost impossible not to think of the answer. I don't know whether this trait is hardwired, or whether we are conditioned this way. The fact remains that when asked a question, we inevitably think of the answer. To illustrate, I'll ask you a question, but I want you *not* to think of the answer: how old are you?

If you're like most of us, you thought of the answer, even after I indicated you should not. Now, consider where the decision to buy your products or services takes place. It happens in the mind of your customer. Therefore, a good question from you can help to focus and influence the direction in which your customer's mind works. For example, suppose you're shopping for a new car, and the salesperson asks, "Which is more important to you, good fuel economy or quick pickup?" Until you were asked, you probably hadn't thought of it that way. The salesperson's question helps you understand what you really think, directing your mind along a certain course. As you think along that line, the conversation naturally proceeds based on your answer. You perform the same service for your customers when you ask good questions. Your questions guide their minds along certain paths, and help clarify their thinking.

Collect Information to Make a Sale

A good question is your best means of collecting the information that will help you construct a sale. How do you know what a customer thinks, or what his situation is, unless you ask? If you're selling a new surgical glove, for example, you first ask questions to discover the surgeon's concerns, so you can point out the specific features of the glove that meet those needs. Without first asking questions, you are reduced to working on assumptions about the needs and interests of your customers. Good questions help you see into the mind and heart of your customer, equipping you with the knowledge necessary to make the sale. You'll do a far better job of selling your products and services if you first ask questions to understand your customer's needs and interests.

Build Relationships

The act of asking good questions shows that you care about the person and his problems. The more questions you ask about your customer, the more he feels your interest. The law of reciprocity indicates that the more interest you show in a customer, the more likely that customer will be interested in you.

Have you ever attended a reception or cocktail party, and met someone who kept asking you questions about yourself? When you parted, you probably thought, "What a great person!" Why did you think that? Not because of what he said, but because he expressed interest in you. You formed that impression because of the questions he asked you. You can use this same principle—asking good personal questions—to build strong relationships with your customers.

Convey the Perception of Your Competence

Customers see you as competent and trustworthy not because of what you say, but because of what you ask. Suppose you have a problem with your car. You take it to the mechanic down the street and say, "My car is making a funny sound." He replies, "OK, leave it here, and pick it up at five o'clock." Not surprisingly, you are not reassured by his approach. So you take the car to the mechanic across the street and say the same thing. He asks, "What kind of sound?" You reply, "A strange thumping sound." "Is it coming from the front or the back of the car?" "It's coming from the front." "Is it a metallic kind of sound, or a rubbery kind of sound?" "It's definitely metallic." "Does it go faster when you accelerate and slower when you decelerate, or is it the same speed all the time?" "It definitely speeds up when I accelerate." Finally he says, "OK, leave it here, and pick it up at five o'clock."

Which mechanic seems more competent? Obviously, the one who asked more questions. The fact is, the focus and precision of your questions does more to create the perception of competence than anything else you do. Every one of your customers wants to feel you are competent. You create that perception by asking good questions about the details of your customers' needs and applications. The use of good questions is the professional salesperson's single most powerful interpersonal tool. Mastering it in every aspect of your sales interactions will dramatically improve your results. ∎

Dave Kahle is president of The DaCo Corporation. For biographical and business information, see page 269.

Editor's Note: James Maduk has over 20 years' experience in strategic business, sales, and market development. A prolific author, James runs the Online Selling University. An Internet veteran, he was vice president of sales at a venture capital-funded startup. Prior to his online endeavors, James won awards in the Customer Relationship Management (CRM) field as one of GoldMine Software's top sales distributors. Both online and offline, James is an expert in selling.

Terminating the Sales Stall
by James Maduk

Unlike Arnold Schwarzenegger in "Terminator," when prospects say, "I'll be baaack," you know exactly what they mean. Not only will they *not* call you back, the sale isn't going to happen today, and it isn't going to happen tomorrow. In fact, the sale is *never* going to happen, but the prospect won't come right out and say so.

Most people consider the dreaded "Let me think it over" and "I'll get back to you" to be two of the most difficult objections in the entire sales process. And therein lies the problem. Far too often, salespeople mistakenly identify these responses to their sales efforts as objections, when in fact they represent a stall in the sales process, and are not objections at all. More importantly, things will only get worse if you attempt to handle this customer feedback using a traditional objection-handling approach.

What's the difference between a stall and an objection, and how do you get the sale to move forward? A real sales *objection* arises when the customer needs more information to make a decision, and either requests more information or seeks clarification on information you have provided already. A *stall* in the sales process happens when the customer is not really interested in what you have to say. It's a polite way of saying, "I don't think you can help me," or "I don't need what you're selling."

For customers, a problem can only exist when the current situation is not working. A stall simply means you have not found a problem the customer wants to fix. Your role as a salesperson, therefore, is to create an environment in which the customer is not satisfied with an existing situation. When a customer recognizes that what he has today is not good enough, you will have his interest.

Gain the Prospect's Interest

To combat the stall, create a series of interest statements that engage the prospect's focus on a problem you can solve. Each interest statement should contain the following elements:

- **State one of your big fat claims.** This gets the customer to focus on a problem he might be having. How do you know which claim to make? Do your homework before any sales call. Industries and companies all suffer from the same problems; however, the ways they fix them usually are different. Make sure you have a list of claims ready for each customer.

- **Link the big fat claim to a statement of fact.** You just made a claim; now you have to give a compelling reason why. Use the word "because" to tie something about your product or service to the prospect's problem. In other words, what fact or feature of your product or service allows you to make the claim?

- **State a logical benefit.** This answers the question, "So what?" Let the customer know what the fact or feature does. You don't have to be fancy or persuasive at this point. Just give the customer an idea of an advantage he will receive if he uses your product or service.

- **Tie his problem to your solution.** What does this really mean to him? Let the customer know he can expect some real benefits by finding out more. This is the part of the interest step that makes your product or service personal. It answers the question the customer always asks: "What's in it for me?"

- **Make it real, give an example.** Do you believe everything you hear? Of course not! To build credibility into your claims, give a relevant example. Has a past customer benefited from your offering? What results did he experience? A recognized third party reference is a great way to build trust into any sales call.

Do your homework. Before your next sales call, research the customer, his industry and his market. Make a quick list of the potential problem areas, and design five to ten interest statements that give the customer a reason to continue the sales call. Here's what an interest statement looks like when it's finished.

> "We can reduce the time it takes to complete your payroll each week by 20%, because our online Payroll Calculator allows you to calculate a pay statement quickly and accurately using the most up-to-date Federal and State tax regulations. The tax tables are always current and accurate, no matter what part of the country you are located in. What this means to you is increased productivity, and reduced costs for your payroll department. Some of our other clients, like XYZ Company, have already seen savings just like this."

Don't make the mistake of jumping into the presentation without first gaining the prospect's interest in hearing what you have to say. Without an interest statement, anything you say goes in one ear and out the other.

This relationship between buyer and seller is based on a win-win philosophy. If the customer has a problem and you have a solution, you can act together to make things better. When you create real interest up front, and remove the stalls from your sales process, customers will be hungry to hear your presentation, and will have a real sense of urgency about buying. ■

James Maduk is founder of the Online Selling University. For biographical and business information, see page 271.

Editor's Note: Art Sobczak's direct, tell-it-like-it-is style delivers a much-needed wake up call to many salespeople and their managers. He's got a very useful list for you of dialing "do's and don'ts."

Cold Calling Do's and Don'ts
by Art Sobczak

As an outside salesperson, your income probably relies on getting in front of new prospects. Yet many reps would rather have their fingernails slowly pulled out than make cold calls. It's no wonder. With all the resistance-inducing techniques out there, most salespeople set themselves up for failure. Like everything else in sales, successful cold calling depends on knowing what to do and when, then following through in a consistent manner. Here are some commonsense "do's" and "don'ts" to help you set more quality appointments on cold calls.

- **Do get information first.** The more you know about your prospect before placing a cold call, the better your chances of securing an appointment. Information helps you prepare a customized opening, and ask better questions. Plus, you impress the prospect by showing you've done your homework. If you have to ask, "Uh, what do you guys do there?" you label yourself as a time-wasting, self-interested peddler.

How do you gather this information? By working with the screener, or anyone who answers the phone. To get that person on your side, try the following approach:

> "I hope you can help me. I'm looking for the name of the person who handles exterior maintenance and landscaping for your building. (After getting the name, continue.) Thank you. So that I'm better prepared when I speak with him, there's probably some information you can help me with first."

Then ask several questions of the person on the phone, being respectful of his time as well. In this manner, you get most of your qualifying questions answered by people other than the decision-maker *before* making your cold calls.

- **Don't send information before the cold call.** Busy decision-makers toss bulging packages of unsolicited literature with form letters straight into the trash (or hopefully, recycling). No matter how many times you send that package, they're not going to open it. Therefore, starting a cold call with, "I sent you a letter, didja get it?" almost never elicits a favorable response.

- **Don't believe cold calling is just a numbers game.** The lottery is a numbers game. Cold calling for appointments is a *quality* game. Avoid burning through the prospect list as fast as you can, expecting that your number will eventually be drawn. Instead, approach each call with an attitude of accomplishment and desire.

- **Don't ask for a decision at the opening of a cold call.** Never open a cold call by including the goofy phrase, "…and I'd like to drop by Tuesday at two o'clock. Or would four o'clock be better?" People resist making those kinds of decisions before they see any value. Also, avoid the equally inane question, "If I could show you a way to save money, you would, wouldn't you?" No one likes to be "techniqued." The only way people will consider investing time with you is if they see some value in doing so.

- **Do have an interest-creating opening for your cold call.** Here's one you might be able to adapt.

> "Ms. Bigg, I'm John Brown with ABC Company. My company specializes in (fill in with the ultimate result customers want and get from you, for example, helping garden centers generate more business during the off-season). Depending on what you're doing now, and your objectives, this might be something worth taking a look at. I'd like to ask a few questions, to see if you'd like more information."

- **Do ask questions on the cold call.** Some pundits suggest quickly going for the appointment on a cold call, and never divulging information. Bunk! Those are people who probably feel insecure about their inability to communicate by phone. If someone doesn't have potential, I want to find that out *now*, at my office, rather than schlepping across town or country to find out. And if the prospect is qualified and has interest, I can pique his curiosity by phone, and pre-sell him on what we'll speak about when I arrive. For example:

  "Pat, based on what you've told me, it looks like you could show quite a significant labor savings with a system like ours. The best thing for us to do would be to get together, so I can ask a few more questions about your operation, and show you some of our options, to see if we have a fit. How about next week?" (Then narrow down a time that's convenient for both of you.)

- **Do make a confirmation call after the cold call.** Some might suggest this gives prospects a chance to back out and cancel the appointment, which is true. However, if they are of this mindset, either they will not be there when you arrive, or they will not give you the time of day. A follow-up phone call gives you a chance to address either situation, and save time.

Above all, *do* keep cold calling, and don't let a "no" get you down. The last call has nothing to do with the next one, unless you let negative feelings strangle your attitude. Talking to people generates income; avoiding the phone, stuffing envelopes, and walking around do not. To maintain a positive attitude, set a secondary objective, such as simply qualifying someone as a prospect, so you can achieve a success of sorts on every call. ∎

Art Sobczak is president of Business By Phone Inc. For biographical and business information, see page 274.

Editor's Note: Tina LoSasso has over 20 years' experience in publishing, marketing, and business development. She has taught marketing and business planning for one of the fastest-growing real estate companies in the United States. She was vice president of sales for a publishing company with a national bestseller. She will give you expert advice on how to convert Internet inquiries into paying customers.

Making the Most of Internet Inquiries
by Tina LoSasso

When someone calls to ask about your product or services, you know *exactly* what to ask, what to say, and how to follow up. Are you as confident, and effective, responding to an Internet inquiry? Without the benefit of talking with the prospect directly, the contact can feel colder than a cold call. As more consumers and businesses research and purchase via the Internet, you can't afford to mishandle these inquiries. To respond in a professional manner, and convert more Internet inquiries into customers, keep these guidelines in mind:

- **To call, or not to call?** Some salespeople don't respond to Internet inquiries because they think they're a waste of time. Others reason, "They emailed me, so they must be expecting me to email them back." When someone asks for information via email, you should respond via email. But what's stopping you from calling them as well? Imagine the impression you'll make: responsive, helpful, and efficient. A word of caution: you must have a *valid* reason to call. Restating the information provided in the email, or interrogating the prospect about his company, budget or time frame, are *not* valid reasons: they're harassment. Telling the prospect all about your company won't cut it either. Instead, consider carefully what you need to know in order to propose the best solution, then ask about that information.

- **Respond in Internet time.** Internet time is roughly equivalent to the speed of light. Thanks to email and instant messaging, people expect everything right now. Accordingly, prospects expect a quick response to their email inquiries. If you don't have enough information to propose a solution, let the prospect know that you're working on it, and when he can expect to hear from you. No one wants to be left hanging.

Customers also expect "24/7" response—day or night, every day of the week—and automated replies don't count. You probably check emails while on the road, over the weekend, and late at night. If you're receiving inquiries after-hours, chances are your buyers are working, too. They will appreciate a response from you, even if you're only acknowledging their inquiry. Let them know when you'll get back to them with the requested information.

- **Don't be too quick on the draw.** Wanting to respond quickly is no excuse for poor grammar, misspellings, and bad form. Proofread your response carefully before sending it. It's easy to miss errors on a computer screen. Try this: print out your draft and read it aloud to catch any mistakes, missed words, or poor syntax. Your email response will create your prospect's first impression of you, so make it a good one!

- **Be detached.** An Internet inquiry is a dream come true: an interested prospect contacting you! You probably can't wait to email a proposal, product specifications, company brochure, comparison chart, product brochure and lists of happy customers. But if you send all those attachments, your email may not get through the prospect's spam filter; it could take forever to be received, and even longer to download. To avoid coming across like an inconsiderate klutz, send a brief reply. If you have a short proposal, include it in the body of the email, not as an attachment. Let the prospect know that you'll send the collateral material he requested in a separate email. If he didn't request it, don't send it!

- **Make an impression.** Buyers who email inquiries are probably searching numerous websites besides yours. After awhile, they blur together. Make it easy for the buyer to recall your site, and why he requested information from you in particular. Remind him who you are by including your company tagline, and a link to your site. If the inquiry came from an industry bidding site, take additional steps to distinguish yourself, keeping in mind that the prospect knows nothing about you, not even your company name. To stand out from the potential dozens of replies the prospect will receive, bypass your normal form-letter response, and personalize your reply. Focus on your special ability to meet the prospect's particular request, and give him a reason to remember you.

As a salesperson, you probably feel more comfortable speaking with prospects directly, because you can easily establish rapport and rely on instant feedback to guide the conversation. Email communication robs you of those advantages, but it does not have to rob you of opportunity. Follow these guidelines, and you will convert more Internet inquiries into customers. ∎

Tina LoSasso is managing editor at SalesDog.com. For biographical and business information, see page 270.

Editor's Note: The first time Tom Freese exceeded his sales quota by 200%, his bosses were sure it was a fluke, so they raised his quota. Tom doubled it. In fact, he doubled his quota for the next seven years straight. After 17 years of working in the trenches of corporate sales and sales management, Tom packaged his unique sales approach as Question Based Selling. He's spent 10 years teaching his method to clients like Cisco Systems, Hewlett-Packard, IBM, and Sun Microsystems. Let him teach you how to refocus your sales approach.

Why Sales 101 No Longer Works
by Tom Freese

Ironic, isn't it? Over the last 15 years, the selling environment has changed dramatically for most companies, but the world of strategic sales training has stayed pretty much the same. It's like the whole country has started speaking Chinese, and we're still teaching English. Consequently, salespeople have to work much harder to penetrate new accounts, while prospective customers are working even harder to keep salespeople at bay.

Don't blame the customer. In the past decade, downsizing and acquisitions have burdened corporate decision-makers with greater responsibility, often without the benefit of additional resources. Meanwhile, workloads continue to increase, competitors are getting hungrier, and the overall pace of business has quickened. Even if they wanted to, customers simply cannot afford to spend time with every salesperson who comes calling.

Customers are also less accessible. In the past, salespeople could build relationships with the gatekeeper in their target accounts, knowing that these relationships would eventually get them in to see the decision-maker. In today's world, however, electronic devices have replaced most gate-keepers; you can't build a meaningful relationship with a voicemail system. Technological innovations such as email, cellular phones, digital pagers, and the Internet have given customers the freedom to execute their job functions away from their desks, which means potential customers are less likely to pick up the telephone when you call.

Many prospects are reluctant to pick up the telephone at all. The recent economic expansion means more vendors offering more solutions than ever. Consequently, decision-makers are inundated with a barrage of sales callers all competing for the same thing: a chunk of the prospect's budget, as well as a slice of his time and attention. Some sales organizations address this problem by encouraging their salespeople to be more aggressive. "If the going gets tough," chants the sales manager, "then we, as salespeople, need to be even tougher." *But people don't like to be pushed.* If our telephone rings during dinner and a salesperson on the line tries to be "more aggressive" with me, he will irreparably harm any chance he had of making a sale.

Clearly, the business world has changed dramatically in the last 20 years. And in my opinion, many old-school selling techniques no longer apply. Most prospects are onto the tricks, such as calling after hours to avoid the gatekeeper, or leaving voicemail messages saying, "So-and-so told me to call." They also know the Ben Franklin Close, the Alternate Choice, and Feel-Felt-Found. Salespeople and sales managers are increasingly frustrated with traditional methods. Teaching them to be just like everyone else puts them at a competitive disadvantage. When a salesperson is perceived to be the same as everyone else, he is, by definition, merely average, and his chances of winning are significantly diminished. Prospects and customers usually do not buy average products from average salespeople.

While the business environment has changed, the following fundamentals of selling remain the same:
- Salespeople must uncover needs before they can provide solutions.
- The product or service being offered must be cost-justifiable.
- The salesperson with the best relationship has the greatest chance of winning the business. People still buy from people.

However, the paradigms of the strategic sale have shifted significantly, and *differentiation* is now the key.

Everyone wants to have good relationships with lucrative prospects in order to uncover needs, present solutions, and secure commitments. However, establishing mutual relationships with new prospects has grown increasingly difficult. Just because a salesperson wants to ask questions does not mean his prospects and customers will want to respond. What makes prospects and customers want to respond? Salespeople must first earn the right to engage. If credibility is the key to building effective relationships, then the question becomes: *What are you doing differently than your competitors to establish credibility in your targeted prospect accounts?* Claiming to have the best product won't work, because everyone claims to have the best product—which, once again, makes you average.

Leveraging curiosity to fuel the sales process is another paradigm shift, but one that makes absolute sense. If a prospective customer is not curious, it becomes very difficult to secure his time or attention. On the other hand, a curious prospect will want to engage in a conversation about his needs and your solutions in order to satisfy his curiosity. Now the question becomes: *What are you doing to leverage curiosity in the sales process?*

If you're still using Sales 101 strategies in an advanced sales world, don't be surprised if you fail to earn a passing grade. Instead, focus on differentiating yourself from the competition and leveraging your customers' curiosity—and you'll go straight to the head of the class. ∎

Tom Freese is founder and president of QBS Research, Inc. For biographical and business information, see page 267.

Editor's Note: Dianna Booher was teaching a novel-writing course when she discovered that most of her students weren't taking the course to write a romance novel, but to learn how to write a simple business letter. She went on to get her Masters, and authored her first book on business writing. Once she taught her students to write letters, she realized they needed help with proposals, so she wrote that book. Then they needed help with presentations—and 42 books later, Dianna's sharing with you her secrets of persuasive presentations.

Ten Tips for Persuasive Presentations
by Dianna Booher

"Well, good morning. We appreciate the opportunity to meet with you today. My name is Simon Shultz, Business Development Manager for Intuit World, and I'd like to start by introducing the rest of my team to you. Starting from my left is Angela Hospitch, systems engineer for the TZ500. Next is Saynar Beneviden, project manager for several current client projects, and then Nancy Lauterbach, our COO. They're here to help me answer any specific questions you have today. Now, with the introductions out of the way, what I'd like to do first is tell you a little about who we are and what we do… ."

Another day, another proposal, another supplier, another *boring* presentation. And if the parade has been going on for a couple of days, or even a few hours, you can understand how buyer weariness quickly sets in. Clients and prospects will never come right out and tell you, "I'm bored!" But if you pay attention, you can easily sense their frustration. How can you make your presentation stand out from the crowd of competitors clamoring for the same business? Try the following suggestions:

- **Influence, don't just inform.** One of the biggest hindrances to selling success is being informative rather than persuasive. Information overwhelms people. Your role as a salesperson is to take available information, and make it come alive for your buyers. This requires using all five "Prongs of Persuasion":

1.) **Word choice.** Use positive, specific, precise words.

2.) **Rhetoric.** Powerful phrasing and graceful grammar pack a punch on a buyer's memory.

3.) **Feelings.** Strive to evoke feelings of pleasure, fear, safety, discomfort, pride, acceptance, rejection, or prestige in the client.

4.) **Reasoning and conclusions.** These are drawn from facts, information, opinions, or ideas.

5.) **Trustworthiness.** To influence people, you must create trust in you and your organization's principles, values, and integrity.

Effective persuasion requires using the best words, establishing credibility for you and your organization, and identifying the best strategies for each buyer, whether that is an appeal to emotion, logic, or a combination of the two.

- **Act against your own self-interest.** Making buyers aware of decisions made in their best interests is a great way to establish credibility and build the relationship. You may make those kinds of decisions routinely, but buyers need to know when you do; this builds trust for larger issues. For example, suppose the buyer is selecting tile for break rooms and restroom facilities throughout his buildings, and has already made it known he likes the best of everything. The color choices are black and beige, with a surcharge of 10% for black. Assuming the most expensive is the best, the buyer selects black. But you know customers have complained that black scratches more readily and requires more care than the lighter color. In this case, you may suggest that beige might be a better choice in high-traffic areas. Such candid advice leads to increased trust, but only if the buyer is subtly made to understand that you decided to share this information at your own expense.

- **Use the "experience" factor.** Buyers can argue about your facts, data, surveys, and research. They can disagree that your products or services outshine the competition. They can even question whether your offering will resolve their problem. But no one can dispute your experience when you state an opinion or respond to a question during your presentation. For example, suppose your buyer asks, "I think customizing the assessment is a waste of time. Why are you thinking we need a customized version added to our intranet before we roll this out to our own customers?" You respond, "The final decision has to be yours, of course. It will delay the project approximately two months. In handling these projects for more than 70 clients during the last two years, I can recall only two clients who skipped that phase. Both regretted the decision, because their own employees proved to be a great cross-section of the population for testing user acceptance. I offer that experience for your consideration." Your experience is your experience. It can be accepted or rejected, but it is still your experience—and as such, is irrefutable.

- **Tell failure stories.** We all have learned to tell success stories. But there is also power in telling case histories about clients who did not enjoy stellar success with your product or service—*if* their lack of success was due to their own decision-making and not your product or service. Failure stories can underscore what other customers did wrong, for example: waiting too long to buy, not using your design team to install and customize their product, not buying a warranty. They also help prospects avoid repeating those mistakes, and add credibility to your success stories. One caution: never use names with the failure stories, because prospects may fear that you will tell others of their own mistakes if they buy.

- **Prefer understatement to overstatement.** When my teenaged son interviewed for a job as a grocery stocker, he had to take an honesty test asking if he had ever cheated on an exam, shoplifted, or done things of that nature. He feared that by answering "no" to all the questions, he might have hurt his chances by sounding like he was too good to be true. He got the job, but his concern showed an astute observation about human nature.

If your product or service seems too good to be true, prospects will automatically discount it. Therefore, it's better to understate the product a bit in order to minimize the prospect's natural skepticism. Always present the range of results you have achieved, and can document. It is generally better to promise only the minimum gains. Otherwise, you set up the client to be disappointed. If clients consider the minimum gains to be worthwhile, the maximum gains will be the extra benefit that turns them into long-term fans.

- **Know when to use exact numbers, and when to round them.** Exact numbers are more credible because they can be verified more easily, and either confirmed or discounted. Rounded numbers are easier to remember. Provide specific numbers the first time you cite results or outcomes, and summarize with rounded numbers when repeating the data.

- **Make statistics and facts experiential.** People digest numbers with great difficulty. Pie charts and bar graphs help, but it pays to go beyond them. For example, randomly survey your committee of buyers by asking them to raise their hands in response to a few questions. Then compare your findings to the random survey you did previously of their entire organization. Are they typical of the rest of the employee population? If so, how? Supporting statistics lend credibility to what you say, but do all you can to help your buyers digest them.

- **Never shy away from the underdog position.** Some people love rooting for the underdog. Consider acknowledging that you are the lesser-known brand and supplier, and focus on the effort you intend to expend for the client because of your one-down situation. Avis has done very well using underdog status as its brand.

- **Plant questions you would like competitors to address.** As you present your solutions, subtly bring up issues that should raise red flags in your buyers' minds about your competitors. Never challenge or attack competitors directly. Instead, mention issues in your key areas of strength that if not handled well, could suggest pitfalls to your buyers. Raising these issues suggests to your buyers that they should ask your competitors about the same concerns.

- **Never just walk through your proposal; give a guided tour.** You have no control over what your buyers hear or pay attention to while you talk. In fact, your proposal will compete with you for attention. For example, while you are on page two, your buyers may be checking out the pricing section on page eight. So carefully select which parts of your proposal to present orally. If you want to refer your buyers to a specific page, do so after making your key point about that page.

Clients are not likely to buy from anyone who puts them to sleep with a dull, boring presentation. Stop giving clients the same tired spiel, and spice up your presentation by using the techniques listed above. Your clients will appreciate the change of pace, and your bottom line will appreciate the increased sales that result from differentiating your company from all the competitors in your field. ■

Dianna Booher is founder of Booher Consultants. For biographical and business information, see page 264.

Editor's Note: A sales strategist and business advisor, Jill Konrath speaks frequently to corporate sales forces and industry associations. Jill shares some insights here on establishing value.

Value is in the Eye of the Beholder
by Jill Konrath

Like beauty, value is in the eye of the beholder. Salespeople often try to inpose their own definition of value in a selling situation. But the reality is that your customers (and nobody else) decide when a product or service has value to them. Customers fall into three categories based on their perceptions of value. For some, value is intrinsic to the product or service. For others, it depends on how the product is used. For a third group, value lies in the strategic relationship between the two organizations. Let's take a look at each of these groups.

Commodity Buyer

Commodity buyers know exactly what they want and how to use it; they don't need sellers to explain the details. They typically value low cost and no hassles. They don't want to pay any more than necessary, and they want the buying experience to be as fast and painless as possible. To succeed with commodity buyers, pull as much cost as you can out of your supply chain, and make it simple, simple, simple to do business with your company. Give these customers an 800 number, send them a quick quote, or make it easy to order online, and they are happy.

When ordering things like contact lenses and office supplies, most people are commodity buyers. As a seller, there is little you can do to create value except make it cheaper and easier to order and deliver goods to their door, with easy returns if necessary.

Strategic Partner

These people are looking far beyond the scope of your products or service toward a strategic partnership with your entire company. Their focus is on how best to leverage their organization's core competencies with yours. These buyers value multi-layered, intimate and strategic relationships between both organizations, with mutual investment in joint projects. By merging systems and processes, they hope to accomplish more than either organization could alone.

Working with both strategic partners and commodity buyers requires a major corporate commitment much greater than the scope of any one seller. If your company cannot or will not streamline operations and cut costs for the commodity buyer, don't waste your time selling to him. And if your company is unwilling to commit to being a strategic partner, no matter how great a seller you are, these buyers will not be interested in working with you. By yourself, you cannot create the value they need. Fortunately, most sellers deal with a third type of buyer, with whom they can personally create the value needed to win the business.

"I Need to Make a Sound Decision" Buyer

These buyers are either spending a lot of money on a decision, or they don't know everything there is to know about what they are buying. Typically, their decision process is complex, involves multiple decision-makers, and takes place over an extended period of time. Sellers can create a great deal of value for these buyers through what they personally bring to the relationship. These buyers value sellers who help them understand their problems in greater depth, and have insight into the challenges they face. They prefer sellers who share relevant information regarding "best practices", and keep them up-to-date on industry trends and how others are addressing them. These buyers also want sellers to help them find ways around the obstacles they encounter, develop innovative approaches to resolving their business issues, and propose new ways to do more with the same investment.

For example, suppose your company handles direct mailing programs for customers. What could you do personally as a seller to create value in the relationship?

- Share ideas about other companies' direct mail programs: what works, and what doesn't.

- Help customers find ways to increase the results of their existing direct mail programs.
- Show customers how to reduce the overall costs of the program while maintaining its effectiveness and integrity.
- Let customers know what their competitors are doing.
- Develop ways to increase the quality of their database.
- Work collaboratively with related vendors, such as agencies and telemarketing firms, to facilitate the handoffs.
- Help customers establish new, important criteria for their vendor selection process.
- Propose ideas for new programs to help them achieve their desired marketing results.
- Act as an advocate within their organization on issues impacting the customer.
- Suggest ways to improve workflow between all companies and internal departments working on the project.

To succeed with the "I want to make a sound decision" buyer, you must bring more to the relationship than just your standard product or service. You must create value with each and every customer interaction, so that even though your customer could buy cheaper elsewhere, he will want to keep you around because your ideas, insights, and knowledge are invaluable to him. This is what selling looks like in the new sales paradigm, and this is what creating value is all about! ■

Jill Konrath is Chief Sales Officer of Selling to Big Companies. For biographical and business information, see page 270.

Editor's Note: When Ron Karr told his bosses he wanted to leave his sales management position to start his training and consulting business, they didn't rant, rave or even beg him to stay: they funded him. (Sounds to me like a guy who knows how to build relationships!) Founded in 1988, Ron says Karr Associates has helped clients like Hertz, HP, and MetLife add over $500 million to their bottom lines.

Do You Believe in Magic?
by Ron Karr

Do you believe in magic? If so, you may need to consider a different profession, because there's nothing magical about closing a sale. Many books have been written and seminars delivered on the development of closing techniques. However, most of the advice regarding these so-called techniques is ludicrous. "Presto, change-o!" they promise. "Say the secret word (or phrase) and people will magically want to buy from you!" But the commitments you win by reciting high-handed or manipulative phrases are likely to be short-lived.

Any experienced salesperson will attest that closing is not a single action or statement, but the carefully cultivated result of a long-term process. Closing really means gaining full participation in a shared objective. The goal in the sales process is for the prospect to invite the salesperson to conclude the deal. When the relationship has been developed properly, that will be the natural conclusion. So how can you improve your closing ratio without resorting to sales hocus-pocus? Three essential steps are necessary to reach the appropriate conclusion to sales discussions.

Don't Get Spooked By "No"

"No" answers arise early and often in our discussions with potential customers, even in situations where we eventually get the business. Why? Because "no" is the answer of lowest risk. When people are not yet convinced to make a commitment to buy, they will say "no." However, that does not mean they will *never* buy from us. Too many salespeople respond to a "no" answer either by withdrawing from meaningful discussions with the prospect, or turning up the heat by chattering endlessly about features, functions, and benefits. In reality, all we need to do when we hear "no" is *find out what the customer perceives as missing*.

To turn a "no" into a "yes," be sure to include the *value proposition*, which is a formal recommendation that satisfies the wants and needs of the buyer while providing the impetus to accept the offer. In order to get a "yes" answer, the value proposition must offer benefits in at least one of these four key areas:

- improving profitability
- improving productivity/saving time
- reducing costs
- gaining a competitive edge.

Always remember that "no" need not be the final answer—especially if you can recreate a value proposition that is attractive to your client.

Ask Issues-based Questions

Issues-based questions focus on a specific kind of challenge the prospect faces in one of the key areas mentioned above. They help clarify what the prospect may think is missing, and encourage him to reveal specifics about that challenge. Let's assume you know a prospect is considering various retirement options, and you want to position yourself as a valuable resource to provide the best retirement solution. Start your interview with issues-based questions like, "Tell me, Ms. Smith: what are the three most important things you want your investments to accomplish for you?" Or, "Tell me, Ms. Smith, what are the three most important characteristics of the lifestyle you'd like to lead once you've retired?"

Issues-based questions garner time and attention, and almost always elicit responses that tell us where the other person wants to go. They focus the conversation on the client instead of on the sale, so we can uncover objectives such as, "I want to do a lot of traveling during retire-ment," or "I want a good college education for my children." Emphasizing these issues opens doors and portrays us as a potential resource, someone who is more interested in meeting the client's objec-tives than overcoming her objections.

Ask Clarification and Consequence Questions

Issues-based questions should be followed by two other categories of questions: clarification and consequence. *Clarification questions* are the ones we ask to make sure we understand the other person's terms. For example, "Ms. Smith, when you say 'a good college education,' what does that mean to you? What schools are you hoping to be able to afford?" These questions ensure that we understand the client's objectives completely, and can respond with the best possible solutions.

Consequence questions point to the perceived value of a solution and highlight the consequences a customer will experience if he rejects the recommendation. They depend on the following formula:

Cost of No Change – Cost of Change = Perceived Value

Consequence questions do not emerge out of the blue. Rather, they are proposed after careful determination of where the prospect wants to go (based on issues-based questions), what he really wants, and how he wants it (based on clarification questions). A consequence question might sound like this: "Tell me, Mr. and Mrs. Jones, what would happen if, for some reason, you were not able to afford an Ivy League education for your children? What impact would that have on their futures?" Uncovering the impact sets us up to make a formal recommendation. The client has clearly stated the problem; now it is our job to provide a solution.

When you have effectively interviewed the prospect using issues-based questions, asking for clarification, concluding with consequence questions, and forming your recommendations as a value proposition, typically people will realize it is in their best interest to move ahead with your proposal, and you can expect to be invited to close the sale. The prospect will either offer to get started, or you will be able to close by saying something like, "Mr. and Mrs. Jones, to start preparing for your children's future, which option do feel more comfortable moving ahead with?"

In the end, there are no tricks to making the close easy. Put away your magic wand, and stop trying to pull rabbits out of your hat. Instead, focus on solid interviewing, careful listening, and presenting solutions that are the most viable course of action for your client. By doing so you will avoid a transaction close and build a long-term relationship, helping your clients make smart choices so they can achieve the outcomes they want. ∎

Ron Karr is founder of Karr Associates Inc. For biographical and business information, see page 270.

Editor's Note: Keith Rosen is a master-certified sales and business coach, corporate trainer, keynote speaker, and the author of several bestselling books on sales. After the devastation of 9/11, it was Keith Rosen who developed an internal executive coaching initiative for leaders in the intelligence community. As the 'go to guy' for advice, guidance, and coaching, Keith continues to reshape the landscape of companies worldwide. Keith has been featured in Selling Power, The New York Times, The Washington Times, Inc. Magazine, *and* The Wall Street Journal.

Are You a Yesaholic?
by Keith Rosen

Have you ever made promises you could not keep, or struggled to honor? Do you have a hard time telling customers the truth about how long a project may actually take, or cost? Is your schedule frequently overbooked? Have you ever withheld information that you knew your customer wanted or needed to hear because you feared a confrontation, or losing the sale? Do you believe you need to please people for them to like you? Have you ever said "yes" when you were better off saying "no"? If you answered yes to one or more of these questions, you may be a "yesaholic"—which means you may be causing far more damage to your important customer relationships than you realize.

When you instinctively say "yes" to someone, without considering whether you can realistically deliver on your timeline or expectations, you always have the best intentions. You sincerely believe you can fulfill your promise, and you have no desire to let the customer down. Yet when you promise to deliver on something (completing a project, meeting with a customer) and are unable to honor that commitment, the ramifications go far beyond the initial disappointment of the broken promise.

A few years ago, my wife and I hired a contractor to build us a new home. Although he did fabulous work, he also failed to honor any of his timelines. As a result, a four-month project turned into an agonizingly long nine-month project. Ironically, the contractor thought he was the only one who accrued expenses for every additional day the job took to complete. In reality, our family paid a much steeper price.

The truth is, the house was always a nine-month project, but our contractor did not want to tell me that. Instead, he thought that telling me what I wanted to hear would make me happy. But thanks to his inability to tell me what I *needed* to hear, I got to extend our stay in temporary housing, pay additional monthly storage charges, and pay my mortgage and utilities bills without living in my home. His need to say "yes" disrupted the lives of everyone in our family, and even though the finished home looked beautiful, his approach to managing client expectations did not make me very happy.

I'm not suggesting that our contractor deliberately lied, or did something illegal or immoral. What I *am* suggesting is that being honest about what you know to be true, and sharing this with your customer—even if the customer may not like what you have to say—is the most effective strategy to manage the expectations of your customers and reduce time consuming problems. You will make more money, have happier customers, generate more referrals, and deal with fewer headaches by telling the truth, and learning to occasionally say "no."

The Courage to Say "No"

Saying "no" is often perceived as a bad thing. After all, no salesperson wants to risk letting the customer down, looking bad, or losing a sale. The irony is, when you always say "yes" (thinking you'll keep the customer happy) and do not follow through with your commitments, you create what you wanted to avoid from the start. In other words, by continually over-committing, you let the customer down and create stressful situations that cost time and money. By contrast, being honest and honoring your boundaries by saying "no" is a very attractive trait. People respect those who have strong boundaries.

The next time someone asks you to do something—including those promises you make to yourself—take the time to process the request and say, "Let me check my schedule and get back to you," or, "Thanks for the opportunity. I will consider it." Then ask yourself five important questions before responding:

- Is this something I really want to do?
- Is this something I have to do? Does it support my goals, responsibilities, lifestyle, and priorities?

- Can I meet this person's expectations?
- Do I really have time for this? Are there other activities I have committed to that have priority?
- What is a reasonable deadline/expectation I can commit to in an absolute worst-case scenario?

By planning for the worst, you build buffers into your schedule that will enable you to handle unforeseen problems while still honoring your commitments. As a result, you look like a hero, and you build trust in the relationship: two very important outcomes for anyone in sales.

How important are these questions? It all depends on how important the customer and/or relationship is to you. In terms of hard dollars, asking these questions would have saved my contractor more than $30,000. More important, they would have maintained the integrity of our relationship rather than destroy it. As things stand now, I would certainly hesitate to recommend him to anyone, even though the quality of his work is excellent.

After practicing this process a few times, you will quickly see the benefits. Your life will become simpler and easier as you eliminate the problems that result from over-committing. So learn to say "no", and start running your own life—or keep saying "yes", and let other people and circumstances run it for you. ■

Keith Rosen is president of Profit Builders LLC. For biographical and business information, see page 273.

Editor's Note: Art Sobczak is one of the premiere telesales trainers in the industry. He's not shy about picking up selling tips wherever he can—and he's sure that listening like a homicide detective will make a difference in your sales calls.

Listen Like a Homicide Detective
by Art Sobczak

Like millions of people, I'm a fan of talk radio. I was listening to my favorite show in the car one day when the featured guest was the head of the city's homicide unit. As he talked about techniques used to question crime suspects, my ears really perked up. At one point, he uttered a statement so profound and applicable to sales that had traffic not been so heavy, I would have pulled over to the side of the road immediately to write it down. Instead, I kept repeating it aloud so I wouldn't forget it. What did this policeman say that made such an impact on me? "When a suspect is talking, don't do or say anything to cause him to stop."

So true! And with potential customers, we have to go beyond the surface level of this statement to realize the inherent danger and potential damage that can be done. It's not just that the prospect stops talking. When you interrupt someone, you psychologically inhibit him from wanting to continue speaking. Do you know someone who dominates a conversation by jumping in with his thoughts before you've finished yours? If this happens frequently, you think, "Why bother? I'll just keep my thoughts to myself." The same thing happens when we continually interrupt customers during sales calls.

How do salespeople cause prospects and customers to stop talking once they've started on a train of thought? Here's how it happens, and what you can do instead.

- **Not responding to an answer with encouragement to continue.** Instead, listen reflectively. Encourage the prospect with statements like: "Go on," "Tell me more," or "Expand on that."

- **Following up the statement or answer with an unrelated question or comment that gets the customer off subject.** Instead, focus on every statement or answer like it is the tip of an iceberg, and your goal is to go deeper. Listen with the rapt attention of a kid entranced by a campfire story. Direct your next question so as to get to the next layer.
- **Responding to a statement or answer with too much of your own experience.** Empathy is good, but one-upmanship—"Well, let me tell you how big a fish *I* caught!"—does not build rapport with clients. Instead, prompt the customer to continue, while resisting the tendency to share your own experiences. You already know your own experiences; focus on what you want to learn from the client.

Interrupting customers won't land you in hot water with the police. But in the sales world, it is definitely a crime, punishable by disinterested prospects and lost sales. ■

Art Sobczak is president of Business By Phone Inc. For biographical and business information, see page 274.

see page 274.

Editor's Note: As semiconductor sales manager for Sprague Electric Company, Steve set company sales records. When he became director of sales and marketing for Vortech Corporation, sales increased by 300% in two short years. An entrepreneur, Steve successfully launched several businesses before opening his sales training and consulting firm in 1994. His clients?   Household names like AT&T, Chrysler, MCI, and United Airlines. Steve shows you how to get to exactly the right people—and they're not in the purchasing department.

Getting Past Purchasing
by Steve Waterhouse

One of the toughest challenges in today's selling environment involves getting past the buyer to the real decision-maker. Solving this puzzle represents one of the most important concerns for today's sales professional, because so much rests on reaching the real buyer. Why is it so important to get through to the true decision-maker? Because the typical purchasing department buyer lives to satisfy the written definitions of others, whereas the decision-maker lives to solve problems for his company and himself.

Only the true decision-maker can understand the total value that your offering brings to their company. Only the true decision-maker can appreciate that a partnering relationship with your company may be the best way to reach their goals. And only the true decision-maker can redefine his own needs based on your input and, as a result, end up buying something completely different from the initial specifications. Fortunately, the task of getting past the purchaser has been made easier as the complexity of the sale has increased. To get in front of more top decision-makers, try the following techniques:

It Would be Irresponsible

Too often, the buyer presents us with an RFP (request for proposal) or specification that someone else wrote. In the mistaken belief that he is doing his job, he attempts to block access to those who actually wrote these documents. However, in order to do *your* job, you must get through.

The first step involves determining what the original decision-maker might have been trying to accomplish when he wrote the specification. Imagine, for instance, that the specification is for new accounting software. While the specification calls out the requirements, it doesn't detail the problems the company is attempting to solve. It may not mention the new SEC requirements, or changes in board policies. Furthermore, the buyer could not possibly answer detailed questions about these issues.

Rather than allowing the customer to perceive you as a vendor of a simple product, define yourself as a provider of comprehensive solutions to complex problems. As such, you and your team are obligated to make the following request: "Since this software covers areas of legal and corporate compliance, it would be irresponsible of me to sell you something that might not comply. For that reason, we are required to conduct a brief needs analysis with the ultimate decision-makers."

This technique can work in a wide variety of situations. The power rests in your honest ability to position yourself as more than a vendor. By creating a situation in which the buyer feels obligated to connect you with the real decision-maker, you gain an advantage over all others. Warning: be sure you make the buyer a hero in the process. Let it be known to the higher-ups that the buyer's astute awareness of the ramifications of this purchase made it possible for you to do a better job for the client.

Muddy the Waters

Another way to get past the buyer involves creating a buying opportunity that requires authorization the buyer does not have. For example, the buyer may be authorized to purchase individual parts but not pre-assembled sub-assemblies. By presenting a compelling case for the purchase of pre-assembled sub-assemblies, you create a situation that requires the buyer to put you in touch with other decision-makers in the organization. You also may create a perfect excuse for going around the buyer. Since the buyer only buys parts, you must make other contacts to sell your assemblies.

This approach is ideal for companies which are combining several divisions with a "Team Selling" approach. Complex multi-divisional offerings usually look more like partnerships than purchases. For that reason, they must be addressed to higher-level decision-makers. What's in it for you? In a market where me-too products are subject to fierce price pressures, differentiation will allow you to stand out from the crowd, giving you an opportunity to sell your value and gain both margin and market share. If the competition continues to sell to the buyer and you sell to the higher-level decision-makers, you win. Higher-level decision-makers always trump buyers.

Complex sales result in unique, longer-term relationships and contracts. These higher-margin deals lock out the competition. Higher-level relationships also lead to broader opportunities and deals. When you are seen as a problem-solving resource, you will be given other opportunities to serve the client. Try these techniques on your toughest client this week. You will be amazed at how well they work. ■

Steve Waterhouse is CEO of the Waterhouse Group. For biographical and business information, see page 276.

Editor's Note: Bestselling author and speaker Tony Alessandra, PhD makes no bones about developing his street smarts growing up Italian-American in New York City. Is his negotiating style "I'll make him an offer he can't refuse"? Hardly. Though Tony indulges his playful side at the speaker's podium, he'll teach you how to bring trust, openness, credibility and honesty to the negotiating table.

Negotiating Win-Win Deals
by Tony Alessandra

Think about the last time you hammered out a deal with a new client. Did both parties leave the negotiations feeling good about the process? Or did each of you walk away muttering under your breath, "I'll never do business with *that* jerk again!" I believe there are two ways to negotiate: manipulatively or collaboratively. One typically leads to win-win results, the other to win-lose. The outcomes you get with customers and clients depend upon which approach you choose.

In manipulative negotiating, the focus is on single answers, and the goal is to win at all costs. The negotiators see each other as adversaries, and as a result, use hardball tactics like exerting power, using subterfuge, and hiding their nonverbal communications. Not surprisingly, manipulative negotiations are characterized by mistrust, tension, suspicion and animosity. They almost always end with hard feelings on somebody's part (usually the loser's). If you don't expect to do business with the other party again, manipulative negotiating may serve your needs. But over the long term, it's not a healthy business practice.

By contrast, collaborative negotiating is based on the notion that there are many ways to satisfy both parties' needs, not just one. Collaborative negotiators see the participants as problem-solvers looking for a mutually satisfactory solution. The focus is on exploring multiple options in order to come away with an equitable outcome for all parties. The process relies on trust, openness, credibility and honesty. At the conclusion of the deal, both sides walk away feeling that neither one was "had."

I also believe that when two people want to do business with each other, they will not let the details stand in the way. However, when two people do *not* want to do business with each other, the details will rarely pull the deal together. If somebody wants to do business with you, they are more apt to compromise, and less apt to seek unreasonable compromises. In that situation, collaborative negotiating always leads to a more mutually-satisfying agreement.

Collaborative Negotiating

Collaborative negotiating involves six basic steps: plan, meet, study, propose, confirm and assure. These steps can occur one at a time, or all together. In some cases, one or more steps may be skipped.

Planning consists of all the behind-the-scenes research and preparation you do before coming face-to-face with the other party. In the *meeting* phase, both parties determine how agreeable they are going to be with each other. Each side jockeys for position while trying to project credibility, authority, power, and the ability to back up promises. Both parties are also deciding, from the way the other looks, talks, and behaves, "Do I want to do business with you?" In the *study* phase, the parties exchange crucial information about what they are trying to accomplish, including end results, goals, needs, and objectives. Each side carefully assesses all the parameters of the other side's current situation. In this phase, the danger lies in missing the big picture by focusing too much on specifics. Parties shouldn't start looking for answers before understanding what the other side is trying to accomplish.

In the *proposing* phase, both sides work together to clarify the specifics: who will do what, when, where, how, and why. This is when contract details are negotiated and some of the fine points of negotiating come into play. During the *confirming* phase, contracts are signed and the first steps are taken towards implementation of the agreement. The *assuring* phase makes sure that everything comes off as planned, everyone lives up to their end of the agreement, the goods or services are delivered as promised, and payment is made in a timely manner.

To get the most from the collaborative negotiating process, use the following steps every time you sit down at the negotiating table:

1. Develop a negotiation strategy that clearly spells out what you will and will not do during the negotiations.

2. Collect as much background information as possible beforehand on the people and companies you will face.

3. Evaluate your competitive exposure. What are the odds that another firm will come up with a better offer than yours? This information can help establish your maximum and minimum positions.

4. Prepare and role-play with colleagues prior to your initial negotiation meeting. This gives you the confidence to face questions and situations you will need to handle.

5. Make sure your clothing, grooming, materials, handouts, preparation, and depth of knowledge project credibility, authority, and strength. This is where you start creating the confidence factor—because people do judge books by their covers. People will not negotiate seriously with you if they do not believe you have the power and credibility to make decisions.

6. Tailor your pace and presentation to the individual differences of the other people. People who are very relationship-oriented and low in assertiveness are called Relaters, and are primarily interested in relationships. Those who are people-oriented and highly assertive are called Socializers, and are interested in recognition. Task-oriented, highly-assertive people are Directors, who are concerned with getting results. Less assertive, task-oriented people are Thinkers, who like structure. A flexible approach to these different personality types will reduce tension and increase interpersonal trust, credibility, cooperation, and productivity.

7. Take time to study all dimensions of the other party's situation. Ask questions and listen with your ears and eyes. Try to determine the real results the other person wants to accomplish, not just his position or demands. Also, strive to uncover his decision-making criteria, his "must-haves," "should-haves," and "nice-to-haves." This will reveal his negotiation limits.

8. When presenting your desires/demands, try to relate them to the end results the other person is attempting to achieve. Show how your requests will also benefit the other party.

9. Negotiate the points of difference. Don't always go for low price unless that is your negotiation philosophy. Look for other points to negotiate.

10. Do not attack the other person's specific demands. Look behind them for objectives/end results.

11. Never defend your position. Instead, invite criticism and advice by asking, "What would you do if you were in my position?"

12. At the conclusion of the negotiations, make sure all parties fully and clearly understand who is to do what, when, where, how, and why.

Following these strategies will significantly improve your negotiating outcomes. Furthermore, your counterparts in the negotiation sessions will feel much better about you, the process, and the outcomes. Both parties will feel that a fair position was reached, one that was in the best interests of both sides. In other words, you will achieve a win-win outcome, which is the real bottom-line benefit of collaborative negotiating. ■

Tony Alessandra is president of AssessmentBusinessCenter.com. For biographical and business information, see page 264.

Editor's Note: Jon Brooks was director of inside sales for Telogy Incorporated, a high-technology financial services company. He grew the inside sales organization to upwards of 50 people across four different inside sales teams. He was responsible for 300% revenue growth in twelve months, accounting for $45M in revenue. Today Jon is a principal in Brooks Dreyfus, a specialized sales consulting firm which helps companies improve their telesales efforts.

Would *You* Return This Call?
by Jon Brooks

Suppose you came home from a hard day at work to find the following message on your answering machine:

> "Hello, Tony. This is your dentist calling. I'd like you to come in sometime next week so we can pull three of your front teeth. I'm not sure if you need them pulled or not, but we're having a special on extractions, and you won't want to miss it. We pull 'em faster and cheaper than the competition—so if you need more than three yanked, we can handle that as well. By the way, we're running a little low on Novocain, so you may have to go without it. But don't worry! It will only hurt for a few days. Give me a call back as soon as you get this message, so we can schedule an appointment. Looking forward to seeing you!"

Obviously, no dentist in his right mind would leave such a message. Nor would any right-thinking salesperson. Yet most salespeople's phone messages have the same effect on the listener as this one. They not only fail to generate interest in returning your call, they frequently cause recipients to actively consider changing phone numbers, so you can never contact them again.

Seriously, though, effective voicemails all have certain elements in common. To leave great voicemail messages that actually motivate prospects and clients to return your calls, I recommend the following:

- **Keep it short!** A voicemail should be no longer than 20 seconds—preferably less. It's much better to leave prospects wondering who you are and why you called, than for them to delete a long-winded message.

- **Arouse curiosity.** This is most important. Your only goal in leaving voicemails for cold prospects is to get them to return your call. If you tell them everything, they don't need to call you back. Instead, spark their interest by having them think about who you are. Sometimes, your vagueness creates interest in the prospect's mind. Pique their curiosity, and they will call you back.

- **Be different.** Think of all the voicemail messages you receive. Do they inspire you to call back? If not, leave messages that are completely different than the ones you receive. Uniqueness will grab a prospect's attention, and be more likely to compel him to return your call.

- **What's in it for them?** If you decide to leave additional information, give only information that demonstrates a clear benefit to the customer. What benefits of your product or service will intrigue him enough to call you back?

- **Warm up the call.** Take liberty in how you warm up the call. Use whatever you know about the company. Do you know other people at the company? Do you know what they do? Do you know their competitors? The more familiar you sound with the prospect and the company, the greater the chance he will return your call.

- **Be confident.** Don't *ask* prospects to call you back—*tell* them. You must believe you are doing them a favor by contacting them, not vice versa. Successful sales calls ensure parity between you and the prospect. Failed sales calls are those in which you assume a subordinate role.

- **Be creative.** Think of new and different approaches every day. Even voicemail messages that seem odd at first may be most effective in getting prospects to call you back.

- **Be prepared.** When customers do call back, make sure you can quickly and efficiently move into your sales pitch. Fumbling around, repeatedly asking their name, putting them on hold on while you bring their name up in the database, or trying to find questions you want to ask, will kill your credibility with customers. You should be able to easily and effectively move into a sales presentation with only pen and paper.

Keep in mind that no matter how much you improve the voicemails you leave prospects, most will not return your call. Therefore, you should not rely on voicemails to dramatically improve your selling results; the time you spend improving voicemails should be but a small part of your telesales efforts.

You may also want to think about other areas of your telesales organization that may be preventing you from maximizing the results of your sales efforts. For example, are you able to establish relationships with gatekeepers so they act as your advocate when you call a prospect? Or do they just dump you into voicemail because they consider you "just another sales guy." Are you improving your selling skills daily with ongoing training? Is your telesales organization designed in a way that identifies the hottest prospects, qualifies those prospects, and converts them to orders in the shortest amount of time?

These (and others) may be areas you want to evaluate in your telesales organization. Continual improvement in all areas from strategic (proper design of your telesales organization) to tactical (sales training) will help dramatically improve your sales results. ■

Jon Brooks is a founding partner of Brooks Dreyfus Consulting. For biographical and business information, see page 265.

Editor's Note: Everything changed for Ari Galper the day he hung up from what he thought was a well-received teleconference with some high-level executives. Instead of hanging up, though, Ari hit the mute button by mistake, and heard what they really thought of him. "So we're definitely not going to go with him," said the vice president. "But keep stringing him along. Get more information so we can get a better deal with another company." Once he got over the rejection, Ari realized he was selling the wrong way—focusing on his own agenda, not the prospect's issues. As a result, he created the Unlock the Game program, which he's taught for over five years to clients including AFLAC, Motorola, Pitney Bowes and State Farm Insurance.

Stop Your Sales Pitch, Start Your Conversation!
by Ari Galper

In baseball, the pitcher can't pitch until the umpire says, "Play ball!" In school, students can't start the exam until the teacher says, "Begin." At a stoplight, the driver can't drive until the light changes from red to green.

Why should it be any different in the sales world? When we first meet prospective clients, something inside us just can't wait to tell them all about the benefits of our wonderful product or service. We launch into a long-winded spiel about what we are selling, acting as if they've said, "So, tell me about your product or service," when, in fact, they haven't. If prospects haven't given us the green light, why do we think talking about what we are selling will engage them? Why don't we begin by talking about *them* first?

Traditional sales training teaches that we must be armed and ready to deliver a sales pitch the moment prospective clients show any interest in what we have to offer. Based on this thinking, many training programs spend a lot of time teaching us how to develop a sales pitch or "elevator speech." To be sure, you need to know all you can about your product or service if you intend to succeed. And you should be proud of what you sell, eager to tell prospects about it because you believe so strongly that everyone needs it. But when you deliver that information too early in your conversation, instead of capturing your prospect's interest, you trigger thoughts like, "Oh no. Here comes the sales pitch. And then he'll probably try to sell me on what he has to offer." As soon as a prospect's guard goes up, the frustrating sales game begins, in which you risk getting rejected, or prospects feel they are being "sold."

This traditional mindset gets us into trouble. Most of us work hard to distance ourselves from the negative image of a high-pressure salesperson. By launching into a discussion about our product before we've established integrity and trust, we create pressure, which inevitably causes prospective clients to retreat.

The solution? Try changing your mindset. Instead of relying on your product knowledge to spark prospect interest, try creating a conversation focused solely on discovering if prospective clients have a problem they want solved, and if they'll consider allowing you to solve it. To facilitate this shift, keep the following in mind:

- Before delivering your sales pitch, gain agreement on the problem to be solved.
- Analyze the reasons why current clients have purchased your product or service, and use those reasons as a basis for discussion with new prospects.
- Be ready to explain to prospects that you have no idea whether your product or service can help them until you both agree that there is a problem to be solved, and that they have the funds to solve it.

When prospective clients say, "Give me your sales pitch," stay centered. Disarm them by replying, "It would be a disservice to us both if I launched into a presentation before we determine if there's a good fit between us." Remember, selling is all about solving your clients' problems, not pitching them your solutions. Launching into a sales pitch too soon will inevitably trigger the cat-and-mouse game that all of us—even our prospective clients—are trying to end. ■

Ari Galper is founder of Reverse Selling. For biographical and business information, see page 268.

Editor's Note: After a twenty-year career in sales and sales management, Will Turner founded Dancing Elephants Achievement Group, an international sales training and consulting company. He is the co-author of Six Secrets of Sales Magnets. *Will is the co-creator of the Sales Magnetism training program, which creates a 56% increase in production in the first year for his average client.*

Does the Opposite Sex Drive You Crazy?
by Will Turner

Whether you believe that women are from Venus and men are from Mars (or someplace else in the solar system), there's no doubt that gender differences have a real impact on interpersonal communications. Men and women exhibit different conversational styles; both styles are equally valid. In the selling world, salespeople need to understand and adapt to these differences, in order to communicate more effectively.

According to Deborah Tannen, author of *Talking From 9 To 5: How Women's and Men's Conversational Styles Affect Who Gets Heard*, men use communication to maintain independence, while women use communication to maintain intimacy. Men often speak to establish status or hierarchy within a group, while women speak to connect, express feelings, and build rapport. Tannen labels these styles as "report-talk" for men and "rapport-talk" for women.

What does this mean in a sales relationship? Simply put, if you are dealing with someone of the opposite sex, you may have different communication styles. To be more effective, adapt your conversational style, or become more open to the style of the other person, making sure that your style fits the setting. As always, listen carefully and clarify. Never assume that you understand, or are understood, without appropriate probing.

Adjusting Your Approach

If you're a female salesperson calling on a male prospect, focus your talk on goal-oriented activities, tangible accomplishments, or problem solving. Observe and listen rather than processing out loud, and be succinct and bottom-line focused. Be careful not to offer help before it is asked for, as doing so may indicate a lack of trust in his ability. Above all, never force a man to talk if he is not ready.

If you are a male salesperson calling on a female prospect, ask what you can do to help, as she will interpret this as a show of support. Understand that women may process out loud as a way of including others and building relationships. Listen patiently to the stories of your prospect, even when you are anxious to get to the bottom line. Never short-circuit the opportunity to get to know your prospect.

As with any communication exchange, if you focus on listening, and follow the other person's signals, you will do fine. ■

Will Turner is president of Dancing Elephants Achievement Group. For biographical and business information, see page 275.

Editor's Note: Mark Shonka and Dan Kosch are co-presidents of IMPAX corporation, a sales consulting and training firm serving big-name clients like 3M, DuPont, Eli Lilly, IBM, and Microsoft. Together, they have more than 40 years' experience in direct sales, sales management, consulting and training. Mark and Dan co-authored Beyond Selling Value: A Proven Process to Avoid the Vendor Trap. *Here they share some up-to-the-minute information on maximizing your use of the Internet.*

Avoiding Internet Flameout
by Mark Shonka and Dan Kosch

When it comes to sales, playing with the Internet is like playing with fire. It sizzles with opportunity, especially for conducting research. With a few clicks of the mouse, you can access key management contacts, company news, annual reports and industry trends. It's all out there online, and accessible to everyone, including purchasing agents. And that's where you can get burned. Years ago, if purchasing agents needed details on product features and benefits, competitive information and industry trends, they had little choice but to call a sales professional. Now, all they have to do is surf the Net. If that isn't enough, they can also conduct online auctions and requests for proposals, where the lowest bidder wins the deal. Or they can execute blind Internet auctions that elevate commoditization to the next level, by making a potential customer completely anonymous.

In light of this, the Internet can easily subtract you from the purchasing equation altogether, and convert you to a mere vendor, whether you sell paper clips, computers or consulting. What's more, your most precious commodity—time—can easily go up in flames, if you answer every RFP and auction that flashes across your screen. That's why it's critical to be choosy about which Internet deals you pursue.

To determine which deals are worth your time, use the following criteria:
- The profile of your best customers. How well does the potential Internet opportunity fit that profile?
- The importance of relationships. Do you have any relationship with

the potential customer beyond the Internet, or are you an unknown?
- Your track record. Which deals do you consistently win, which do you consistently lose, and how does each online auction or request for proposal compare?
- The potential long- and short-term profitability of the deal. Could there be future opportunities beyond the initial sale?
- The logistics of the deal, urgency and budget.
- The organization's reputation. Is it known for being penny-wise and pound-foolish? Do they always buy based on price, even if it's clear they will lose money in the long run? If so, is the potential payback worth doing business with them?

With this information, you can determine which Internet opportunities are worth your energy—and just as important, which are not. Too many sales professionals waste time chasing smoke. Remember: being busy does not equal being productive. So choose your prospects carefully.

Moving From Virtual Reality to Real Life

If you're serious about developing a genuine sales relationship, you must reach beyond virtual reality to real life. This requires gaining access to the decision-makers, those who base their investment decisions on how your product or service benefits their business, not on price. More importantly, you must know how to influence them.

Start by gathering data and information to better understand the prospect's business, a process for which the Internet is ideally suited. Then find someone (usually within the prospect's organization) who has inside information, and is eager to give it to you—because if you win, he wins. Finding these "coaches" requires networking savvy and investigative know-how, but gives you an edge in making the process work. These coaches will provide knowledge you cannot find anywhere else, including on the Internet. Your ultimate goal is to leverage this hard-won knowledge to access key decision-makers. You can then deliver an intelligent, powerful presentation that will conclusively demonstrate how a business relationship with you and your company can help them achieve their business objectives, address key issues, or implement priority strategies.

Used wisely, the Internet can provide the fuel to ignite these opportunities. Used indiscriminately, it can burn up your time—and ultimately, leave your career in ashes. ■

Mark Shonka and Dan Kosch are co-presidents of IMPAX Corporation. For biographical and business information, see pages 273 and 270.

Editor's Note: Jim Domanski has spent the past 20 years helping companies set up telesales units and teaching reps how to be more effective on the phone. Author of four books on telesales strategy and tactics, Jim's back to demonstrate how creating scenarios for your clients gets them to open up with their concerns, and move in a buying direction.

Scenario Selling
by Jim Domanski

What's the most difficult part of the sales process? For many sales reps, it's getting prospects to open up and reveal their real issues, challenges and concerns early on. Without this critical information, the sales rep has no clear direction in which to take the sales call. As a result, demonstrating clear and compelling value to the prospect becomes almost impossible.

In my experience, questioning prospects for key motivators like "points of pain" can be challenging and difficult in two ways. First, not all sales reps are comfortable asking sensitive questions about problems or concerns in the early stages of selling. Either they ignore them, or botch them completely. Second, in the early stages of selling not all prospects are comfortable with baring their souls and revealing their areas of pain. They skirt the issue, or dismiss it completely. While both these challenges can be overcome with time and effort, a technique called "scenario selling" speeds up the process, helping you get to the meatier issues in less time— which means more sales for you.

Why don't prospects open up immediately? When you probe for needs, most prospects are reluctant to divulge areas of pain. This is understandable. The prospect doesn't know you, and may not know your company. Because you're a stranger, he feels a natural hesitancy to open up the floodgates and spill all his issues. On another level, some prospects don't want to admit to anyone that they have a pressing problem. Many consider it a private issue, one that reflects on them personally. Consequently, they keep their problems (which represent your opportunities) hidden, as if they are embarrassed to admit them.

At the same time, many sales reps—particularly new, inexperienced ones—are reluctant to ask prospects tough questions about problems or concerns. Although they've been told to ask, sales reps quickly learn that a prospect will shut them down with curt answers. For example, I recently heard a rep pointedly ask a prospect, "So, do you have any challenges in your business?" Not surprisingly, the prospect bluntly replied, "No." Responses like this can intimidate reps so much that they avoid asking tougher questions, and never get down to the heart of what concerns a prospect.

Of course, some sales reps aren't intimidated in the least about asking sensitive questions. They go to the opposite extreme, wielding questions like a club, and smashing the client with them. For instance, "So, Ms. Bixby, to get started—do you have any cash problems?" Questions like this catch prospects completely off guard, encouraging them to shut down rather than open up with their concerns.

How it Works

Scenario selling is a process that makes it easier for sales reps to ask tough questions, and easier for prospects to respond. It involves questioning for areas of pain or gain by describing a situation or event, then determining if it applies to the prospect. For example:

> "Ms. Bixby, much of our client research shows that cash flow is sometimes an issue, particularly with the fluctuating price of oil. Let me ask you—what has been your experience with cash flow over the last year or so?"

> "Anne, at our seminars we hear that collecting overdue accounts is sometimes a challenge, particularly with clients who have been long-time customers. Tell me, what has been your experience with collections over the last few months?"

> "Mr. Edgerton, one of the things we've learned with new practices is that marketing their services is a challenge, because the owners are doctors and not marketers. Let me

ask, what has been your approach to marketing, and what type of results have you been experiencing?"

"Scott, we are getting more and more feedback from IT directors and managers of large corporations regarding the misuse of licensing agreements. It's creating some concerns about compliance. Let me ask you, what has been your experience with this so far?"

"Chris, one of the things we're seeing in the market today is the growing frustration of investors trying to get a reasonable return on investment. This is impacting their retirement strategies. Let me ask, what has your experience been on ROI over the last year or two?"

You can see that scenario selling is formulaic, and divided into two parts. First, the sales rep broaches the problem/concern/pain area by using a statement or story that describes a specific situation experienced by others. In effect, the rep creates a scenario as a pretext for asking a sensitive question. Next, the rep uses an open-ended trigger phrase such as, "What has been your experience?" that invites the prospect to elaborate. This is important, because a closed-ended question can still shut down the prospect. Once the prospect begins to open up, the sales rep can probe further and deeper if necessary.

Why it Works

Scenario selling works on two levels. For the prospect, scenario selling works very well because it is based on the principle "misery loves company". When you describe a situation others are experiencing, the prospect does not feel quite so alone, and conscious of his dilemma. This makes it easier to open up; the prospect doesn't feel like he has been put on the spot. Your scenario is almost hypothetical in nature, so the prospect feels somewhat removed and objective. In effect, it becomes okay to acknowledge a similar pain. For the sales rep, scenario selling makes broaching awkward topics a little easier. It uses a subtle approach to deal with topics that clients might find sensitive or delicate. More importantly, it eases the sales rep into deeper questions, effectively inserting a wedge in the door.

Not every situation calls for scenario selling. For example, if you sell office products, you probably don't need to create a scenario. However, the more complex and sensitive the issue, the more strongly you should consider using this technique. To get started, sit down with your manager or fellow reps, and identify the points of pain that your product or service can resolve. Develop a scenario or two that highlights these points of pain, and script them so they truly hit your prospects where they live. Practice presenting your scenarios until they flow naturally. Finally, deliver them, and watch the impact they have on your sales results! ■

Jim Domanski is president of Teleconcepts Consulting. For biographical and business information, see page 267.

Editor's Note: Patricia Fripp was once the top men's hairstylist in San Francisco. She later traveled nationwide representing a leading line of hair care products, and garnered praise for her unusually effective presentation style. This led her to launch a new career as a speech consultant. She studied the principles of copywriting, screenwriting, and comedy, to create what she calls "conversational selling." Today Patricia is one of the leading executive speech coaches and presentation trainers, showing sales teams not just how to say it, but what to say, to win business.

Power Pitching for the Personal Edge
by Patricia Fripp

When pitching your product or service to clients, dozens of factors figure in the final decision of your prospects. But if everything is equal, you'll have the edge if you can establish a personal connection with them. As a salesperson, you may have been trained to address the analytical side by presenting all the facts, figures and supporting evidence in a logical, rational manner. *Power pitching* involves connecting with your prospects intellectually *and* emotionally, so they like and trust you more than your competitors. How do you make that connection, and get your prospects to like you? Try these tips:

- **Focus and be sincere.** If you appear nervous or unsure, clients may perceive you as devious or incompetent. If your sales presentation does not respond to their concerns, and you grind on with a prepared pitch, they will decide you don't care about them or their problems. Look people right in the eye and convince them that you stand 100% behind the ideas, products or services that you sell. Pick up on their concerns, and directly address them.

- **Divide and conquer.** When giving a sales presentation, shake hands with everyone as they enter the room. Connect with and see them as individuals, and you will become more memorable to them, too. People are usually shyer in groups of strangers than in one-on-one contact.

- **Don't rely on technology to make an emotional connection.** Use technology to enhance your sales presentation, not drown it. PowerPoint can keep you on track, but it can't establish trust.

- **Keep it simple and memorable.** When your prospects have a debriefing, you want them to remember your presentation more than anything your competitors pitched to them. Break your talking points into snappy sound bites that are easy to write down and remember. Make them interesting and repeatable.
- **Steer clear of technical language and jargon.** Rehearse your presentation in advance with your spouse or an intelligent twelve-year-old at the dinner table. Anything they don't understand is too complicated for the client.
- **Tell great stories.** People are conditioned to resist a sales pitch, but no one can resist a good story. Suppose you're trying to get money to fund your software company. Tell a story about how the prospective investor's life will change when you bring the product to market. "Imagine that a year from now, you come to work and use this software to do in five minutes what now takes you 45 minutes. I don't know what that would do to your life, but in all our test markets or pilot programs, people tell us... ." Then add more stories. If you're pitching a product that has not yet been produced, build a story around what it will be like for someone using it.
- **Take a lesson from Hollywood.** Give your stories interesting characters and dialogue, plus a dramatic lesson your prospects can relate to. Don't say, "Certain companies have used our software." Don't even say, "IBM has used our software." Instead, say, "Joe Smith at IBM told me, 'If we don't increase sales turnover by 20%, we won't make our projections.' We guaranteed him they would, if they used our software. Six months later, Joe called and said, 'You guys saved us.'"

Facts, figures and empirical evidence are important when pitching clients. But everything else being equal, you will come out way ahead of the competition when prospects like and trust you. ∎

Patricia Fripp is founder of Fripp & Associates. For biographical and business information, see page 268.

Editor's Note: Dave Kahle is a master sales expert. For 30 years, Dave's been obsessed by getting salespeople to practice good time management. See if you recognize yourself in this article—and if you do, follow the steps he suggests for making some changes.

The Four Biggest Time Wasters
by Dave Kahle

Do you make the best use of your time? Or do your bad habits cause you, like so many people, to waste time and accomplish less than you should? Getting salespeople to practice good time management has been an obsession of mine for three decades. Over the years, I've seen some patterns and tendencies in salespeople that detract from their effective use of time. Here are the four most common time wasters I've observed.

The Allure of the Urgent and Trivial

Salespeople *love* to be busy and active. We have visions of ourselves as people who get things done. No idle dreamers, we are out there making things happen. For most of us, a large part of our self-worth and personal identity depends on being busy. At some level, we believe that being busy means we must be important. One of the worst things that can happen to us is to have nowhere to go and nothing to do. So we latch onto every task that comes our way, regardless of its importance.

For example, a customer calls with a backorder problem. "Oh, good!" we think, "Something to do! I'm needed! I can fix it!" So we drop everything, and spend two hours expediting the backorder. In retrospect, couldn't someone in purchasing or customer service have taken care of that task? Couldn't they have done it better than we did? More importantly, did we just allow something that was somewhat urgent but trivial prevent us from making sales calls? And would those potential sales calls have been a much better use of our time?

Or suppose a customer hands us a very involved "Request for Quote." "Better schedule a half-day at the office," we think, "in order to look up specifications, calculate prices, compile literature, and all that other stuff." Immediately we become involved with working on this project for our customer. But couldn't we have asked an inside salesperson or customer service rep to do the legwork? Couldn't we have communicated the guidelines to someone else, and reviewed the finished proposal? Once again, we succumbed to the lure of the present task. And once again, it prevented us from making sales calls, and siphoned our energy from the important to the seemingly urgent.

I could offer page after page of examples, but you get the idea. We salespeople are so enamored with being busy and feeling needed that we grab at any task that comes our way, regardless of how unimportant it is. Each time we do, we compromise our ability to use our time more effectively.

The Comfort of the Status Quo

Many salespeople have established habits and routines that make them feel comfortable. They make enough money, so they don't want to expend the energy it takes to do things in a better way, or become more successful or effective. Some of our routines work well for us. However, our rapidly-changing world demands new methods, techniques, habits, and routines. Just because something has worked for us for a few years doesn't mean it will continue to do so. When we're so content with the status quo that we haven't changed anything in years, we're not as effective as we could be.

For example, you still might be writing phone messages down on little slips of paper, when entering them into your contact manager would be more efficient. Perhaps you continue to keep track of vital customer information manually, when contact management software makes that task easier. These are simple examples of a principle that extends to the most important things you do. Are you using the same old routines for organizing your workweek, determining who to call on, understanding your customers, and collecting information? Or do you look for new and better ways to perform these essential activities? Contentment with the status quo almost always means you'll never realize your full potential.

Lack of Trust

Salespeople have a natural tendency to work alone. We decide where to go and what to do, and are pretty much on our own all day long. It's no wonder we generally prefer to do everything ourselves. In most cases, this is a positive personality trait for a salesperson to have. But when it extends to tasks that could be done better by others, it becomes negative. Instead of soliciting aid from others in the organization, many salespeople insist on "doing it themselves", no matter how redundant and time-consuming the task. The world is full of salespeople who don't trust their own colleagues to write an order, source a product, deliver a sample or literature, research a quote, submit a proposal, et cetera. But many of these tasks can be done better or cheaper by other people in the organization. When salespeople refuse to release these tasks because they don't trust others to do them, the result is a tremendous waste of good selling time and talent.

Lack of Tough-Minded Thoughtfulness

Ultimately, time management begins with thoughtfulness. In fact, I like to say that good time management is a result of "thinking about it before you do it." Good time managers invest in this process. They set aside time each year to create annual goals; they invest planning time every quarter and every month to create short-term action objectives; and they plan every week and every sales call. Poor time managers do not dedicate sufficient time to the "thinking about it" phase of their jobs.

Not only do good time managers invest in the planning process, they are disciplined and tough-minded about how they think. They ask themselves good questions, and answer them with as much objectivity as they can muster. For example:

- What do I really want to accomplish in this account?
- Why aren't they buying from me?
- Who is the key decision-maker on this account?
- Am I spending too much time on this account, or not enough on that one?
- How can I change what I am doing in order to become more effective?

In addition to regularly asking these kinds of tough questions, good time managers don't allow their emotions or comfort zones to dictate their plans. They go where it is smart to go and do what it is smart to do. They do these things because they've invested the necessary amount of quality thinking time.

There are hundreds of time-wasting habits in the sales world, but these four are the most common. Correct them, and you will be well on your way to dramatically improved results. ■

Dave Kahle is president of The DaCo Corporation. For biographical and business information, see page 269.

Editor's Note: Jim Meisenheimer was a U.S. Army officer serving in Germany and Vietnam before becoming vice president of sales and marketing for the Scientific Products Division of Baxter International. He's been a sales trainer, speaker and coach for over 18 years. Jim prides himself on the fact that over 80% of his training business comes from repeat clients like Alcoa, Allstate, General Motors, and Teledyne.

Are You Getting the Cold Shoulder?
by Jim Meisenheimer

What happened the last time you showed up unannounced at a prospect's office? Did you manage to finagle an appointment with the decision-maker? Or, as so often happens, did the gatekeeper give you the cold shoulder and show you the door? Making your way past the gate-keeper is one of the most important steps in the sales process, because if you can't get through to the decision-maker, you can't make the sale. Yet in my experience, most salespeople have no idea how to win over these critically important people.

For starters, most salespeople view the gatekeeper as an adversary, rather than a potential ally. As a result, they come in expecting to do battle, rather than make a friend. Secondly, they do nothing to distinguish them-selves from every other salesperson who walks through the door. Finally, they fail to give the gatekeeper a good reason to agree to the requested appointment.

To get a warm reception (rather than a cold shoulder) from the gate-keepers you meet, try the following approach:
  • Recognize that gatekeepers are not really gatekeepers: they're people just like you and me. Too often, salespeople get off to a poor start because they treat the gatekeeper like an inanimate obstacle to be overcome, rather than a human being.
  • Understand that the gatekeeper has many responsibilities, none of which include sending babbling, unprepared, disorganized, unfriendly, and self-centered salespeople in to pester, and possibly annoy, senior managers.

- Recognize also that most gatekeepers are anxious to help their senior managers identify cost-saving opportunities, as well as new products, services, trends, even new contacts that could add value to their organization. Therefore, getting past the gatekeeper requires demonstrating value, and doing it in just the right way.

People Skills 101

Let's begin from the gatekeeper's perspective. In general, gatekeepers don't like pushy, aggressive salespeople. They don't like salespeople who talk too much. They don't like salespeople who have all the answers (especially before they ask any questions), and they *really* don't like salespeople who treat them like invisible servants.

Now let's go back to People Skills 101. Most people (including gate-keepers!) respond well to people who are courteous. They respond well to people who speak softly. They respond well to people who ask questions, and/or ask for help and advice. And most respond well to people who have a sense of humor. (Are you starting to see a pattern here?)

Next, let's consider the nature of the task. If you routinely, or even occasionally, drop in to see people without appointments, we can classify that as a recurring task. A fundamental rule of selling states that all tasks should be prepared in advance, especially recurring ones. There are many ways to approach a gatekeeper, and if you don't prepare *your* approach in advance, chances are you will duplicate what other salespeople have done. With that in mind, here's how to approach the gatekeeper in a manner that sets you apart from everyone else:

As you open the door to the office, make sure you're smiling, and your chin is up and in the locked position. Speaking softly, introduce yourself. For example, "Good morning, my name is Jim Meisenheimer, and I'm with the Superior Products Company." Then say, "I need your help." Remain silent until the gatekeeper says something like "How can I help you?" After she responds, say, "I need your advice on what would be the best way for me to get five minutes with Bill Anderson." If she responds with, "You'll have to make an appointment," simply ask, "Who should I see to arrange one?"

At this point, the gatekeeper is likely to ask, "What is this regarding?" Now is the time to launch into your elevator speech, a well-practiced, 30-second pitch briefly describing what you do, and how you add value. If your speech goes on longer than an elevator takes to get from the lobby to the 15th floor, shorten it. Then say (softly and subtly), "I'm not sure what we offer is what Bill Anderson needs." Pause for a moment, then follow up with, "After five minutes with Bill Anderson, he'll either want to know more, or show me the door." There is no risk to the gatekeeper with this approach, because if you do not add value, you will be out the door in five minutes.

Take a moment to re-read this example. In fact, read it out loud. Conventional wisdom suggests that most salespeople "show up and mess up," usually because they sound canned and unprepared—which means they sound like every other salesperson. By contrast, knowing what you're going to say before you say it differentiates you from 90% of all salespeople. More importantly, it creates a hard-to-resist conversation between you and the gatekeeper, and gets her working *with* you rather than against you.

So put down your club, and stop trying to bludgeon your way to an appointment. Instead, softly ask for advice, and five quick minutes with the decision-maker. You'll get the cold shoulder much less often if you warm up the gatekeeper in this manner. ■

Jim Meisenheimer is the creator of No-Brainer Sales Training. For biographical and business information, see page 271.

Power Tips
by Michael Dalton Johnson

Everybody likes to buy, because buying is fun. If you don't believe this, try to find a parking space at a shopping mall, or a seat at an auction, this weekend. However, while buying is fun and exciting, nobody likes to be sold. The truth is: the best salespeople don't "sell" their customers; they help them buy.

- **Get emotional.** When presenting your product or service, do not attempt to appeal strictly to the buyer's rational mind with a list of perfectly logical reasons to buy. Instead, fire their imaginations, and appeal to their emotions. Stress the benefits and rewards of owning your product or using your services. If possible, have them hold your product in their hands. Use colorful verbal illustrations that stress benefits. Sprinkle in some brief case histories. Be likeable. Have some fun. Above all, let the customer do most of the talking. Take the pressure to buy out of the experience, and the successful close will come naturally.

- **What buyers want.** In most business-to-business sales situations, the central question on buyers' minds is, "What's in it for *me?*" Take note: the question is, "What's in it for *me?*" not, "What's in it for *my company?*" Let prospects know how your product or service will help them to:

Make their jobs easier	Look good to management
Gain respect and prestige	Advance their careers
Be appreciated	Save time
Have some fun and excitement	Stay ahead of the competition
Minimize their personal risk	

Remember, the central question you must answer for the prospect is, "What's in it for me?"

- **Respect your buyer's intelligence.** Speak to your potential customer as if you were talking with an intelligent, yet uninformed friend. Do not insult your prospect's intelligence with inane leading questions such as, "We all want to save time and money, right?" Instead, simply state, "Our product will save you both time and money," and immediately follow this statement with a brief example or two. Allow the prospect to respond to your time and money-savings premise. A high-pressure "What's there to think about?" approach doesn't work in today's business environment. Your buyers are smart, and deserve your respect.

- **What's in a name?** There is no sweeter music than the sound of one's own name. Try to use your prospect's name a couple of times during your sales presentation. However, don't overdo it, or you'll sound insincere and patronizing. If your buyer's name is difficult to pronounce, get the correct pronunciation from the receptionist or secretary. Write it out phonetically, and say it aloud a few times before your meeting.

- **The nose knows!** Do not overwhelm your client's olfactory sense. It is a major turnoff for buyers when a salesperson reeks of perfume, cologne, or aftershave. Prospects will often cut the meeting short just to escape the smell. Rule of thumb: use only enough fragrance that if a loved one were nuzzling your neck, the scent could barely be detected.

- **Be on time, but don't come early.** While this seems painfully obvious, you might be surprised to learn how many sales folk show up late, with some lame excuse. Arriving too early for a meeting is nearly as bad. Never arrive more than ten minutes before your scheduled appointment. Being punctual shows respect and good business form, and will get your meeting off to a good start.

- **Create powerful imagery.** Instead of saying to a business owner, "Your employees will really appreciate this program," consider saying with a smile, "Your employees will stand up and applaud you for giving them this program." Don't worry; the buyer will allow this bit of poetic license. Even though he knows his employees won't really stand up and applaud, the mental image of them doing so is powerful.

- **Beware the time bandits.** Everyone needs a break from the action. However, 20 minutes a day wasted on office small talk, surfing the Net, or personal phone calls adds up to two full weeks a year in lost production. How many sales could you make in two weeks? Eliminate these time bandits, and watch your productivity climb.

- **Don't interrogate buyers.** A recent article in a leading sales publication advised "intense questioning" of prospects to determine their needs. The writer included a laundry list of questions that were both intrusive and transparent. Sophisticated buyers perceive too many probing questions, especially in the first stages of a meeting, as a pitch-tailoring sales tactic—which, of course, is exactly what it is. If you get prospects talking and follow the 80/20 Rule—you listen 80% of the time and talk only 20% of the time—many of your questions will be answered before you even ask them. Sure, you still have to ask questions and seek clarification. But your fact-finding process should flow naturally in response to buyers' comments and conversational pauses. Do not put them on the hot seat.

- **Breaking the ice.** Some telephone cold-call gurus will tell you to offer a pleasantry or two after introducing yourself. They are wrong. Avoid the opening, "How are you?" When spoken over the phone to a stranger, the phrase reeks of insincerity. You might as well scream, "I am a salesperson!" Instead, employ a more businesslike opening, such as, "The reason I'm calling you this morning is to learn about your company's personnel needs, and to see if we can be of help." In other words, after introducing yourself, state the reason for your call. Prospects will appreciate your honesty and respect for their time and intelligence. Only ask, "How are you?" after you've progressed beyond the initial contact, and a relationship has been established.

- **Don't answer a question with a question.** Again, contrary to conventional sales training wisdom, never answer a question with a question. This tactic is usually perceived by the prospect as evasive. For example, if your buyer asks, "When can you ship?" do not respond, "When do you need it?" This strategy diminishes your credibility. Simply tell him your average shipping time, and ask if that works for him. If not, go to bat for him, and if possible, get it for him when he wants it.

- **Look sharp.** The old cliché about dressing for success especially holds true in sales. Your clothes and personal grooming speak volumes about you to buyers, co-workers, and management. If you are looking good, you are undoubtedly feeling good, and you will close more sales. Take a critical look at your appearance, keeping in mind that shoes are one of the first things noticed. Your working wardrobe should be made up entirely of the following materials: cotton, wool, silk, linen and leather. That's it. For men, facial hair is generally a negative. (Name the last politician elected to the presidency who had a moustache or beard.) There are several good books on sharp dressing and good grooming. *John T. Molloy's New Dress for Success* is an update of the classic.

- **Never thank anyone for taking your call.** This seemingly polite gesture immediately puts you in a subordinate role—and subordinates are easily dismissed. For the same reason, when you finally make contact with a difficult-to-reach prospect, never open with, "You're a hard person to get hold of!"

- **Mood follows form.** When you feel in winning form, you smile, stand up straight, and walk with confidence. On some gloomy, depressing day, try this: smile, stretch, and strut. You will feel your mood begin to lighten as your physical actions mimic those of a winner. The same thing goes for your phone personality. If you sit up straight and smile, you will begin to feel self-confident and purposeful. Your voice will reflect those qualities, and you will enjoy more successful contacts with prospects and clients.

- **Let the buyer lead.** While you always want to maintain subtle control of your conversations with prospective buyers or clients, modify your pace and style to match theirs—sort of like dancing. If your customer likes to chat, by all means indulge in a little small talk. Conversely, do not ask Mr. Down-To-Business about his weekend plans. If a client has a breezy, big-picture personality, do not bog him down with details. This personality type loves to hear, "I'll take care of everything for you." However, if a prospect has questions about every detail, take the time to carefully review the nuts and bolts with him. Reading your buyer's personality and conversational style will pay big dividends in increased sales.

- **Buyers are like cats (and you're probably a dog!)** Just like our feline friends, buyers can be a difficult lot: suspicious, wary, finicky, independent, aloof. If you chase after one, it always runs. If you attempt to coax it, it invariably ignores you. However, if you sit quietly, letting the cat take its time and make up its own mind, before you know it, it's purring on your lap. ∎

Michael Dalton Johnson is founder and president of SalesDog.com. For biographical and business information, see page 269.

Editor's Note: As publisher of the popular newsletter, Telephone Prospecting and Selling Report, *Art Sobczak has been teaching effective telesales techniques for over 22 years. Here he shares his secrets for dealing with a bad luck situation.*

What to Do When Your Regular Buyer Leaves
by Art Sobczak

It's been a rough day. Hours of prospecting have yielded zilch, and you're staring at a helium-filled quota number that's floating farther out of your grasp by the minute. Paging through your tickler system, looking for a member of the 20% club of your account base that represents 80% of your business, you search for a slam-dunk that will book you some quick numbers, so you can at least bob up to quota sea level.

Ah-ha! Here's one. Looks like it's time for him to reorder. You pick up the phone and eagerly punch in their number.

> "Quality Industries, may I help you?"
> "Yes," you respond confidently. "I'd like to speak with Kyle Johnson."
> "I'm sorry, but Mr. Johnson is no longer with our company." Your heart sinks faster than a high-rise elevator as you search for an intelligent response.
> "Uhhhh," is the first sound you can muster. "What happened to him?"
> "He's just no longer with the company." (Code for 'he got canned.')

Wonderful. Here's a guy you had a great relationship with, who always had time to shoot the bull (maybe that's why he's no longer there), who loved your products, and could always be counted on for an order. Oh well, better find out who the new guy is. So you get the name of Jennifer Stevens, hang up, and regroup.

Ever been in that situation? Most of us have. Here's what you do *not* want to say.

"Hiya, Jennifer? Hey, I'm Dale Wilson with Complete Supply. I hear you took ol' Kyle Johnson's place. Well, Kyle used to buy all his fittings and bearings from me. I know it's getting about time for you guys to reorder, and I'm sure you'll want to do the same thing. I'd like to talk with you a bit about the way Kyle did things, and get you going on your next order here."

That would only be funny if it hadn't been done before. By the time you call, Jennifer has heard it so many times you're lucky she doesn't slam the phone in your ear. Let's look at some better alternatives for working with new buyers.

- **Do not assume anything.** Keep in mind that the new buyer had a life before taking this position and might have existing relationships with other vendors, maybe even a stronger one than the one you had with her predecessor. A cocky attitude will surely get you crossed off the list.

- **Send a welcome note or card.** When you learn the new person's name, send a handwritten note, congratulating her on her new position. Do not sell in the note. Mention you're look forward to speaking with her, and sign your name and your company's name. She will not get much mail personally addressed to her during her first few weeks on the job, so your gesture will be memorable.

- **Learn about the new buyer.** It's likely you have allies in the department. Snoop around. Learn where she came from, her personal interests, and what she has been doing in her first few days on the job.

- **Call to introduce yourself, and add value.** Here is where you need to make the best impression. "Hello Ms. Stevens, I'm Dale Wilson with Complete Supply. First, congratulations again on your new position with Quality Industries."(Pause, chit chat.) "I've had the opportunity over the past several years to provide Quality with bearings and fittings that the engineering department says works superbly in your line of wheels and components. I know you're probably quite busy in your new position, so I'd like to arrange a time when we could take about 20 minutes to discuss by phone how you like to deal with vendors, your preferences, and anything that I can do to make your job run more smoothly."

Notice this approach is focused entirely on the new buyer, not on the caller. Granted, you're coming in with the status of a longtime vendor. But you're not flaunting it, or ramming it down the new buyer's throat, as in "This is the way things have been and always will be done."

By the way, after cementing your relationship with the new buyer, find out where your old buyer went. Call him. It pays to stay in touch with old friends. ■

Art Sobczak is president of Business By Phone Inc. For biographical and business information, see page 274.

Editor's Note: Mike Schultz is a principal with the Wellesley Hills Group, a consulting and marketing firm. Mike is also founder and publisher of RainToday.com, a content site with research and tools for growing a service business. A frequent speaker and worldwide consultant to service firms on topics such as service firm branding, marketing, lead generation, e-marketing and rainmaking, Mike's current and previous clients include firms such as Bank of America, Fidelity Investments, John Hancock Financial Services, and Ryder System.

Transforming Customer Complacency into Urgency
by Mike Schultz

You know the drill. You've just completed the final sales meeting with a prospect who seems very interested in your product or service. He promises to call you Tuesday with a decision. Tuesday comes and goes, and the phone doesn't ring. Wednesday and Thursday, still no word. Finally, the prospect calls on Friday to say how impressed the client team was with your presentation, but they've decided to delay any action for at least a quarter. There is no competitor on the account, no major assumptions or situations have changed, and they don't plan to solve the problem themselves. They're just going to sit on it awhile.

As you hang up the phone, you think to yourself, *"What happened?"* Properly assessing this situation requires an understanding of the client's true options. When faced with the decision whether to buy your services, clients can take one of three paths: buy from you or a competitor, do it themselves, or do nothing at all. Often the sales rep will demonstrate strong value, and the client will agree the value proposition is solid. However, for some reason the client has no sense of urgency, and chooses to do nothing at all. At this point, we don't know what could have turned the situation around. What we *do* know is that the client has chosen to table the issue, and the current window of opportunity on this sale has closed.

Overcoming the Lack of Urgency

Clients often need a little prodding to overcome their lack of urgency. The next time you're preparing for a final presentation, meeting or proposal submission, use the following steps to help your client get in gear:

- **Ask yourself, "What won't happen?"** By the end of the sales process, you should have a very clear idea how your services will provide value to the prospect if he buys. Your next step is to get the client to understand the implications of not choosing to engage your services. Start by building a case (to yourself) for the negative implications if the client chooses not to solve the problem or address the issue using your services. Armed with this analysis, you're ready for the next action.

- **Ask the client, "What won't happen?"** At the appropriate time in the sales process, ask the client, "To help me understand your situation so I can craft the best solution for you, can you give me a sense of what will happen if you choose not to move forward in this process and engage our services?" Like a good trial lawyer, you already know from your earlier analysis what those implications will be. However, the point is to get the client to state those implications out loud, in his own words. If the client fails to enumerate them as you might like, lead him with further questions. For example, the middle of the conversation might go like this:

Sales Rep: "Yes, I can see what you're saying about monthly revenue generation taking a potential $7,000 hit if you don't take care of this. (Sales rep punches calculator.) That's $84,000 per year. I am also wondering what will happen to your customer retention. Since you're retaining 50% of your customers per year, and we've already discussed how engaging our services can get you up to about 70%, what might happen if we don't go forward?"

Client: "Well, I'm not really sure. I guess we've been losing a little ground to competitors, which is, of course, why we're talking here. So I guess we'd lose a little more. But I don't know how much."

Sales Rep: "It's impossible to know for certain, of course, but do you think it's more than 2%? 5%? Higher?"

Client: "I'd guess—no, I'm pretty sure it would be more than 5%, but I'm not sure how much."

Sales Rep: "OK, then, we'll use 5% as a benchmark, to be on the conservative side. One last question about pricing: what do you see happening there?"

Client: "Well, if we move forward, we'd like to raise prices, of course. But if we don't move forward, we'll continue to have price competition pressures. I think we'll find our prices either hold steady, or fall by up to 3%."

- **Quantify the results.** Just as you quantify the benefits and value of moving forward, quantify the implications for the customer of not moving forward. Make sure your case is clear before going on to the next step.
- **Demonstrate the results.** Most good salespeople enumerate or quantify the value and benefits of engaging their services. When demonstrating your value in the presentation or proposal, also demonstrate the results of the "What won't happen?" analysis. For example, suppose you demonstrate that revenue will go up by 3% and customer retention 20% if they purchase your service. Now show them the flip side. Demonstrate that if they choose not to go forward, revenue will stagnate or drop and customer retention will drop by at least 5%. Emphasize that these are their numbers and assumptions, not yours. Do your best to translate percents and other metrics into specific dollar amounts, keeping in mind that the best metrics are the ones your client is already using or agrees upon.

By employing a "What won't happen?" analysis in your sales process, you will find a consistent increase in the sense of urgency of your clients, resulting in measurably increased closing rates. ■

Mike Schultz is principal of Wellesley Hills Group. For biographical and business information, see page 273.

Editor's Note: I'm infamous around the office for interrupting hapless salespeople and long-winded staff members by saying, "Bottom-line me here!" Like most business owners, I have no time for tedious sales presentations, rambling stories, or lengthy explanations. I want you to get to the point—now. If you're getting cut off halfway through your presentations, you're talking too much. Michelle Nichols knows how to get to the point. A popular BusinessWeek Online *columnist with over 10 years' experience in technical sales, she started, ran, and sold two companies before launching her own sales training and consulting company.*

Help – I'm Talking and I Can't Shut Up!
by Michelle Nichols

Are you guilty of committing the crime of TMI -- too much information? You know what I mean. Someone asks the price of your product, and you launch into a long-winded discourse on every feature, a competitive comparison, financing options, and more. Meanwhile, all the client really wanted to know was if the cost would be closer to $20K, or $40K. Ouch! One of the most frequently committed "sales crimes", TMI can be hard to spot because offenders actually think they are being helpful. In fact, they're being the opposite. All that excess information slows down the sale, possibly even killing it.

A while back, I was speaking at an association of sales reps for promotional products. The event was so inspiring I thought I'd write a column on clever promotions, so I asked one of the trade magazine editors for some ideas. She generously agreed to send me two years of back issues (24 magazines) and signed me up for a subscription, too. When the magazines arrived, I was so overwhelmed with all the information I put them aside, intending to study them later. As you can guess, I never opened them, and that column never got written. In retrospect, I could have picked out one magazine with the most potential for column fodder and pitched the rest, but I didn't. TMI ruined that sale.

Pascal's Formula

There are many varieties of TMI. I heard about travel-weary attendees at an insurance convention being greeted with a four-hour, nonstop information dump on everything that was new and improved since they had gathered a year ago. That is *way* too much information before the first glass of chardonnay! On a smaller scale, we have all experienced "Death by PowerPoint," presentations that go on much too long, in far too much detail. Electronic slides should provide just an overview. If you have a lot of details to cover, put them in a handout or reference guide. TMI also crops up in the form of long-winded brochures, emails, sales letters, even phone calls. Whatever the method of delivery, TMI always has the same result: it weakens the connection with the other person.

The seventeenth-century French mathematician Blaise Pascal wrote, "I have made this [letter] longer, because I have not had the time to make it shorter." I understand his pain. When I released my latest sales CD, I was so excited I immediately sent copies to my key customers and prospects. The problem was the accompanying sales letter was two pages long. I *knew* I was committing TMI. But like M. Pascal, I didn't take the time to make it shorter. I should have sent a brief summary that said, "Thank you for your business. Please order copies of my new CD. Please hire me to speak. Let's keep in touch. Love, Michelle." Who knows how many CDs I didn't sell because of that letter?

Information is like food: some is good, but too much is not necessarily better. Let the customers decide. When they ask you a question, respond with an overview, then ask what they'd like to know more about. For example, if you provide copying services and receive an inquiry, you could explain that you offer a wide variety of solutions, including A, B, and C. Then you might ask what copying services the prospect uses right now, and outline how your offerings are similar or different. Later, you might ask if he has ever considered using some of the services you offer that he didn't mention. Pace yourself.

Use the Goldilocks Strategy

If you offer 50 different types of products, hearing them explained one by one can be downright painful for your client. Instead, group your offerings into a handful of categories. Review the categories with your customers, and go deeper only into the ones that interest them. Yes, that means you won't get to talk about all 50 products on the first sales call. But that is not only okay—it is *good*.

If you have to send a catalog, take a moment to highlight pages of special interest and include a personal note on the cover. Customers do not want to look through your entire catalog to find the handful of items they want to buy. Granted, a few customers love to sort through boatloads of data. For them, there is no such thing as too much information. They will ask to see the warranty, manual, brochures, your last five annual reports, and more. But they are the exception, not the rule. For all the rest, use the Goldilocks strategy. She didn't want things too hot or too cold, too big or too little. She wanted everything just right! Give your customers just the right amount of information and you will sell more and close faster.

I hope that was just enough information on TMI. ∎

Michelle Nichols is principal of Savvy Selling International. For biographical and business information, see page 271.

Editor's Note: Tom Richard is a syndicated weekly business columnist and sales speaker. Tom began his successful sales career in high-end retail, before moving to outside sales. His company presents sales seminars, CSP certification training, and sales coaching for individuals and teams.

A Picture is Worth a Thousand Sales
by Tom Richard

It's the question every husband dreads. You're just about to sneak out the door to pick up some chips and dip before the big game, when a voice calls out from the kitchen, "Honey, are you going to the store? Could you pick up some (long, detailed list of miscellaneous items)?" Forget about the extra trips down the aisles, or spending a few more bucks. The real problem is getting the exact items our wives want: the light (*not* fat-free) French vanilla ice cream, the newest version of baked (*not* regular) chips. Every time we husbands dutifully set off to acquire the proper goods, and every time we come home with at least one wrong item.

Fortunately, my wife discovered a valuable trick to ensure I get exactly what she wants: she shows me the empty box. Why is producing a visual cue the easiest way for her to explain, and for me to understand, exactly what she wants? Why is it easier for me to remember that product when I get to the store? It's simple: we think in pictures. Because our minds use pictures to digest and remember information, communication works most effectively when we use images.

Unfortunately, most salespeople spend more time choosing their words than creating images for their customers. They use words like "best," "quality," and "service" to describe their company or product. But these words are used so frequently they've become meaningless to customers. In addition, they mean different things to different people. When salespeople depend on these words to convey an image or idea, the message is unclear, and the sale is lost. Only you understand what these words mean to your business, because you have firsthand experience with your company. How did you get this wonderful understanding? By seeing the examples, hearing the stories and talking with customers who love you. Because of this, you have pictures to accompany these otherwise empty words.

Your customers, however, do not share these associations. They don't understand these words the way you do because they don't have the same mental pictures. They don't know about the customer you saved from a difficult situation by rushing a service team to his office on a holiday to fix his equipment, no questions asked. They don't know about the time your customer won a large account because of the impeccable quality of the products he bought from you. They don't know these things; only you do.

Your job as a salesperson is to share these pictures with prospects and customers in order to fully illustrate what you can do for them. Too many salespeople rely on lists, brochures, FAQs, and comparative charts to aid them in the sales process because they don't understand the power of a good story. Using stories to illustrate the quality and service of your company engages your customers, and makes it easy and entertaining for them to digest all the wonderful information you give them. By visualizing your stories, they will get a clear understanding of what your product and company is all about.

Creating images also leaves a memorable impression in your customer's mind. Just as it is easier for me to remember a product by its box, it will be easier for your customers to remember you by your stories. The next time your customer is in a meeting and is asked which vendor to go with, you and your story will be uppermost in his mind.

The great thing about using pictures is they help customers not only understand you, but relate to you as well. Because stories and images are clearly understood, customers feel more at ease when salespeople use them. Understanding your message clearly makes your customer feel good about you, your company, and your product. With pictures, it is easy for customers to understand and remember how you and your product exemplify the qualities other salespeople only talk about. So grab that paintbrush, and start painting! ■

Tom Richard is an author and sales trainer. For biographical and business information, see page 272.

Editor's Note: I've told you Jill Konrath was born to be a sales trainer. She excels at demonstrating exactly what doesn't work, spelling it out so you can see yourself in a similar situation. Even more helpful, she shows you what will work, with real-world examples and dialog. Here Jill explains how to escape the "Tell me more" trap.

Passing the "Tell Me More" Test
by Jill Konrath

Establishing a business relationship with a new prospect is a lot like walking a balance beam: every move you make has consequences. Executing a move flawlessly puts you in perfect position for the next one. One misstep, however, and you immediately go into recovery mode. Sometimes you manage to bounce back and continue your routine. Other times, you fall off the beam, and are out of the competition. To make it even more challenging, stone-faced judges ruthlessly evaluate how well you execute each move, as well as its level of difficulty.

Sounds a lot like sales to me! The early stages of the sales process are fraught with difficulties. Prospects assess your every word to determine whether it is worth their time to meet with you. One misstep can cause the entire sales process to fall off the beam. That's why so many sellers get excited when prospective customers say, "Tell me more" thinking it means they have scored a perfect 10 on their first routine. Then, without thinking, they launch into their second routine. What most sales reps fail to realize, however, is that they must first pass this "Tell me more" test before they can advance in the competition.

Recently I worked with a large services firm. Like most, they constantly struggle to crack into new accounts. We worked on crafting strong value propositions, creating enticing voicemail messages, and engaging customers in a discussion. I could tell what we'd created would work, so I asked how they would respond if a customer said, "Tell me more." They replied, "Our company has been in business since 1997. It was formed by four separate firms—each with its own expertise in the communications field—that came together to address the greater challenges faced by global companies today. Since our merger, we've been growing at the rate of 28% annually, making us the leading provider nationwide. We offer a full range of services... ."

They flunked the test. It was a nice answer, but not the right answer. This kind of stuff bores clients to death. This approach is all about you, you, you. Believe me: clients couldn't care less about your self-serving pabulum.

Okay, now you're confused. The prospect wanted to know about your company. In fact, he *asked* you to tell him more. Yet here I am, saying not to tell him more. We'll get to the answer soon; first, I want to illustrate another way to flunk the test.

Shortly after working with the large services firm, I had the same conversation with a Six Sigma consultant. He gets really excited when corporate decision-makers say, "Tell me more" because he interprets this as a sure sign that they want to know all about his methodology. Typically he responds with the following:

> "The process we use to achieve these results involves pulling together a team of people from several different functions, to analyze and address your critical business challenges. First of all, it's absolutely imperative to have senior level commitment in order to make this work. So before any session, I conduct thorough interviews with key executives and other stakeholders. Then, when we get together, we use a variety of proven tools, such as customer value mapping and process mapping, as well as a systematic, integrated tactical approach to help you achieve objectives... ."

As he droned on, my eyes glazed over. Eventually it became too painful for me to listen, and I let him know that his long-winded description was not what prospects wanted to hear. He, too, became confused. They wanted to learn more, so he explained his process to them. But he recognized that his response wasn't getting the results he wanted, so he agreed to consider any and all suggestions.

Here's what I told him. When you're in the early stages of working with a prospective customer, the answer to "Tell me more" is not an overview of your firm, nor a description of your process, methodology or products. The people you're talking to are sitting at their desks, struggling to get everything done with fewer resources and in less time: an impossible, never-ending task with no relief in sight. *That* is what you focus on—the challenges or issues your product or service addresses.

In responding to "Tell me more," your primary goals are to develop credibility as someone intimately familiar with the issues the prospect faces, and demonstrate your ability to deliver results. Expand on how tough it is for companies to achieve their objectives using outdated systems or processes. Talk about all the difficulties that arise, the bottlenecks and the workarounds, the frustrations. Mention the ramifications on other areas of their business. Share a story about a customer you recently worked with, how he was operating when you initially started working together, the problems he faced, and the impact of these problems on his business. Then briefly summarize the outcomes. Wrap it up by asking a question that engages your prospect in discussing the issue in greater depth.

For example, if you say to me, "Tell me more," I will respond:

> "The biggest challenges facing sellers today is cracking into corporate accounts. Decision-makers never answer their phones. They automatically roll all calls to voicemail, and never call anyone back. Most direct mail goes into the trash, and emails from strangers are treated as spam.
>
> "You may have the greatest product or service in the world, but if your people can't get their foot in the door, it's all academic. Most sellers I work with are extremely discouraged. They've tried everything they know, and nothing is working. I help them figure out what it takes to succeed in this crazy business environment. How big an issue is this for your company?"

That is what you need to say to pass the "Tell me more" test. However, these words don't just roll off the tongue effortlessly. You need to practice and prepare like everything depends on them—because it does. Your prospect is the ultimate judge of your "Tell me more" response. If you fail to advance to the next step, your routine needs fine-tuning. But when you get that next meeting set up, you'll know you scored a perfect 10. ∎

Jill Konrath is Chief Sales Officer of Selling to Big Companies. For biographical and business information, see page 270.

Editor's Note: Julie Thomas has been using, teaching and coaching ValueSelling techniques for over 15 years. She learned the system as a technology sales rep and subsequently taught it to her company's sales force. Later she joined the ValueSelling team at ValueVision Associates and became CEO. Julie's clients include Cisco Systems, Novell, and Siemens Group; she is also the author of ValueSelling: Driving Up Sales One Conversation at a Time.

Gotta Have It
by Julie Thomas

When times get tough, most companies scale back on spending. Some even try to stop spending altogether. Fortunately, a frozen spending situation can't last forever, as daily needs must be addressed. What do these companies do when expenditures must be made? They prioritize based upon the value to the business, and often, the value to the buyer personally. As the salesperson, your challenge is to help prospects recognize the value of your product, so that your sales campaign ends up on their short list of "must-have" purchases.

To sell value, we need to assess the customer's business issues and help resolve his most important challenges. To do this, we need to connect four topics:

- an unresolved business issue
- problems that make the business issue tough to resolve
- solutions which overcome the problems, thus resolving the business issue
- the significance of the problems and/or business issue in terms of measurable consequences and personal impact.

Every company has unresolved, yet important, business issues. All are related to the twin objectives of increasing revenue and profits, and may include cost management, competitive challenges or losses, quality, time to market, and time to revenue. Each of these issues may have its own set of problems, such as iterations in process steps, lack of skill or training in new areas, difficulty securing personnel or resources, changes in technical or regulatory support requirements, and mistakes common to manual processes.

Finally, every problem and every business issue has a cost or impact. The challenge is to help the customer see the value from his perspective, not ours. This means asking questions such as:

- How would you quantify the impact of these rework steps?
- How much time do you spend chasing inventory information?
- How much delay does that cause, and how does that translate to revenue production?
- You mentioned quality issues; what is your customer return rate?
- How does this affect you? Are you impacted by this personally?

Only after we have identified the critical business issue, its underlying problems, and the value of solving these problems, are we in a position to help the prospect move our solution to the top of the list of must-have purchases.

Anything short of revealing the connection between these subjects means we are handing the selling over to the prospect. Chances are he doesn't have the time or the inclination to finish the job for us. So we end up with a stalled sale, or a loss to a competitor who did a better job than we did connecting these subjects. ■

Julie Thomas is president and CEO of ValueVision Associates. For biographical and business information, see page 275.

Editor's Note: Tina is affectionately known around the office as Lady SalesDog. Having been responsible for selecting and distributing gifts to thousands of clients, she is the consummate gift-giver. Gift giving can be a tricky business, but follow Tina's tips, and you'll do fine.

The Salesperson's Guide to Gift-Giving
by Tina LoSasso

Finding the perfect gift for family or friends is no small chore. Business gift-giving is even more challenging. While you may be able to get away with Starbucks gift cards for your staff, thanking your clients for their business requires more time and thoughtfulness. How do you go about selecting exactly the right gift for that important client? Here are some time-honored rules of thumb:

- **Thoughtful gifts will earn you huge dividends.** If you're working a large account, check your notes on the key players. What are their hobbies? Do they golf, cook or play sports? For example, if you know someone loves to fish, send him a book on fly-fishing America's rivers.

- **The ultimate in thoughtfulness is a gift you make yourself.** This is especially true around the holidays. Unless your customer is a Martha Stewart type, she probably has little time to make much of anything. Gifts of homemade cookies, candy or preserves will be greatly appreciated. Packaging is important with homemade presents, so make them look pretty!

- **Women love chocolate.** In this case, think quality, not quantity. A small box of exquisite, handmade truffles will be appreciated far more than a big box of run-of-the-mill chocolates. Gourmet coffees and teas, crystal items and potted plants are usually a hit. A sales-*woman* may send more personal items—aromatherapy candles, a spa kit—to her stressed-out female buyers, but sales*men* should not be so familiar. Sorry guys—that is life. You are not in the club.

- **Men love gadgets, toys and food.** Think of the latest electronics, or a clever desktop novelty. High-quality pens, nuts or jellybeans also score highly with men. Cigars are a great idea *if* you know he smokes them. Once again, think quality, not quantity. It's far better to send a few of the very best than a box of duds he will throw away.

- **Think regional.** Consider sending a gift from your region of the country: Ghirardelli chocolate from San Francisco, smoked salmon from the Northwest, cheese from Wisconsin, citrus fruit from Florida or California, authentic Cajun fixin's from Louisiana, or barbecue sauce from Texas. Cleverly packaged, these unique local gifts (and you) will be remembered far longer than a generic tin of cookies.

- **Do not overspend.** Many companies have strict rules on the value of gifts that employees may accept. When in doubt, send a fun gift that can be shared by the whole office, rather than one expensive gift for your client.

- **Stay away from the booze.** Alcoholic beverages are usually risky business. The one exception is when you *know* someone loves a certain brand of Scotch, or a hard-to-find microbrew. Never send a bottle of champagne to that key account in Salt Lake City (or for that matter, a ham to an Orthodox Jewish firm). Don't laugh— it's happened!

- **No advertising!** When is a gift not a gift? When it comes with your company's logo on it. Save the logo-embossed pens, paper- weights, mouse pads and calculators for trade shows. And gift certificates from your own company are not really gifts. They're promotions that make you look stingier than Scrooge. Instead, send a gift certificate from a national department store or e- commerce site. Many sites, such as Amazon.com, offer corporate gift certificate programs.

- **Everyone gets a card.** All clients, large and small, should receive a holiday card. Avoid religious themes (stick to "Happy Holidays" or "Season's Greetings"), and again, *no* advertising. You'd be surprised how many people can't resist putting their business tagline or logo on a greeting card!

- **Think New Year's.** If you run out of time to plan or shop for the holidays, get the cards in the mail and send an appropriate New Year's gift. Think pens, desk clocks, or paperweights, packaged with noisemakers and streamers. Timing your gift to arrive right before New Year's is a great way to stand apart from everyone else.

Giving All Year Round

Keep in mind that gift-giving opportunities arise all year, not only at the holidays. Perhaps you want to send a token gesture of thanks to a key player in a newly-landed account. Or maybe you have representatives from a large prospective account flying in to tour your facility, and a welcome gift would start the visit off right. Foregoing the familiar bottle of wine or basket of fruit in the hotel room for a well-chosen, individualized gift will make a big impression. You might also consider presenting a gift to visitors as they leave. Something reminiscent of the area makes an ideal memento of their time with you.

How Sorry Are You?

When your company fouls up and creates a major headache for your customer, you have another opportunity to send a gift. In these situations, a mere phone call or letter often is not enough to undo the damage. As a sales professional, you are the face of your company, so you need to say you're sorry (regardless of whether it's your fault). An appropriate gift will go a long way toward soothing ruffled feathers.

What should you send? Flowers always say it best. For female customers, send a floral arrangement in a vase. Stay away from roses, no matter the color, as they spell romance in any language. Avoid lilies, because they are often used at funerals, and have an overpowering fragrance. An elegant mixed flower arrangement can be pricey, so if funds are tight, opt for a tasteful bouquet of just one variety of flower for maximum impact. Irises, dendrobium orchids or gerbera daisies work well. For the men, send a healthy-looking potted plant, preferably not a blooming one. A bonsai plant, bamboo, or money tree will hit just the right masculine note, and look great on his desk. Remember: you can also send flowers to say "thank you."

A carefully-selected gift shows your customers how much you appreciate them. Give your giving the time and effort it deserves, and you will impress your customers, and be fondly remembered when it is time to buy again. ■

Tina LoSasso is managing editor of SalesDog.com. For biographical and business information, see page 270.

Editor's Note: Jim Domanski is a leading telesales consultant and trainer in both North America and Europe. He's been featured in numerous business publications, including Advertising Age, Sales and Marketing Management, Selling Power, *and* Tele-Professional. *Jim's back to share a secret that will help you make every call more profitable.*

Cash In On Every Contact with Add-On Selling
by Jim Domanski

It happens far too often in the selling world. You've spent countless hours punching in telephone numbers. You've battled dozens of hard-nosed secretaries and left voicemail message after voicemail message. You finally break through and reach the decision-maker, the one who has the money and the authority to say "yes." It was a long, tough haul, but you finally have him on the line.

Here's the problem: at this point, *most salespeople do absolutely nothing to leverage the moment.* After all the toil and trouble to reach the decision-maker, they do nothing more than make a sale. That's like scaling Mount Everest, and not taking any pictures at the summit. You're asking, "What's wrong with making a sale? Isn't that what we're *supposed* to do?"

Absolutely! But if you leave it at that and walk away feeling like you've accomplished the mission, you miss out on a tremendous opportunity to leverage the sale.

The fact of the matter is you *can* do more. Virtually every call you make, or take, has added potential. It might be more revenue, or another opportunity, such as a garnering a lead or a referral. Whatever the case, you need only scratch the surface to see what lies beneath. How can you take full advantage of your calls? Through *add-on selling*, the process of leveraging a customer or prospect contact by generating additional revenues or a marketing opportunity. In simpler language, add-on selling is a way to maximize every dialogue you have with a client, a way to grab and squeeze every single ounce of opportunity from an inbound or outbound call. As the name implies, add-on selling is something you add to a call or a sale. It comes at the end of a call, after the call objective has been completed, and will lead to some interesting benefits if applied on a regular basis.

What kinds of benefits? For starters, expect the average value of a sale to increase, which means more revenues. Add-on selling also means less work. If you can achieve your objectives without calling as much, you save yourself time while experiencing less frustration and burnout. When performed well, add-on selling typically pleases customers, who are more inclined to reward you with referrals. And as we all know, good referrals close at a higher rate, with less time invested by the salesperson.

Add-on selling can be applied in virtually every calling situation, including cross-selling, up-selling, getting a referral, generating additional leads, selling on an inquiry, converting a cancellation, selling on a complaint, and gathering market intelligence. Done correctly and professionally, it will almost always increase the value of the sale.

A Four-Step Process

Simple and easy to use, add-on selling consists of four basic steps. Master these, and you will quickly make more money in less time.

- **Step #1: Handle the initial request or task.** Remember that add-on selling comes *after* your initial objective has been met. So before applying add-on selling, first handle the inquiry, get the order, close the sale, deal with the cancellation or complaint: whatever the situation calls for. An old adage says "A bird in the hand is worth two in the bush." First, get the bird in hand.
- **Step #2: Bridge to the add-on.** A bridge is a transition phrase that alerts the client to the fact that you are about to provide some additional information. For example, "Mr. Ford, thank you for your order. Oh, by the way, while I still have you... ."
- **Step #3: Present the add-on with a benefit.** State the add-on. It might be a cross-sell or an up-sell. It might be a request for a referral, or to gather some market information. Whatever it is, state the add-on and provide some sort of benefit to the customer.
- **Step #4: Close.** Conclude the process with a close, so the client can take action.

Add-on selling is easy—and it works. Unfortunately, most salespeople don't apply it on a regular basis. The next time you find yourself at the top of the mountain, talking to the decision-maker you worked so hard to reach, try this simple technique. It will allow you to leverage the moment and make the most of *all* your selling opportunities. ■

Jim Domanski is president of Teleconcepts Consulting. For biographical and business information, see page 267.

Editor's Note: Bill Stinnett began his career in retail sales, and spent several years making direct sales to private consumers before moving into corporate sales to Fortune 1000 customers. Along the way, he founded four profitable private companies, including a high-tech startup, an executive search firm, and two training and consulting companies. Since 1990, Bill has specialized in high-technology solutions. Today Bill is a speaker, coach, and consultant, whose clients include American Express, GE, IBM, Microsoft, and Verizon.

Means, Motive, Opportunity: Making a Case for the Sale
by Bill Stinnett

It's the question most salespeople dread more than any other: *Is this deal qualified?* What is it about this question that causes even experienced sales reps to tremble? One, it's difficult to answer, because qualifying sales opportunities isn't merely a step in a process that gets checked as "yes" or "no." Two, it takes a lot of time and energy to reach the point where you can give a yes or no answer with reasonable confidence. And three, once you get to that point, the answer can easily change from day to day. Qualifying is an integral part of the ongoing sales process, and as conditions change throughout a sales campaign, an opportunity that would be considered qualified one day might not be qualified the next.

Determining the quality or "closeability" of each opportunity in your pipeline enables you to prioritize your efforts, and properly allocate sales resources. Answering a question like, "How many do they want to buy, and when do they want to buy them?" hardly scratches the surface of what you need to know. What you really want to know is *why* they would want to buy something in the first place, and *how* they could buy it if they wanted to. Obtaining this "why" and "how" information requires qualifying prospective customers for motive and means.

Understanding Motive

Understanding motive requires knowledge of the client's business, his business goals and objectives, and how the business is performing against those goals and objectives. A business need, which precedes a motive to buy, shows up as a discrepancy between where he is today, and where he wants or needs to be in the future. Whether the buyer discovers his need on his own or with your help, the next step is to help him find a suitable solution.

Sales qualification starts with a powerful, one-word question: "Why?" To fully understand motive, we need to ask questions like:

- Why does this discrepancy you've discovered constitute a problem?
- Why does this discrepancy exist?
- Why haven't you done something about it before?
- What good would come from solving this problem?
- Why would you invest money in solving this problem rather than in addressing a different need?
- What are the risks involved in tackling this issue?
- Why couldn't you let someone else in the company worry about solving this problem?
- Why not do nothing, and hope the problem works itself out?

The answers to these questions reveal not only corporate motives to buy, but individual motives as well.

Determining the Means

In order to determine whether the prospect has a motive to buy, we need to qualify for means. Specifically, we need to know:

- Can the prospect afford the solution we will propose?
- How will he justify the purchase?
- How will it ultimately be approved?
- How does he plan to pay for it or finance it?
- Will a lending party be involved?
- Who will execute the contract or release the purchase order?
- Who must give approval before the deal can be signed?
- Does the prospect have the resources to fully utilize our solution?
- Can the prospect really derive the value he is seeking?
- Once he buys, will he be willing to act as a reference?

Unless we have a clear understanding of all these elements, we have not fully qualified the deal, because many of these elements can significantly impact our ability to close the opportunity. It is common to discover a buyer has not yet considered all these factors. But to conduct a bulletproof sales campaign, we must understand all these variables, and many more.

Qualifying the Opportunity

If the prospective customer has the motive to buy *and* the means to buy, you can provide the opportunity to buy. But this should be done only in proportion to his motive and means. In many industries, providing a client the opportunity to buy involves a significant investment on the seller's part. Beyond time and effort—both of which cost money—there may be travel required, products to demonstrate, proposals to prepare, and reference clients to talk to or visit. A dozen or more people could be involved. An investment of this kind should be approached as any other investment: by carefully weighing risks versus potential rewards.

Understanding a prospective client's motive and means involves a little research, and a lot of questions. But having the information with which to analyze and prioritize opportunities, and thereby optimize the investment of valuable resources, is well worth the work of collecting it. Once it has been collected, you can use this information to communicate the quality of an opportunity throughout your organization, to everyone who needs or wants to know. ■

Bill Stinnett is president of Sales Excellence, Inc. For biographical and business information, see page 275.

Editor's Note: Dave Kahle is a selling expert with plenty of real-world experience, who understands and appreciates the problems salespeople face. He knows one of the biggest obstacles salespeople encounter is having enough qualified prospects. Dave has some practical ideas for filling your prospect pipeline.

Jumpstart Your Prospecting
by Dave Kahle

Customers are like an old-fashioned gumball machine. In the beginning, the clear round globe is filled to the brim with colorful gumballs. But as people put in their quarters and turn the handle, the number of gumballs gradually declines. Eventually, unless you add new gumballs, the machine becomes empty.

Well, the same thing happens in business. The constant churn in the marketplace means that some of your customers will be acquired, and some will go out of business. Others stop doing business with you because they find a better solution, or are dissatisfied with your service. Regardless of the reason, customers do leave, and most of them never come back. Unless you regularly replace lost customers with new ones, your business pipeline, like the gumball machine, will inevitably empty.

How do you avoid this gradual erosion of your customer base? Through effective prospecting. Prospecting refers to the front end of the sales process. This essential activity involves identifying companies and institutions that could buy your products, then arranging a first appointment with them. As with every other stage of the sales process, some methods of prospecting are more effective than others.

In today's economy, it's not enough to simply identify a prospect; you must identify a prospect who is likely to buy. This first step plays a major role in your long-term success, as it keeps you focused on those who are most likely to do business with you. The more information you obtain about a prospect, and the closer you bring him to doing business with you in the early stages of the relationship, the further ahead you will be. Following is a two-step process to jumpstart your prospecting efforts.

Step 1: Buy a List

This is so simple and obvious, yet relatively few people do it. Study your best current customers, and develop a profile of what they look like. How many employees? What SIC codes? Where are they located geographically? Who are their customers? Once you have a profile, go to the Internet or Yellow Pages and look up "mailing list brokers." Call two or three, tell them what you're looking for, and ask them to quote you the count and cost for a list that includes the name, address, phone number and employee size of the businesses that meet your criteria. For a cost of $.20 to $1.50 per name, you can obtain a list of those companies who look most like your good customers. This is a great place to start.

Step Two: Use an "Enticer"

Offer an "enticer" to your prospect list. An enticer is an offer for something prospects are probably already buying, but it's such a good deal that they can't refuse it. For example, if a certain type of imprinted pen costs 55 cents, offer a one-time purchase for 25 cents. Yes, you'll lose money on the deal. But if someone takes you up on it, you move the sales process forward considerably. You will now be on that customer's computer vendor list, you will have a reason to call on him, and he will be predisposed to spending some time with you. In other words, you will have lost a little money, and gained a customer for it. Think of this as buying a customer at a very good price. The few dollars you lose on the initial order makes it a bargain.

Employ this simple, two-step process, and in a matter of a few weeks, you'll have a handful of high-potential prospects who are open to doing business with you. ■

Dave Kahle is president of The DaCo Corporation. For biographical and business information, see page 269.

Editor's Note: Wendy Weiss is known as the Queen of Cold Calling. She is a virtuoso of voice, who will show you how to use your instrument more effectively.

Your Voice Is Your Instrument
by Wendy Weiss

What do the following occupations have in common: surgeon, painter, navigator and salesperson? Answer: all use an instrument to practice their craft. The surgeon uses a blade of razor-sharp titanium steel to make precise incisions. The painter uses a brush made with the finest bristles to put color on canvas in new and exciting ways. And the navigator uses a sextant to chart his position against the stars.

What does the salesperson use? On an introductory call, your voice is your instrument. During a face-to-face meeting, visual cues and body language are available to add layers of meaning, in addition to charts, graphs, handouts, PowerPoint slides, and sales literature to support your verbal communication. But on the telephone, you have only your voice and your words. How you use this most delicate of instruments can make or break your conversation.

To tune your instrument for a great performance, do the following:

- **Monitor your tone.** Imagine you're telling a bedtime story to a child. You wouldn't drone on in a bored tone about the Big Bad Wolf. No! You would put fear and passion into your voice to make the story come alive for the child. Think about your introductory calls in the same manner. In essence, you're telling your story to your prospect, and tone of voice plays an important role in determining what the prospect hears, feels and sees.
- **Pay attention to voice inflection.** The emphasis on a particular word can totally change the meaning of a sentence. Let's take the phrase, "She is not a thief." If you emphasize "She," the sentence means that she is not a thief, but someone else is. If you emphasize "not," the sentence is a defense. If you emphasize "thief," the

sentence implies that she is something else that you have not named. Think about the emphasis you wish to convey, and use your voice accordingly.

- **Rehearse your delivery.** Look at each sentence in your sales pitch to determine what you're trying to convey, and the best way to do so. Try out different line deliveries until you are satisfied with the result.
- **Hear yourself as others hear you.** Use a tape recorder to listen to how you sound. When speaking, you hear yourself differently than others do. By listening to your taped voice, you will hear yourself as others hear you.
- **Listen for clarity, tone and energy.** Listen for warmth and passion in your voice. Do you sound interesting? Convincing? Confident? Is your speech clear, professional and pleasant? Or do you sound angry, tired, tentative or bored? Is your speaking voice nasal, a monotone or singsong? Do you speak too quickly or slowly? Do you mumble? Most of all, do you sound like someone with whom *you* would like to have a conversation?

Once you've determined what you wish to convey to your prospect, practice your script until it flows easily. The worst phone faux pas is to sound like you are reading straight from a script. Call your friends and pitch them. Perhaps you can work with a colleague who is also making introductory calls. This way, when you have your prospect on the telephone, you will be prepared to voice the message you want to voice, and can use your instrument like a true professional. ■

Wendy Weiss is known as the Queen of Cold Calling. For biographical and business information, see page 276.

Editor's Note: Joe Heller has been building multi-million-dollar revenue streams for over 17 years. He can directly track $237 million in revenues for companies in which he's controlled sales—and countless millions more for his consulting clients. He travels worldwide speaking to international CEO groups, and considers himself a revenue consultant. Here Joe identifies your real competition.

Who Is Your Greatest Competitor?
by Joe Heller

Throughout the history of selling, sales professionals have faced worthy adversaries competing for the same highly-coveted piece of business. Some salespeople point to the large multi-national company, with deep pockets and seemingly endless resources, as their most difficult adversary. Others identify the small boutique firm, the one that somehow always manages to sneak under the radar and call on their best customers, as their staunchest foe. In reality, the most formidable competitor that has haunted salespeople for decades is an invisible competitor: *the unseen attitude of customer indifference.* An old saying warns "You can't fight what you can't see," which is why it is so important to uncover this daunting foe before it delivers a knockout punch to your selling opportunity.

What makes indifference such a challenging competitor? Psychologically, indifference is rooted in our belief system. It is an endemic attitude or viewpoint held by your customers, one that you must change in order to close sales. While you may be able to compete head-on against the visible products of your toughest competitor, the balance of power shifts when you're forced to compete against the human mind.

Indifference is not based on logic, but lies embedded in your client's perception. Many factors contribute to client indifference, including
- familiarity with an existing product
- false satisfaction with a competitor's product
- failure of the buyer to notice additional needs
- failure to recognize the unique benefits of your product or service.

However, the most prevalent factor by far is simple complacency, as in the familiar refrain, "But that's what we've always bought." Indifference comes from the client's opinion that what you are selling is a commodity with relatively no distinction or value over their existing product or service.

How does the successful salesperson confront the competition of indifference? By attacking the issue strategically, armed with a thorough evaluation of a potential client's current business practices. Indifference is overcome when the salesperson maps out a plan to resolve a customer's hidden frustrations by uncovering previously unidentified needs. When approaching indifference, the sales professional must understand the psychological considerations tied to changing an attitude, because the client needs to be motivated to change.

Adopt a Questioning Strategy

To combat indifference, first acknowledge that it affects your customer, then get their permission to ask probing questions that increase your understanding of their specific needs. By adopting a questioning strategy, you help the customer gain an awareness of the needs and problems your product can solve. Probing questions permit you to explore problems that may have been lying dormant or hidden, buried for years by the initial adoption of poor business practices. They also allow you to understand the customer's core business, including any new business strategies the client is planning. Most importantly, they allow you to define the competitive pressures within a market niche or segment, with the goal of helping the customer recognize problems or needs of which he was unaware.

A questioning strategy designed to overcome indifference allows you to identify other suppliers currently doing business with your prospective customer. By evaluating how satisfied the customer is with these suppliers, you uncover business needs he would like to improve. Additionally, strategic questioning provides an opportunity to investigate the customer's strategies and goals, allowing you to align your product or service with the achievement of those business objectives. Once a customer's objectives are in the open, you can determine how your product can assist in meeting them.

Effective probing that links questioning and strategy allows you to become consultative in your selling approach, while focusing on the customer's business needs. Probing also allows you to gain insight into how your customer is positioned in the market. Then you can evaluate how effectively he is competing, identify his main competitors, and determine whether he is gaining or losing market share respective to the specific products and segments served.

Making the customer aware of his satisfaction or dissatisfaction shows the consequences of leaving things unchanged, promoting the need to change. When your questions are carefully crafted by your understanding of his business, the customer sees the immediate cost of not acting in a timely manner. This helps break down the indifference barrier. Learning to recognize indifference and applying appropriate strategies to combat it advances the sale, leading to greater sales success. Sometimes you can overcome indifference immediately, but in most cases, conquering customer indifference requires long-term commitment.

To combat indifference, your questions must enable both parties to gain understanding of the prospect's needs, and drive a business solution. For example:

- How do you feel about the results you're getting now?
- Are you on track to achieve your one-, three-, and five-year goals?
- Are there any competitors in the market impeding your growth plans? How does that affect your business operations/sales? What impact is that having on new client acquisition? Customer retention? Product quality? Productivity? Cash flow?

Keep in mind that an effective questioning strategy involves more than just asking open- and closed-ended questions. It needs to include questions designed to capture account information, help the customer recognize problems, and more importantly, understand what the problems will cost if not addressed. It should also include questions which help the customer recognize that your product is the right solution, one that will drive results to reach his business goals. Indifference is a formidable psychological competitor in the attitudes of our customers. But with the right questioning approach, you can turn customer indifference into customer enthusiasm for your product, service or solution. ■

Joe Heller is founder and president of Trust Cycle Selling. For biographical and business information, see page 268.

Editor's Note: Bill Caskey has over 19 years' experience coaching hundreds of sales professionals and executives. The author of Same Game, New Rules, *Bill has presented over 3,000 workshops in more than 150 business-to-business industries, and invested over 14,000 hours training these companies. Bill distills that experience here to give you the essence of what makes a top performer.*

Success Is An Inside Job
by Bill Caskey

Contrary to the old adage, I believe great salespeople are *made*, not born. Furthermore, the "making" of a great salesperson involves more than just going to the right training classes or having the right coaches. It also requires developing the attitudes, attributes and inner discipline that allow you to maximize what you've learned in those classes and coaching sessions. What are these qualities? Following is my list of the top five attributes of a high-performance sales professional.

- **Mental toughness.** This is skill number one for all salespeople, yet typically it hovers below the radar screen of most conventional sales trainers and recruiters. The top 5% of sales professionals achieve at a higher level than 50% of the rest. Some might attribute these results to superior closing, probing, or territory management skills. In reality, they're a result of mental toughness: the inner ability to know what to do, coupled with the mechanical ability to execute it.

- **Profound communication skills.** Effective communication involves more than just matching and mirroring prospects. Profound communication skills enable you to create an environment of trust in which prospects become willing to share and reveal the truth about their problems. Ninety percent of sales processes are based on lies, misinformation and gamesmanship. In order to get prospects to open up and reveal their problems, you must understand how to communicate in a way that elicits truth. Then, and only then, will you be working on the right problems.

- **Knowledge of value.** Some would say this is not a skill. But if not, what is it? If you don't understand the core tenets of your value proposition, how can you expect to articulate them effectively to the marketplace? In fact, most salespeople have a weak understanding of what a value proposition is, which is why they typically convey only a small percentage of the value their company really offers. Communicating real value requires study, practice, and shedding preconceived notions about what selling really is.
- **The ability to deal with humans.** Those pesky humans! Wouldn't it be nice to not have to deal with all their insecurities and pains? But then, who would write the checks, approve the deals, and have the motivation? When you accepted life on earth, you accepted the challenge of relationships. The better you are at having a relationship with yourself, the better you will be at external relationships. This applies to relationships with your superiors, clients, prospects, vendors and anyone else you come in contact with.

If you're in sales, you signed up for relationships, and lots of them. So your skill at dealing with people is essential. Do you have a good psychological understanding of why people do the things they do? Do you know why most prospects lie about their true motives when a salesperson shows up? Do you know why a prospect gets excited about the presentation, only to disappear two weeks later? Do you know why some prospects simply cannot pull the trigger to buy? People who study this stuff get real good, real quick. They make a great deal of money because they are dialed into their profession at an entirely different level than their competitors.

- **Process thinking.** This essential skill keeps you from spending too much time with the wrong people in the sales process. Time is an active asset, ticking away each day. Do you spend it talking with true prospects who understand and believe in your value, or with average prospects who have to be convinced of the value in your services?

Ideally, it would the former: potential clients who see your value. But that's not what usually happens. Because of insecurity about their own value, most salespeople will spend time with anyone who extends an invitation.

Then, instead of telling the prospect that it doesn't appear to be a good fit, they continue trying to force a fit, ending with confusion, frustration, and possibly a small deal that was hardly worth the time. When you understand up front what a good prospect is, how he thinks and acts, you will spend more time with the right people.

Success is an inside job. By focusing on developing these five attributes, you will acquire the positive attitude and mental discipline necessary to be a high-performing salesperson, and accomplish all you desire in the field of sales. ■

Bill Caskey is president of Caskey Achievement Strategies. For biographical and business information, see page 266.

Editor's Note: For over 15 years, Colleen Francis sold in some pretty tough fields: life insurance and technology. She led one of her sales teams to increase its average per-sale size by 50%. In another instance, she grew her corporate customer base by 300% in just over a year. She's going to demonstrate how you might be training your customers to treat you badly.

Are You Teaching Your Customers to Mistreat You?
by Colleen Francis

Nobody wants to be treated with disrespect. Why, then, do we so often train the people around us, including our customers, to do just that? The fact is, we (and nobody else) are responsible for what happens in our personal and work lives. More importantly, we have a lot of power to change the things we don't like. But if we neglect to pay attention to the messages we send, we are usually rewarded with unintended consequences.

Consider the following real-life example: at one of our seminars, a public relations consultant named Maria related a story about how her husband, Raymond, had begun building a shed in their backyard. Suddenly, for no apparent reason, he decided to stop. Maria repeatedly complained to her husband that the unfinished shed was an eyesore, and asked him to finish the project. When he failed to take immediate action, she did what any right-thinking wife would do: she gave him a deadline to complete it. When the deadline came and went, Maria yelled at her husband, then gave him a new deadline. Maria became incensed when Raymond ignored the second deadline, and stepped up her demands that he finish the project. She gave him a final, this-time-I-really-mean-it deadline, which he promptly ignored.

Maria concluded that it was impossible to train and condition someone to do what you want them to. My response was that Maria had actually trained and conditioned her husband with great success. The problem was, she had trained and conditioned him to believe that her word meant nothing. Obviously, Maria had not intended to condition this response.

But by failing to follow through on her deadlines, she sent a powerful message to her husband that he could continue to ignore her demands.

Silence Equals Consent

Throughout my career, I've seen countless companies and salespeople make this same mistake with their prospects and customers. Sales and discounts are an example. Many companies offer their customers special discounts for placing an order before the end of the month. Their salespeople then exert pressure with statements like, "I can only offer this discount if you buy before April 30th. After that, it's back to full price!" The truth is, if the customer calls on May 5th with a nice, big order and wants the discounted price, nine out of ten companies will give it to her. What these companies fail to realize is that by going back on their word regarding the time limit, they are training their customers to expect they will always get the lower price. In effect, they're conditioning customers to believe that the so-called limited time offers are available for the asking.

We all teach the people around us how to relate to us, whether or not we realize it. Like Maria, if we fail to recognize the messages we send through our action or inaction, we will encounter responses we didn't expect, and probably don't want. What's the best way to counter these mixed messages in sales? Never say anything you do not mean, or do not plan to carry out! For example, suppose you say a report is due by 3:00 p.m., your rep turns it in at 5:00 p.m., and you say nothing about it. You have just trained this person to understand that your deadlines are artificial, and you do not mean what you say.

Maintaining silence is one of the most powerful ways we train others to respond with undesirable behaviors. This was precisely the problem that John, a banker attending one of our seminars, was having at his branch. Whenever his employees did something he disliked, John made a point of not saying anything, believing his silent treatment would let them know how he felt. Unfortunately, his silence had the opposite effect, and his employees kept repeating the undesirable behaviors.

This cause-and-effect relationship holds true with customers as well as employees. If a customer yells at you and you say nothing, you have just told him it is perfectly acceptable to treat you this way. And believe me, he will repeat that behavior with increasing frequency. Customers generally interpret silence as agreement, even if your intention is just the opposite. This is why so many people who hate conflict and avoid addressing troublesome issues end up creating major conflicts anyway. If we say something is "no big deal" when it is a big deal, we train ourselves and others to deny the truth.

Mean What You Say and Say What You Mean

The way we conduct meetings is another great example of the power of our actions to condition those around us. Laurie, a government sales rep for a major software company, was responsible for overseeing the implementation of a new software system at her client's site. The project required weekly meetings, which would be effective only if the entire project team from both companies attended. At almost every meeting, someone arrived late. At first, Laurie accommodated this problem by waiting until everyone arrived before she started the meeting. This put a serious strain on both productivity and client relations. It also trained the other attendees to expect Laurie's meetings always to start late, prompting more and more of them to show up behind schedule.

How did Laurie solve the problem? First, she told her customer that she was responsible for the meetings always starting late. Second, she promised that in the future, meetings would always start on time, regardless of who was present. Third, she kept her word, starting all meetings at the designated time, even if hardly anyone was there. Then she went through the agenda, without backtracking for those who arrived late. When late arrivals requested a review of the information they'd missed, Laurie politely refused, and continued with the agenda as scheduled. In other words, she retrained everyone to believe that the meetings would start on time, and that she meant what she said. Sure enough, it took only a handful of meetings before everyone began showing up on time.

The next time you find yourself faced with responses that strike you as surprising or unreasonable, ask yourself, "How am I training my colleagues and customers to deal with me?"

By realizing how we train and condition other people to deal with us, we can gain control of difficult situations, as well as our careers and our success. ■

Colleen Francis is president of Engage Selling Solutions. For biographical and business information, see page 267.

Editor's Note: Craig James has over 12 years' sales and sales management experience, primarily in technology and software. He holds an MBA from the University of Chicago's Graduate School of Business. In addition to training, coaching, and consulting, he teaches at New York University's School of Continuing and Professional Studies. Craig has been published and quoted in several business publications, including Business Week, Sales and Marketing Management, *and* Selling Power.

Commitment is a Two-Way Street
by Craig James

From day one, asking for commitment from the buyer is drilled into salespeople. Unfortunately, too many of us interpret this as simply asking for the order. Thus we feel the only time to ask for commitment is during the close—when we ask for the ultimate commitment. A far more effective approach involves asking for commitments at various points in the sales cycle. Anyone who has ever experienced the "Things were going great, why won't he call me back?" syndrome will understand why.

First, a prospect's unwillingness to agree to even the smallest request sends up a serious red flag about his level of interest. Second, the more commitments your prospect makes and keeps, the more he has invested in the deal. The more he "sticks his neck out," the more difficult it will be to walk away from the deal. Think about it. Suppose your contact has invested a lot of personal time, and has gotten others, including his boss, to do the same. If this is a high-profile, company-wide investment, it becomes very difficult for the prospect to pull out and say, "We're just going to stick with the status quo," without getting a lot of egg on his face.

Ask for a Reciprocal Commitment

Out of an eagerness to please, salespeople often commit to doing something for the prospect without asking for something in return. Keep in mind that commitment is a two-way street. You have as much right to ask a qualified prospect for help in getting what you need as he does to ask you for help in getting what he needs. For example, the next time your prospect asks you to send some literature, reply with, "Sure, I'll be happy to. To allow you enough time to review it, shall I give you seven or ten days before I call to continue our discussion?" Or the next time your prospect asks, "Can you bring your team in to do a demo?" reply, "Sure, and who will you be inviting to the demo? May I ring them and introduce myself?"

If you aren't getting reciprocal commitments from your prospect equal to or greater than the ones you're being asked to make, address the situation immediately, before even thinking about proceeding. You're much better off ferreting out an early-stage prospect who is unlikely to play ball with you, and who is likely to waste your precious time in the end. Instead, move on to one who will work with you to achieve his objectives through an investment in your product or service. ■

Craig James is founder and president of Sales Solutions. For biographical and business information, see page 269.

Editor's Note: Tom Reilly is one of the industry's foremost authorities on value-added selling. After becoming top salesman at Mallinckrodt Chemical Works in his first year, he started his own successful chemical company. As president of Tom Reilly Training, he speaks to thousands of salespeople, managers, and employees each year at companies like Apple, Ford, and Schlumberger.

When You Can't Compete on Price
by Tom Reilly

If you left your company tomorrow and went to work for a really good competitor, how many of your customers would go with you? (Be honest!) If your answer is a few or none, I've got to tell you that you're not bringing much value to the customer. Think about it. Your competition sells good stuff; you sell good stuff. Their service is acceptable; your service is acceptable. Their prices are competitive; your prices are competitive. In other words, the buyer looks at your package and the competitor's package, and sees parity along both the product and company dimensions.

When products are the same or similar, and the suppliers' services rival each other, the only way to differentiate a solution is through you, the salesperson. In fact, when two Fortune 500 companies asked how much value their salespeople bring to the table, they discovered that 35% to 37% of the value customers receive comes from the people with whom they do business. Do you bring that much value to the table?

A business owner told me he routinely wants to be 10% higher than the competition. "If the buyer doesn't feel I'm at least 10% better than the competition, I need to know about it," he said. If you were in this situation and could not sell at a lower price, how would you communicate your value to the customer? If you could not argue that your service was any better than the competition, how would you sell? If you could not rely on product differentiation, what would you use as an advantage? You'd have only yourself left to sell. Therefore, you must be able to answer the customer's question: "Why should I want to do business with you as a salesperson?"

You are the product over which you have the most control. You may not be able to do anything about your product's quality or your company's service level, but you *can* do something about your performance. One study found that the salesperson's competence is the number one factor accounting for customer satisfaction. All other things being equal, would the customer pay to do business with you as a salesperson? You can increase your value to the customer by doing the following:

- **Study.** Become a serious student of our profession. Increase your knowledge by studying the market, your company, the customer, your products, and our profession. Become an expert; learn so much about your craft that the customer can't afford *not* to do business with you. Become the benchmark by which all other salespeople are judged.

- **Follow up.** The number one complaint buyers have about salespeople is a lack of follow-up. Guarantee your follow-up. Advise buyers that it is part of your added value. Assure them you will be there after the sale to guarantee their complete satisfaction with your solution. Promise your accessibility before, during, and after the sale. Promise a lot, but always deliver more than you promise.

- **Seek to add value, not cost.** Diligently look for ways to add value with your performance. The customer must perceive you as a profit center, not a cost center. Help the customer achieve greater efficiency and higher productivity. Help the buyer gain maximum performance from your solution. Work as hard to keep the business as you did to get it. Look for ways to re-create value at every turn.

When you can't compete on your price, your product, or your company's service, all that's left is you. In fact, you may be the most significant competitive advantage your company offers. In our commodity-based world, selling success often comes down to a basic question: "Are your customers willing to pay more to do business with you, the salesperson?" ■

Tom Reilly is president of Tom Reilly Training. For biographical and business information, see page 272.

Editor's Note: Since 1989, Kevin Davis has trained tens of thousands of sales-people and sales managers. He is president of TopLine Leadership, a sales training and consulting firm. Before starting his company, Kevin was a sales representative, account executive, sales manager, and district general manager during his distin-guished career with Lanier Worldwide. In each of his positions, he earned annual awards for ranking in the top 5%. As a sales manager, Kevin hired, trained and coached over 250 salespeople. Kevin Davis is the author of Getting into Your Customer's Head.

Going Beyond Show and Tell
by Kevin Davis

The sales presentation is your best opportunity to "show and tell," but there's more to it than just showing and telling. You also need to think strategically about the customer's buying process and his needs, your competitors' offerings, and why your solution is best.

To plan and deliver winning sales presentations, try the following approach:

- **Find out in advance how much time you have.** Have you ever had a key decision-maker leave in the middle of your presentation because he was out of time? You can't hold someone's attention when he's looking at the clock! At the beginning of the call, ask how much time the prospect has set aside, then adjust your presentation to take no more than 60% of the allotted time. Why only 60%? Because your prospects' decisions to act typically occur at the end of a meeting. Adjusting your presentation will allow enough time to resolve any remaining issues, and reach an agreement.

- **Check in.** Another good question to ask at the beginning of every sales presentation is, "Since the last time we met, has anything changed?" If your competitor gave a presentation yesterday, you may have a few new hurdles to overcome. The sooner you identify those hurdles, the more time you have to plan a response.

- **Take his temperature.** The next question you want to ask is, "Where are you in your decision process?" If he tells me he's scheduled presentations with three suppliers and I am the first presenter, I know the chances of him agreeing to a decision at the end of my presentation are virtually nonexistent. For starters, it would take the prospect more time, energy and stress to cancel the appointments than to go ahead with them. More importantly, the prospect wants to hear all three presentations, because comparison is necessary to recognize value. Never go for the close if you're the first presenter. You're asking for something you can't get, and customers will think you're pushy. Instead, come up with a legitimate reason to come back after the other presentations, when the prospect likely will be in a position to make a decision.

- **Try to be the last presenter.** The last presenter has a significant advantage, because he is closest to the customer's point of decision. If I am the final supplier to present, and have shown why I am the best choice, it's only reasonable to ask for a commitment to buy. It also creates an opportunity to address any lingering concerns that may prevent a sale.

In one of the largest sales opportunities I ever worked on, I was the third of three presenters to a committee of seven decision-makers, the most senior of whom was the executive vice president, Mr. Burns. Ten minutes before the conclusion of my presentation, the phone rang. Mr. Burns had a plane to catch, and his cab had arrived. As he stood up, I said, "Mr. Burns, before you leave, may I ask you one final question?" He said, "Sure." I asked, "Now that you've evaluated all the options, is there any reason why my solution is not your best option?" He said, "Yep!" And out came his final concern about my solution. It was a concern I was ready for, but I never got the chance to respond because his comment triggered a firestorm of conversation around the conference table. Mr. Burns missed his cab, but several other decision-makers drove him to the airport so they could continue their discussion.

- **Arm your contacts.** A few weeks later, I learned that in the car on the way to the airport, a lower-level decision-maker had resolved Mr. Burns's concern—and I won the sale! This example shows that today, as much as 90% of the sale takes place without you in the room. So it's essential to make sure that the prospects championing your cause have the tools to sell other decision-makers for you.

- **Start with a quick review of the customer's goals and objectives.** On a flip chart, list each of the customer's buying criteria. (This list is your outline for an effective sales presentation.) Next, show how your solution meets and exceeds each criterion. Throughout your presentation, get a reaction from your prospect. For example, after demonstrating a capability you could ask, "How would this be an improvement?" or "How would this help?" Interactive presentations keep prospects more involved and interested.

- **Communicate all your unique strengths.** Today's customers want to know two things: can you do what we need done, and how can you do it better than the other options we are considering? It's not enough to show that you can meet their needs. You must also have some reasons why you are their best choice. To ensure that my strengths are understood, I always prepare a flip chart titled "Why We're Your Best Choice," which lists at least three reasons why I'm the customer's best choice. Often, I list seven or eight reasons. The more reasons you have, and the more compelling those reasons are, the better your chances of winning the sale.

- **Use visuals.** A picture is worth a thousand words. Support your important ideas with a picture, or show images on an overhead, flip chart, or laptop computer. Keep your visuals simple: one idea per image. Make the presentation interesting, relevant and readable.

- **Be willing to reschedule.** If your customer is not in a position to make a decision at the end of your presentation, schedule another appointment. Come up with a reason to get back in there.

- **Be yourself.** Last, but not least: have fun and be yourself. If you want to persuade other people, you must first connect with them on a personal level. To put more impact in your sales presentations, connect with your prospects just by being you.

In sports, when two teams are evenly matched, the winner is the team that makes the fewest mistakes, and executes its plays the best. To deliver a winning sales presentation, you must do the same. When you implement these ten tips in your sales presentations, you will win more sales! ∎

Kevin Davis is president of TopLine Leadership Inc. For biographical and business information, see page 266.

Editor's Note: Art Sobczak is a renowned leader in telesales training. He's back to share his real-world tips for making effective follow-up calls.

Follow-up Calls That Work
by Art Sobczak

Want to throw cold water on a hot prospect as quickly as possible? Then start your next follow-up call with one of the following approaches:

- Ask for a decision: "I was calling to see if you're ready to buy now."
- Be reactive: "I was just checking to see if you had any questions."
- Perform a quality test of the U.S. Postal Service: "I wanted to see if you received the material I sent."

Most salespeople never give a second thought to their follow-up calls. As a result, many never get a second chance at earning the prospect's business. If you want to fan the flames that keep prospects interested in learning more about your product or service, pay close attention to how you conduct your follow-up calls.

To begin with, your follow-up calls should always be based upon a specific objective. For example, the prospect agreed to do something between the last call and the scheduled follow-up: something that would make this call worthwhile. Or a future event was to take place, one that would make the follow-up more appropriate, such as the beginning of a new budget year. Either way, there must be a good reason why you and the prospect agreed to a follow-up call. (The standard "Call me back in six weeks" is *not* a specific objective, and rarely leads to a productive follow-up call.)

Secondly, the opening of your follow-up call needs to smoothly bring the customer's state of mind back to where it was when you ended the previous conversation. Specifically, it needs to bring him into a conversation that readdresses the hot points which fueled his interest during the last call, and move the process closer to the ultimate outcome you are seeking: the sale. Unless you accomplish both goals in the opening, your prospect will lose interest, and the follow-up call will go nowhere.

Opening Format

To create strong openings for your follow-up calls, use the following formula:

- **Identification.** When introducing yourself, a good rule of thumb is "the less familiarity, the more formality." If you have spoken only once, include your first, last and company names. If you are well-acquainted, use your judgment as to what sounds appropriate.
- **Bridge.** To bring the prospect back to the desired emotional state, remind him of his interest and the previous call. Use phrases like: "…calling to continue our conversation of two weeks ago…," "I'd like to pick up where we left off…," "…calling to resume our discussion of (mention what his main interest was)," or " …where we went through the savings you'd show with internal management of your… ."
- **Agenda.** This part of the call should be proactive. For example, "I'd like to go through the material I sent you to point out the specific cost-cutting features that apply… ." Other proactive words and phrases include "discuss," "analyze," "cover," "review," and "walk through."

Remember, you're not calling just to check in, or hit him with a goofy question like, "Well, what'd you think? Are you ready now?" You must also bring something new to the table, some value-added reason for this call beyond what was covered last time. That way, if his interest has waned since the last contact, and/or he didn't follow through with what he said he'd do (which happens often), you still have a basis for continuing this contact. For example, "I also did some research, and came up with a few examples of something you showed interest in the last time we spoke, how other engineering firms have used this process."

The opening is a small but integral part of the follow-up contact. When well-prepared and executed, it enables you to rekindle the prospect's interest, and move him to the next phase of the call, which is your questioning. ∎

Art Sobczak is president of Business By Phone Inc. For biographical and business information, see page 274.

Editor's Note: Jill Konrath is a product launch consultant, specializing in the handoff from marketing to sales. She's back again, to show you how those glossy new brochures derail your sales efforts.

Collateral Damage: How New Product Brochures Kill Deals
by Jill Konrath

When companies introduce new products and services, everyone is excited and upbeat—especially the sales force. They have a new reason to go back to old customers, an opportunity to knock out competitors, and the potential to have a great year. Yet all too often, things don't work out quite as planned. Customers are hesitant to embrace the new product or service. Sales come in more slowly than projected. As the tension rises, marketing and sales start pointing fingers, blaming each other for the lackluster results.

Sound familiar? I can't tell you how many times in my years as a consultant I've seen this scenario unfold. Many factors are involved, some of which are beyond the salesperson's control. But there is one important factor over which you have total control.

Recently, I worked with a company that had just introduced a new technology product. This product was way ahead of the competition, and offered a strong value proposition. To gain a better understanding of the company's sales process, I spent a day in the field with one of their salespeople. "Dave" was a real nice guy. He had been with the company for 13 years, and had always done a decent job. We had an appointment with a good prospect, someone he'd called on before, but with whom he had never done business. Dave's plan was to leverage this meeting into a full-blown needs analysis.

Though he started out fine, Dave was in deep trouble within 10 minutes. It started when he mentioned his excitement about the new product. The buyer asked some techie questions that Dave understood, and they talked some more. Then the buyer asked the near-fatal question, "Do you have a brochure?" You're probably thinking this was a good sign: Dave was doing a great job, and the prospect had a real interest in the new product. That's exactly what Dave thought. And his next move was his undoing.

Dave pulled a glossy, full-color brochure from his briefcase, and laid it on the desk between them. The buyer leaned forward and started reading. "Can it do this?" he asked, referring to a specific capability. "How about that? What speed? How does it connect?" The barrage of questions continued for what seemed like an eternity. As the prospect peppered him with questions, Dave grew even more excited. He pointed out features that had been discussed at the launch meeting, highlighting how much better the product was than anything else on the market. All the while, the buyer nodded his head as if in agreement. I knew the sales call was going downhill fast, but could do nothing to stop it. My role was to listen and observe.

Finally, the killer question emerged: "How much does it cost?" Trying to deflect the question, Dave explained that a full assessment was needed to configure the system properly. He suggested that as the next step—but the damage was already done. "You'd be wasting your time," the buyer said. "There's no way we can spend that kind of money right now. Besides, it can't...," he said as he proceeded to pick apart some minor detail about the system. Dave looked puzzled, not understanding why this obviously-qualified buyer would so quickly reject the new product, especially when it had such a financially attractive value proposition. Though he tried valiantly, Dave couldn't get the meeting back on track, and we left with no follow-up planned.

It seemed like Dave had done everything right. What went wrong? It was that darn brochure! By bringing it out so early, Dave lost control of the sales process, and essentially dug his own grave. He failed to uncover any of the customer's problems, difficulties or dissatisfactions with his current system, and did not explore any business ramifications, or find any payoffs for making a change. No wonder the buyer said it was too expensive. The worst thing was this: everything that happened was totally preventable.

The moral of this story is that the untimely use of brochures and other marketing collateral can quickly derail the best sales efforts, even with highly-qualified prospects. If your sales process requires multiple calls and involves a variety of decision-makers, keep your new product or service brochures in your car on the first call. Instead, use early sales calls to focus on the customer's goals, processes, challenges, issues, bottlenecks, and needs—and save your brochures until later. Who knows? If you do a good job of uncovering the client's pain, and demonstrating an appropriate, cost-effective solution, you may never even need them! ■

Jill Konrath is Chief Sales Officer of Selling to Big Companies. For biographical and business information, see page 270.

Editor's Note: Linda Richardson was the director of a private school in New York City before heading the training department of a major New York bank. Over 25 years ago, she founded Richardson, a leading sales training and consulting firm. Her thoughts on a prickly subject will have you looking at the competition differently.

Asking Customers About the Competition
by Linda Richardson

Smart salespeople use a variety of methods to gather important information about their competitors: newspapers, magazines, trade shows, the Internet, marketing and promotional materials. Surprisingly, though, the simplest and most effective method for gaining competitor information is often the most overlooked: *asking the customer.*

Why don't more salespeople ask their customers about the competition? Some consider it inappropriate. Others may not want to hear what could be bad news. Some get so caught up in learning about the client's needs that they forget to ask. But most salespeople, it seems, are simply not disciplined enough to make it a critical part of their sales dialogue.

As a professional salesperson, it is vital that you ask about competitors. Most of the time, clients will readily tell you about competitors giving you important information to plan a competitive strategy, and properly position your solution. A small percentage of clients may refuse to answer. For them, a simple acknowledgement like, "I can understand," then moving the conversation along, works well. Or you can ask, "I know you don't want to share names. How does (your idea) compare to what else you are hearing?"

Try using the following strategies to learn about your competitors:

- **Time it.** Don't ask about competitors too early in the meeting. Instead, identify the client's objective, needs, and current situation before raising the competitor issue. The best time to ask about competitors is after you ask about the client's criteria, but before you position what you offer. This can help you preface your competitive question with a client benefit. For example, "To help me understand the approaches you are considering, can you tell me who else you are talking to?" When the client mentions the competitor, you have a perfect opportunity to probe the topic.

- **Probe it.** Once the subject comes up, acknowledge what the client says. When you learn who the competitor is, ask for details: What is their approach? What are they offering? How does the customer feel about it? After positioning your ideas, ask the client, "How do you feel we compare?" and drill down to gain specifics. Find out who the competition has met with, what the relationship is, and what they are offering. These questions will enable you to gain very important competitive data for this and other sales. However, if the customer is reluctant to answer these questions, tread gently.

To obtain multiple viewpoints, ask other contacts in the client's organization for their perspective on the competition. Once, a salesperson was told by a prospect that her experience with the company's top competitor would be detrimental. However, after speaking with two other decision-makers in the company, she learned that the company considered her relationship with the prospect's competitor to be a big advantage, and she went on to use that knowledge to win the business.

- **Offset it.** Know your competitors, but never denigrate them. To point out competitive weaknesses, ask questions that strike at the competitor's weakness. For example, if you know the competitor has poor distribution capabilities, ask about that and then position your capabilities to highlight your advantage. Sometimes you can raise a point that the customer has not previously considered. Always ask your client for feedback on what you have positioned.

The most compelling reason to ask about the competition is to uncover the information you need to create a competitive strategy. Asking about competitors provides you with competitive data that is critical not only to your deal, but to your organization. Remember, just knowing who the competitors are is not enough. As you debrief, ask yourself, "Who are the competitors? How do my offerings stack up? How does the client feel about them? How does the client feel about the competition compared to my company?"

No matter who the competitor is, don't underestimate yourself, and never assume that you can't compete. Instead, remain confident, ask questions, and get specifics. In doing so, you can get the competitive information you need to differentiate your offering, and win the business. ■

Linda Richardson is president and founder of Richardson. For biographical and business information, see page 272.

It's a Jungle Out There
by Michael Dalton Johnson

Whoever coined the phrase, "It's a jungle out there!" must have been a sales rep. Why? Because some days you'll encounter more difficult customers than there are animals in the jungle. When hacking your way through the dense underbrush to get to the sale, the trick is to stay cool, calm and in control. See if you recognize here some of the creatures you must deal with from time to time. Then follow my simple instructions for a successful sales safari.

- **The Monkey.** This quarrelsome and inconsiderate buyer goes out of his way to make trouble. The Monkey likes to fume, argue and misrepresent facts, and particularly enjoys trying to derail your presentation. This type must be treated politely, patiently, and without direct counterargument. Ignore his antics, keep your presentation on track, and, above all, be firm! When Monkey sees he is not getting to you, Monkey will calm down.

- **The Sloth.** This ultra-deliberate client is painfully slow-moving, slow-thinking, and indecisive. Speak to the Sloth slowly and clearly, taking up just one point at a time. Do not confuse him with superfluous details or complex concepts. The upside is that once the Sloth truly gets it, he is usually sold!

- **The Magpie.** A most talkative customer, the Magpie chatters without stopping, often forgets what he started to say, and without prompting, cheerfully launches into his family history, holiday plans, or stories from his college days. Treat this type with tolerance and self-control. Be watchful for opportunities to bring him back. Lead the conversation, be businesslike, and keep him focused on your sales message.

- **The Crab.** This crabby prospect may be tired, ill, unhappy, nervous, or just chronically irritable. Ever moving sideways, the Crab is contradictory, jumpy, and must be met with patience and a calm, soothing voice. A warm smile coupled with agreement, understanding, and respect, will usually win him over.

- **The Peacock.** A self-important and snobbish decision-maker, the Peacock fans his tail feathers and looks down his regal beak at you and the goods or services you offer. The Peacock often makes haughty or derisive remarks, which requires rigid politeness and good temper from you. Your best bet is to ignore his preening, posturing, and snooty behavior, and pleasantly move on with your presentation.

- **The Cat.** The Cat is your most suspicious contact. This animal doubts the sincerity or accuracy of your representations, is cynical about your claims, and demands clear, detailed proof of benefits backed up by hard, documented facts. Your deference and unruffled temper will pay off. Do not be intimidated or insulted by his sometimes rude remarks, which question your product's worth, or your honesty and sincerity.

- **The Rooster.** This decisive, smart-aleck customer is cocksure, impatient, and intolerant. Since the Rooster rules the roost, this type wishes to make his own decision without appearing to yield to a mere salesperson. Rooster should be permitted to strut his way to a decision while you practice good humor, respect, and patience.

- **The Dodo.** With a room-temperature IQ and the attention span of a three-year-old, the Dodo is the airhead of the sales animal menagerie. Don't be surprised if, at the end of your presentation, this poor soul is still unclear on exactly what you're selling, and what he's supposed to do. Don't bother starting over, because the Dodo probably doesn't have the buying authority anyway. Instead, diplomatically locate someone who does.

- **The Mouse.** We all have met the indecisive or timid prospect who does not know his own mind, and is vague and uncertain. This type needs to have the facts presented confidently and clearly, and his mind literally made up for him. With tact and understanding, give the Mouse what he wants, which is to be led gently by hand to the buying decision.

- **The Crow.** Here is the stingy, close-to-the-chest buyer, who is interested not so much in benefits and features as in picking your price apart. The loud and repeated cry of this bird is "too high, too high!" Dealing with him calls for concentration on price justification, backed up with solid, documented proof. Stick to your guns to win the Crow's respect, and his order.

- **The Beaver.** This super-busy type hardly has time to hear you out. Given to taking—even making—phone calls and conducting other business during your presentation while continually looking at his watch, this type needs a highly visual and entertaining presentation to grab his interest. Be quick to get to the bottom-line benefits of your product or service. Once sold, show Mr. Busy Beaver where to sign on the dotted line, so you can be on your way and he can get back to being busy.

As you can see, the sales world has its share of wild and wooly creatures. Put on your pith helmet, study the habits of these sometimes cantankerous creatures, and learn how to respond to their individual idiosyncrasies. You'll have more fun while preserving your sanity and closing more sales. ∎

Michael Dalton Johnson is founder and president of SalesDog.com. For biographical and business information, see page 269.

*Editor's Note: Early in life, Jacques Werth discovered his passion for sales. When his wife asked him to retire in 1990 after 40 years, he found retirement bored him out of his mind. So he wrote that book he'd always wanted to write—*High Probability Selling. *Now Jacques has made a new career out of studying the top 1% of sales professionals, and modeling their techniques for the rest. His analysis takes the difficulty out of high-tech selling.*

Is High-Tech Selling Really That Difficult?
by Jacques Werth

True or false: selling high-tech products and services is much more difficult than selling most other products and services. The answer is "both." Selling anything that is not a known commodity can be difficult. However, most of the difficulty stems from a traditional selling methodology that *creates* obstacles during the sales process rather than *removing* them. Here are some of the reasons why high-tech sales seem so difficult.

- **Most salespeople are unable to clearly and briefly describe their product or service.** Most people take 20 to 30 seconds to decide whether they want what a salesperson is selling. As a result, prospects get frustrated and annoyed when the salesperson fails to communicate with immediate clarity. An effective prospecting offer should be no more than 45 words. Top salespeople can take up to two hours to design an effective and concise prospecting offer. Most salespeople do not even know where to start.

- **Pressing prospects for an appointment before they are ready to buy greatly reduces the probability of ever getting the sale.** Most salespeople believe they should convince any prospect who has an apparent need for their products and services to buy. However, most prospects are not ready to buy the first time the salesperson calls. Driven by the mistaken belief that he should be able to convince the prospect, the salesperson presses for an appointment. Instead, the best route to ultimate success is to call each prospect every three to four weeks (limiting each prospecting call to a maximum of 45 seconds), changing the wording of your offer each time. That will condition the prospect to take your calls until he is ready to meet and specify or buy your type of product or service.

- **Premature selling efforts leave a lasting negative impression, and dramatically reduce the odds of ever doing business with that prospect.** "Forced" appointments and communications result in closed sales less than 14% of the time. When they feel pressured, prospects who don't commit to doing business on the first visit are even less likely to ever buy. The probability of eventually getting that sale drops to 5%.

- **Most high-tech salespeople first approach a prospective customer at the end-user level.** Most line managers do not have the authority to buy, and usually do not have access to the funds. Instead, they are "influencers" who make recommendations. The top 1% of the salespeople we studied usually initiates their sales process at the vice president level, which requires a specifically-tailored approach.

- **High-tech salespeople are fascinated with the features and benefits of their products and services.** Most prospects only want to know what your products and services can do for them. Once they determine that what you have is what they want, they will want to know how your particular product works (its features). Most salespeople honestly—and mistakenly—believe that prospects need to be educated before they can make an intelligent decision.

- **Most high-tech salespeople focus on concrete product specifications, and ignore their prospects' two primary motivators: trust and respect.** In high-tech sales, a common mistake is dealing with prospects on the basis of specifications, good presentations, logical arguments, convincing documentation, and factual economic justifications. Most prospects, including engineers and senior managers, have different motives. Their first priority is to deal with a salesperson they fully trust and respect. Only the top 1% of salespeople knows how to establish that kind of relationship in the first half-hour of meeting a prospect, and continuously reinforce it.

- **Most high-tech salespeople acknowledge that they are weak closers.** Salespeople assume that with enough education and information, prospects will logically determine that their product or service is valuable and worth buying. The top 1% of salespeople closes a sale after the prospect has effectively closed them. Starting with agreements made during the initial prospecting call, they arrive at dozens of mutual commitments throughout the sales process. The sum of those commitments is a closed sale with absolutely no pressure on either party.

High-tech salespeople who are strong on product knowledge and weak on the one-to-one sales process help perpetuate the myth that high-tech sales are difficult. The truth is that selling high-tech products and services is easy, when an effective selling process is utilized with each and every individual involved in the buying decision. ∎

Jacques Werth is president of High Probability® Selling. For biographical and business information, see page 277.

Editor's Note: Joe Guertin began his training career when an advertising sales client asked him to share his selling philosophy at their sales meeting. Joe was happy to oblige, and a new career was launched. Today, Joe is a leading sales trainer, specializing in developing new business and selling value versus price. Here are some of Joe's secrets to closing.

The Lost Art of Closing
by Joseph Guertin

Closing a sale is nothing more that leading the process to a conclusion. It involves laying all the groundwork, and asking the prospective customer to proceed with the action plan. But if closing is so easy, why is it so difficult to accomplish? According to NASCAR driver Kurt Busch, "Winning a championship requires having your preparation meet the opportunities, whether it's out on the racetrack or behind the scenes." In sales, winning starts at the beginning. Do the right things throughout the process and you'll be better positioned for success.

The steps in the sales process may vary. But in talking to hundreds of successful salespeople about what gets in the way of effectively closing a sale, three critical errors are mentioned over and over again:

1. We do not ask for the sale.
2. We ask the wrong person.
3. We try to close before the prospect is sold.

Let's take a look at why these common closing mistakes occur, and what we can do about them.

"Good" Advice, Bad Results

Often, we don't ask for the sale because of the "feel good" advice given in recent years that "good salespeople don't close the sale, they let it happen." In other words, make your presentation, stop talking, and the sale will close itself! That's like telling an airplane pilot not to worry about landing because the plane will get to the ground one way or another.

Even the sharpest businessperson can be indecisive. If I make a terrific presentation, then wait for the prospect to say "yes," I will likely never hear that word, and will ultimately lose a once-promising sale. Why? *Because I have not asked him to make a decision.* In addition, my lack of action might plant a seed of doubt in the prospect's subconscious mind.

Early in my sales career, a senior co-worker urged me to "go out and get as many 'no's' as you can." His message didn't sink in at first, but I soon understood what he meant. If you want to avoid rejection, not asking for the business is the way to go. But if you want to close as many sales as possible, ask for the order—and ask for it often!

Don't Take "No" From Someone Who Can't Say "Yes"

The second criterion involves making sure you ask the right person. Have you heard the phrase, "Don't take 'no' from someone who can't say 'yes'?" This definitely applies to closing a sale. We sometimes find ourselves boxed into a situation where our primary contact is not the final decision-maker. This person—often a buyer—has the power to say 'no,' but isn't empowered to say 'yes'. He meets with suppliers to gather information and prices, but the ultimate decision is made by committee, or in budget meetings.

To resolve this dilemma, start by making connections at the top. Call the company president first, and set up a meeting by explaining, "An opportunity to work with your company is very important to us, and I want to make sure I've got a complete understanding of your goals." You'll be surprised at how easily executive doors open to salespeople who show a genuine interest in helping company presidents solve their problems. Once that connection is made, continue to follow up. Send a summary of your proposal and a thank you note, to keep the door open and yourself in the president's mind.

At the same time, give your direct contact everything needed to sell the proposal internally. For example, a company I consult for was considering a new software package. I sat in on a meeting where the IT manager tossed copies of three proposals on the table and asked everybody to choose one. Effective questioning would have helped the vendors see that this manager did not want to make the decision alone. A smart salesperson would have offered to attend the meeting and give the group an overview of the proposal. That is our job as salespeople; but too often, we fail to follow through with this important step.

You might think these strategies apply only to large companies with deep management structures. But the same rules apply to small businesses. They even apply to in-home selling, where the presence and commitment of a spouse often makes the difference between closing the sale and closing the door.

Make Sure They're Sold

Finally, make sure that the prospect is convinced. This might sound like Sales 101, but making sure the prospect is sold often represents the greatest roadblock we face. Today's fast-paced business climate forces us to conserve our time and the prospect's time. It is not unusual for a sales call to consist of a phone call, an invitation to visit a website, and a price quote sent via email. I believe in using tech tools to save time, but I also continually remind myself that efficiency in time does not always lead to efficiency in selling.

Improve the Odds

To immediately boost your closing ratio, ask yourself four key questions:

1. **Does the customer have a burning need for my product or service, or just a mild interest?** I've always been good at selling meetings and convincing people to give me a piece of their time. I figured all we had to do was talk, they would see the need to act, and I'd have a sale. Wrong! I quickly learned that when a prospect doesn't see me as a solution to his problem, my chances of making a sale are nil. Moreover, their burning needs are not always obvious. For example, a retailer might want to draw more store traffic. But if the deeper need is to position his store against large discount retailers, he might see spending more money as throwing good money after bad.

2. **Is this a fast-track decision or future exploration?** We need to know in advance if the prospect plans to make a decision soon, or is merely looking at pricing for future consideration. Sometimes we add a prospect to our pending list without knowing his timetable or intent.

3. **What is their status with other suppliers?** Comfort levels make people do strange things. The buyer might have a good relationship with you, and may even be signaling "yes." But buyers often find it more reassuring to go with their existing supplier, because the known is always more comfortable than the unknown.

4. **Have I presented my case based on their needs and goals?** A "one-size-fits-all" presentation has far less impact than one custom-tailored to the customer's exact needs. For instance, if I sell accounting software and learn that the company's office manager dislikes long learning curves that bog down productivity, my proposal will include a strategy for getting the staff trained and acclimated within a specified timeframe. That might not be a feature of the software, but my presentation will be more customer-centered, which increases my probability of closing the sale.

The final step in any sale, which has nearly become a lost art, is *asking for the sale*. It sounds simple—and it is! Asking for the sale can be a simple question or statement like, "Should we go ahead and get started?" or "Let's get the paperwork done so we can start shipping next week." The worst thing that can happen is the prospect might not be ready, and he will tell you why.

In reality, closing is a beginning, not an ending. Our job is to take the time to understand the customer's needs, demonstrate a sincere desire to be of service, then confidently lead the sales process to a mutually beneficial conclusion. Though that may be where the transaction ends, it is where real customer relationships begin. ■

Joe Guertin is president of The Guertin Group. For biographical and business information, see page 268.

Editor's Note: Tony Alessandra has a streetwise, college-smart perspective on busi-ness, having fought his way out of New York City to success as a graduate professor of marketing, an entrepreneur, business author, and keynote speaker. He earned his MBA from the University of Connecticut, and his PhD in Marketing from Georgia State University. He is a widely published author, with 14 books trans-lated into 17 languages.

Juggling After-Sale Customer Care
by Tony Alessandra

Not too long ago, every circus or traveling road show had a juggler, a gifted performer who amazed and delighted audiences by keeping all manner of objects flying through the air with apparent ease. For sales-people, attending to established clients while trying to win new ones some-times seems like a juggling act. The juggler's fear is that if any of the whirling balls drops, the act fails. The bad news is, if the balls drop too often, that fear will be realized. The good news is that if a ball or two occa-sionally drops, the act usually can be salvaged. Like a juggler, the successful salesperson needs to balance and organize his performance so the move-ment continues in a positive, exciting direction—a task often easier said than done.

How do you, the modern salesperson, go about accomplishing this? Maintaining all your accounts requires scheduling them for periodic calls. The timing and logistics of calling on your accounts should be planned but flexible. Monitor your customers, be sensitive to their needs, and stay alert to the following warning signals of client dissatisfaction (the drop-ping of one of those gravity-defying balls):

- Changes in purchase volume. Unless external variables have a bearing on a product's sales, a decrease in volume should be inter-preted as a warning signal.
- An increase in the number and frequency of complaints about your product, customer service, company policies, pricing or delivery.
- Repeated comments about the merits of the competition.

- A decrease in rapport. A less cordial atmosphere during your sales calls indicates a breakdown in the relationship.
- The hiring of managerial personnel unfamiliar with your product or service, who seem to have no desire to become familiar with it.
- The absorption of your client's company by a larger firm. Companies often start over by accepting bids on different products or services, and you may find yourself back at square one.

When it comes to your attention that an account is unraveling, conduct an immediate and thorough investigation. Contact the client and respond to any complaints in a calm, realistic fashion. If you're lucky, that will effectively handle the complaint. At other times, winning back lost customers takes you once again through the process of establishing trust, identifying needs, determining solutions, and assuring the customer that things will improve in the future. This is time-consuming; you must decide if the account is worth your time and effort.

Annual Client Reviews

Annual or periodic client reviews provide a valuable tool for looking at the activities of an account, an industry in general, competitors, company strengths and weaknesses, and so on. In addition to determining this information for yourself, meet with your accounts to discuss where you've been and where you're going together. This special meeting will give you feedback about your customer's level of satisfaction, and provide an opportunity to introduce new products or services. It will also convey that you care, and strengthen the trust bond between you.

To set the stage for an effective meeting:

1. Arrange a breakfast or lunch meeting at your customer's convenience.
2. Select a place that is well-lit, and conducive to conversation.
3. Invite all the necessary participants on the account. If there are two buyers, invite them both.
4. Bring all records necessary to discuss the previous year's business.
5. Allow an adequate amount of time for the meeting.

6. Be prepared and organized. Know what you want to talk about, and proceed in a logical manner. Take notes if necessary, and send a typed copy to the participants within one week after the meeting.
7. Listen carefully for implied needs and concerns.
8. Reiterate your desire to be of service and to maintain an open, trusting relationship.
9. During your conversation, look for opportunities above and beyond the client's immediate horizon. Ask for referrals and letters of testimony if appropriate.
10. After the review, offer a new idea, service, product or special promotional offer. This is an excellent opportunity to spark interest in something new.

Diamonds in the Rough

It is not enough merely to service your present clients. Smart salespeople are continually looking for new sources of business within their current customer base. There's a famous story about a nineteenth-century farmer who sold his farm and traveled the world in search of his fortune. After exhausting all his resources, he lost hope and threw himself into the ocean. Meanwhile, acres of diamonds were discovered on his farm, which yielded an incredible fortune! The moral of the story is that opportunities are in front of us every day, but we miss them in our anxious search for new horizons. The professional salesperson recognizes that current clients represent the best source of new business. If you have a strong relationship with your customers, you can feel comfortable asking them for referrals, which may bring additional accounts. Here are several ways to expand your business through your customers:

- **Referrals within their company.** Whenever you talk to clients, keep one eye open for clues that indicate needs within their company, for example, a new office or branch that may need your product or service. Ask your customers for a referral, either verbally or in writing.
- **Referrals outside their company.** Ask your clients if they know anyone else who may have a need for your services. If possible, get

clients to write or endorse a testimonial letter. Testimonials are much more powerful than simply saying, "Bill Jones of Real-Time Systems sent me." Always ask clients for permission to use them as references.

- **Sell more of the same.** While servicing an account, suggest that they buy more if you see they have the capacity to use larger volumes of your product. Under no circumstances, though, should you try to sell them more if they do not need it.

- **Sell additional products or services.** If you see a need, offer new products and services to your present customers. If they like your original product, they will listen to your ideas about expanding into other products.

- **Upgrade your clients.** If a client uses a medium-priced product, you may be able to upgrade him to a higher-priced, higher-quality product, especially if his company is growing and its needs are changing. For example, a company using a copying machine may need one with more capabilities, such as photo-reduction and collating. If you are aware of their increased needs, suggest the upgrade—before your competitor does.

Follow-through after the sale is a never-ending balancing act. It requires communication, sensitivity to the other person's needs, and a commitment to grow together. As a salesperson, exert an extra measure of effort to ensure the continuation of your performance. Remember, clients can walk out on you anytime they feel dissatisfied or don't like your performance. So visualize yourself as a command performer for your customers, and you will find they appreciate you more because of it. Undoubtedly this will result in numerous encores—with your current clients, and with their referrals. ■

Tony Alessandra is president of AssessmentBusinessCenter.com. For biographical and business information, see page 264.

Editor's Note: Prior to starting her sales consulting firm, Jill Konrath was a highly successful sales executive, regional sales manager, and product launch manager for leading technology companies. Jill's back with some timely tips on handling objections.

Sometimes the Best Defense is a Good Offense
by Jill Konrath

In the field of sales, there's a school of thought that says objections are a good thing, and that salespeople should welcome them as a sign that the prospect is interested.

Riiiight. That's like saying you should welcome getting a flat tire on a long road trip, because changing tires builds character. Objections are trouble, pure and simple! Anyone who tells you to embrace them because they mean you're one step closer to the sale is living in the past. Customers who have an objection about your product or service are functionally unable to listen to you. While you're busy asking them questions or sharing information, their attention is focused elsewhere. Customers with objections have an invisible CD player inside their heads. It keeps playing the same disk over and over again, telling them things like:

"Her prices are much higher than the competitors."

"This won't integrate with our current systems."

"I can't do business with a company that's in financial trouble."

"We can't afford a $400,000 system right now."

"They've never worked with a firm like ours."

With messages like these playing at full blast, there's no way prospective customers can concentrate on what you're saying. Finally, toward the end of your meeting, they blurt out, "That's pretty expensive!"

Now you're stuck, because you have to justify your price, experience, capabilities or whatever else the customer is objecting to. And you have to do it really well, in order to convince someone that he should agree with you. But people hate being convinced. You're caught in a double bind:

either way, you lose. How can you avoid this thorny situation? Bring up the ugly objection yourself, and deal with it at the beginning of your sales call. This may sound counterintuitive, but if you do it right, it works every time.

In my consulting practice, I often help companies figure out what differentiates their top performers from their average ones. I recently finished such a project with a company selling medical insurance, whose co-payments and initial out-of-pocket hospitalization costs are higher than their competitors in some areas of the country. For many sales reps this was a showstopper, something they just could not overcome. But not for the top sellers. Every one of them dealt with this objection up front, and in most cases it became a non-issue.

For example, after building rapport with the customer, the sales rep would say something like:

> "Ms. Customer, your decision on your health care coverage is a critical one. It shouldn't be made on whether there is a $5 or $10 co-payment. I want to give you the correct impression. Our company is different; not equal to the other plans out there. And if you don't understand why, you won't go with us."

> "Our health plan is focused on keeping you out of the hospital. It includes many, many services you don't get with the competitors—at all. We include free annual physicals, free blood testing, free chiropractic care, and (many other differentiators)."

> "Yes, our initial out-of-pocket hospital costs are more expensive. But with us, you're far less likely to go to the hospital, and you'll be much healthier. So don't get caught up in the numbers thrown around by the competition. Their plans are not equal to ours. Ours protects your health much, much more. Now, would you like to understand more about our benefits?"

The ability to confidently and factually address objections early in the sales call prevents customers from causing trouble. In fact, by raising the objection yourself, you build trust with the prospect and add credibility to your presentation.

In my own business, I charge more than many consultants. As a result, people have concerns about whether they can afford me. So I always tell prospects up front, "I'm not cheap. In fact, I'm far from it. But I'm darn good at what I do. More importantly, my depth of knowledge and expertise in the sales field will yield a very high return on your investment. We'll figure out how to make it work with your budget." This is a true statement, spoken with confidence and self-assurance. People believe it, thus eliminating the objection.

Now, what about you? What objections are you running into each and every day? Most likely, the same ones keep popping up over and over again. So put on your thinking cap and figure out how you can raise and resolve those issues early on in your presentation. Then start experimenting with your next sales call. My final words of wisdom: stop worrying about "objection handling" techniques, and get rid of your objections by bringing them up before your prospects do. You'll close more sales, and your customers will feel better about their decisions to buy from you. ■

Jill Konrath is Chief Sales Officer of Selling to Big Companies. For biographical and business information, see page 270.

Editor's Note: Art Sobczak held telesales and management positions with AT&T Long Lines and American Express before he launched his own telesales training business. He writes and publishes a popular newsletter, Telephone Prospecting and Selling Report, *since 1984. Considered the grand master of telesales training, Art is back to share with us more secrets of selling success.*

Are You Suffering From Premature Assumption?
by Art Sobczak

Do you continually find yourself unable to close a sale, even though the prospect was interested? Is your closing ratio lower than it should be? If so, you may be suffering from "premature assumption," a common condition that plagues salespeople who assume the sale before the prospect has reached the point of making a buying decision.

I know that old-school, tactical methods of selling insist you should assume the sale as soon as the prospect shows any degree of interest. But in today's world, assuming the sale not only annoys the prospect, it comes across as "salesy," cheesy, and in most cases is flat-out wrong. Yet many salespeople continue to employ this dinosaur of a closing technique, and their closing ratios suffer because of it.

Despite its ineffectiveness, assuming the sale remains popular, so much so that you've probably had it used on you more than once. Suppose you're at a car dealership scouting out your next ride—or worse, sitting through a timeshare sales presentation. You're not even close to buying, yet the sales rep is filling out something that appears to be a contract! Of course he tries to disguise it as "just taking down some information", but you know *exactly* where things are headed. A sales rep at a high-end electronics store used the assumptive close on me. Seemingly out of the blue, he inquired, "Where will we be delivering this?" To which I replied, "I never said I even *wanted* it." In these situations, the prospect had not yet crossed the emotional buying bridge, and felt uneasy being subjected to the tactic. Needless to say, the assumptive close did not lead to a sale in either case.

The "Buying Bridge" Theory

When people buy, they pass over a bridge that takes them from indecision to the decision to purchase. Try to assume the sale before they cross that bridge (or even get close to it) and you had better bring along a life preserver, because you'll end up dead in the water underneath the bridge. In some cases, the prospect has already crossed the bridge before you show up, e.g. calling you to place an order. Or he may have one foot on the bridge, but hesitates to go any further due to uncertainty about the safety and stability of the crossing. Our job as salespeople is to recognize where people stand in relation to the bridge, help them cross it, and get the final commitment.

When making a sales call, the prospect's proximity to the bridge determines how you should handle the call. Look for the following signals, then take the appropriate course of action.

- **Close to the bridge.** In this instance, the prospect not only talks about having a need, but actually mentions doing something about it. For example, "We've been considering making a change in this area." Your task? To get the prospect thinking more about his reasons for "doing something about it." You might ask, "What are some of the reasons why you're considering changing?" Any question that stokes the fire underneath the problem/need helps move the prospect from being close to the bridge to actually stepping onto it.

- **On the bridge.** A prospect who is on the bridge will speak of what he hopes to get in the future as a result of what you're offering, for example, "I believe this is something all of our employees would benefit from." At this point, your action involves asking more questions to strengthen the prospect's beliefs, such as, "In what ways do you think the employees would benefit?" Getting the prospect to state the value impels him to make the journey across the bridge on his own, which leads to a much stronger sale.

- **Across the bridge.** The key is to listen to the prospect for indicators of mental possession. In other words, look for signs that indicate he has mentally already begun enjoying the results of what you can deliver. For example, the prospect might say, "I think we would bring all of our reps into town for the training." Your action here should reinforce the prospect's mental possession by solidifying the details. Now is the time when you can safely assume the sale, because the prospect has. You might say, "That sounds like a great idea! Do you have a specific location in mind?"

The more you can help the prospect visualize owning and using the results of what you sell, the closer he gets to the other side of the bridge. Try saying, "And when you use the new machine you'll notice...", or, "...and who do you think you would designate as the main user?" or, "Where do you think you'd put it?"

The moral of the story is that you *can* assume the sale, but *only when the prospect has.* So look before you leap: determine where the prospect stands in relation to the bridge. Guide prospects across the bridge by asking questions that get them to visualize the benefits of using your product or service. Then look for signs that indicate mental possession of the benefits you have to offer. You'll avoid the perils of premature assumption, and start closing a much higher percentage of your sales calls. ■

Art Sobczak is president of Business By Phone Inc. For biographical and business information, see page 274.

Editor's Note: Since 1994, Steve Waterhouse's sales training and consulting firm, The Waterhouse Group, has helped thousands of sales professionals. Coming from over 20 years' experience in sales, sales management and sales training, Steve reveals a key to making your proposal seal the deal.

Make Your Proposal Sell
by Steve Waterhouse

Are you tired of friendly rejections? You know, the ones where the meeting ends with smiles and handshakes, and you walk out the room thinking you've clinched another one. The next day you get the bad news—usually on the phone—that you lost the deal. As you look back on the situation, one thought keeps going through your mind: *what went wrong?*

Believe it or not, the answer might be your proposal. Most of us are pretty good at selling. We do it face to face. We do it over the phone. Some of us are even fairly talented at selling via letters. But how many of us sell in our proposals? I realize the purpose of a proposal is to summarize the agreement already reached by both parties. And I understand that it should contain no surprises. So where does the selling come in?

With the hidden buyer.

Selling the Hidden Buyer

As a professional salesperson, you're trained to map out the customer's buying process, and make sure you know every person who will be influencing this deal. So you ask all the right questions of all the right people. You double-check what one person says against what the others say. You even ask other reps to tell you who was involved in their deals. By now, you should have all the bases covered, right?

Not! The hidden buyer lurks in every large company, and many small ones. This is the person who gives the purchasing team full authority to cut the deal and write the check, but decides not to get involved with the buying decision. He is a master at delegating, except when he changes his mind, or when the team decides that that this person should give it "one last look" before they sign. At that moment, the only salesperson in the room is your proposal.

How scared are you now? If your proposal is to stand on its own, and convince the hidden buyer of the merits of doing business with you, it must contain the following sections:

- **Summary of need.** The customer must be confident that you understand his problem. He must know you are both starting from the same place, and that you understand how he got there, so that you won't dig him deeper into the same hole. This section says to the customer, "I heard you, I understood you, I believe you.

- **Statement of objectives.** The customer wants to know what you are going to do, and that it is the same thing you proposed in your meetings. He wants a checklist to measure your work against, something that begins to justify your price. This is the first concrete evidence that gives the client hope for a better future.

- **Task list or methodologies.** This is your path to the future, one that shows the client how you will connect his need with his objectives. It answers the question, "What are you planning to do?" Accordingly, it needs to be clear enough to help the client build faith in your ability to deliver.

- **Measures of success.** How will the client know when you have succeeded, and how will he measure the improvement? Specifically, what can he see, count or measure? The easier it is for the client to see the result, the easier it is to sell the deal. If you can't measure it, you can't sell it.

- **Relevant experience.** To build trust, you need to show that you have done this before, and that your company's ability to deliver is like falling off a log for you. The more specific you can be, the better. For example, "We've helped 15 pharmaceutical companies increase sales by an average of over 15% in the first year of our programs." Think of this as your marketing kit and reference letters condensed into a few sentences.

- **Timing.** Time is money, and everyone is late. That means no one is worth what they are charging. You must show you understand and can make the target dates with ease. Your client may have many times the cost of your product or service resting on this deal. If so, he may be much less concerned about your price than your timing.

- **Value statement.** Here's the tough one. How do you articulate your value to the client in the proposal? First, ask a *lot* of questions. Second, work with the client to build a success scenario early in the discussions. Lastly, use his numbers to make the case. This section should be as numeric as possible, and tied directly to the client's bottom line. For example:

  "Based on your assessment that improved information systems of this type will improve output by 10%, this system will pay back $1.9 million in the first year and $34.5 million over the next five years."

Done correctly, the value dwarfs the fee, and makes your price a non-issue. The value case is the one that hidden buyers always jump on. They ask, "Is this worth it?" and, "How are we going to pay for this?" Without a value case, you're at the mercy of the person standing in the room to make your sales presentation for you. (If you weren't scared before, you should be now.) With a strong case in the proposal, however, you have at least a prayer of winning the day.

- **The details.** Somewhere in the proposal you must detail the deliverables, price, terms, and conditions. Again, these should not be surprises, since you worked them out long before you wrote the proposal. I love clients who say, "Send me a proposal." I say, "How about if we talk it through right now, then I'll send you a summary of our agreement?" No one ever objects, and I get the benefit of hearing their reaction to my offerings.

So, why did you lose that deal? Because you forgot that proposals need to be stand-alone sale presentations, not simply pre-invoices. Think of it this way: assume the proposal which is outlined above is sitting next to yours, and the client has never talked with either company. Who do you think has the best chance of winning? Make your proposal sell, and you will build an insurance policy behind every deal you close. ■

Steve Waterhouse is CEO of the Waterhouse Group. For biographical and business information, see page 276.

Editor's Note: Roger Dawson is a top expert in the field of negotiation training. The author of the bestselling audio program "Secrets of Power Negotiating," Roger founded the Power Negotiating Institute in 1982. A full-time speaker and author who travels the world giving seminars to corporations and associations, he was inducted into the Speaker Hall of Fame in 1991.

Don't Give Away $100 When $67.50 Will Do
by Roger Dawson

Want to make more money when negotiating deals with customers? Stop giving it away! Making concessions is an integral part of the negotiating process. Sometimes you have to give a little away in order to satisfy the client and make him feel like he got the best deal. But in my experience, many salespeople give away far more money than they need to in order to close the deal. Why? Because they fail to heed one of the most fundamental negotiating principles: *how much you give away in concessions depends on how you give it away.*

Suppose you want to sell a used car. Your asking price is $15,000, but you're willing to go as low as $14,000 in order to make a deal. This gives you a negotiating range of $1,000, some or all of which you may give away during the negotiating process. Using this scenario as an example, let's look at four of the most common (and costly!) mistakes salespeople make when negotiating price.

Giving a Small Concession to Test the Waters
Giving a small concession to see what happens can tempt even the most experienced negotiators. However, this strategy invariably leads to larger concessions as the negotiations proceed. For example, suppose you initially tell your potential car buyer, "I might be able to shave another $100 off the price, but that's my limit." If the buyer rejects your offer, you might think, "This isn't going to be as easy as I thought!" So you offer a slightly larger concession of $200, but he still doesn't buy the car.

In the next round, you give away another $300: still no sale. By now you have only $400 left in your negotiating range, so in your final concession you give the buyer the whole enchilada. At this point, if he still doesn't buy, you either have to expand your negotiating range, or walk away from the deal. When you start with a small concession and build up to a larger one, you will never reach agreement, because the buyer is conditioned to expect more and greater concessions. Every time he asks for a concession, the price gets better: why should he stop?

Giving Equal-sized Concessions

This mistake involves giving two or more concessions of equal value. In this case, it would mean giving away your $1,000 negotiating range in four increments of $250. Again, this only benefits the other side. When you make concessions of the same size, the other person doesn't know how far he can push you. What he *does* know is that every time he asks, you give away $250. So what does he do? Keeps pushing, of course!

Making the Final Concession a Big One

Now let's suppose you make a $600 concession, followed by a $400 concession. Then you tell the buyer, "That's my absolute bottom line. I can't give you a penny more." The problem is that $400 is too big a concession to be your final offer. The buyer is probably thinking that since you made a $600 concession and a $400 concession, he can surely squeeze at least another $100 out of you.

So the buyer counters with, "We're getting close. Come down another $100 and we can talk." You refuse, saying you can't come down even ten more dollars because you've just given him your final offer. Rather than leading to a deal, this likely upsets the buyer, who is thinking, "You just made a $400 concession, and now you won't give me a lousy ten bucks. Why are you being so difficult?" To avoid creating hostility and potentially sinking the deal, never make your final concession a big one.

Giving It All Away Up Front

Another variation of the pattern is to give the entire $1,000 negotiating range away in one fell swoop. Why would anyone do such a thing?

Suppose someone who looked at your car yesterday calls and says, "We've located three cars we like equally, so now we're down to just price. We thought the fairest thing would be to let all three of you give us your very lowest price, so we can decide." Unless you're a skilled negotiator, chances are you'll panic and cut your price to the bone, even though you've been given no assurance that there won't be another round of bidding later on.

A different version of this tactic is the "we don't like to negotiate" ploy. Let's say you're trying to land a new account. With a look of pained sincerity on his face, the company's buyer says, "Let me tell you about the way we do business here.   Back in 1926, when he first started the company, our founder said, 'Let's treat our vendors well. Let's not negotiate prices with them. Have them quote their lowest price, then tell them whether we'll accept it or not.' And that's the way we've always done it. Just give me your lowest price and I'll give you a 'yes' or a 'no', because we don't like to negotiate here."

Guess what? The buyer is lying to you. In reality, he *loves* to negotiate. He proved it by trying one of the oldest tricks in the book—seeing if he can get you to make all your concessions before the negotiating even starts!

A Better Approach

All these tactics work against you, because they create a pattern of expectation in the buyer's mind. A better approach is to initially offer a reasonable concession that just might cinch the deal. In the used car case, a $400 initial concession would not be out of line. Then, if you have to make more concessions, make sure they decrease with each concession. For example, your next concession might be $300, then $200, then $100. By reducing the size of each concession, the buyer is convinced he has pushed you about as far as you will go.

To test the effectiveness of this approach, try it on your children the next time they come to you asking for money for a school outing. Suppose they ask for $100. You respond with, "No way! When I was your age, my weekly allowance was 50 cents. Out of that, I had to buy my own shoes, and walk ten miles to school in the snow, uphill both ways. I would take my shoes off and walk barefoot just to save money. I'll give you $50 and that's all!" "But we can't do it on $50!" your children wail.

Now you've established the negotiating range—they're asking for $100, you're offering $50. As negotiations progress, you offer $60, then $65, and finally, $67.50. By the time you reach $67.50, you don't have to tell your children they're not going to do any better. By tapering your concessions, you have subliminally communicated that they've reached the end of the line, and won't get any more.

It's always better to hold firm on price if you can. But when it becomes obvious that some concessions will be necessary in order to cement the deal, keep in mind that the way you make concessions creates a pattern of expectations in the other person's mind. Never make equal-size concessions, because the other side will keep on pushing. Don't make your last concession a big one, because it creates hostility. Remember never to concede your entire negotiating range just because the other person calls for your "last and final" proposal, or claims that he "doesn't like to negotiate." Instead, taper your concessions to communicate that the other side is getting the best possible deal. ■

Roger Dawson is president of Roger Dawson's Power Negotiating Institute. For biographical and business information, see page 266.

Editor's Note: Shamus Brown is a Professional Sales Coach and former high-tech sales professional who began his career selling for IBM. Today he coaches high-tech sales professionals for his own company, Industrial Ego. Shamus has some no-nonsense advice on what it takes to be a top performer.

Seven Essential Selling Skills
by Shamus Brown

The top performers in any profession constantly work at improving their skills, and salespeople are no different. The big question for salespeople is, with so many different skills to work on, which areas of focus will yield the greatest return on investment for time and effort expended? I have identified the seven sales skills I believe are most important for professional salespeople to develop on an ongoing basis. Get good at these, and you will make a lot of money, no matter how the economy is doing.

- **Skill #1: Qualifying fast.** Do you chase after your prospects until they tell you "yes" or "no"? Conversely, do you ever tell your prospects "no", as in "No, I am not going to sell to you"? There are many things in selling that you can't control. The one thing you *do* have control over is your time, and how you choose to spend it.

To qualify fast, you must have a set of criteria that clearly describes who you will and will not sell to. Focus on the prospects likely to buy your products, and drop the ones unlikely to buy, so you can find more good prospects. This sounds simple, but too many salespeople let sludge build up in their pipeline, constricting the total revenue that flows out. If someone doesn't meet your qualifying criteria, don't invest your sales time with him.

- **Skill #2: Motivating prospects.** Qualifying goes beyond budget, authority, and need. It involves finding prospects who want to buy from you. Finding prospects who need your products is usually not difficult. However, finding those who *want* your products can be very hard, if you wait for them to come to you.

Products sold by professional salespeople are more complex and offer more value than commodity products offered through stores, catalogs, and brokers. Prospects generally do not know they need such products until they discover that they have a problem. This process takes seconds or years, depending on the nature of the problem, and the prospect. Prospects become motivated to work with you when you help them discover that you can solve their problem better than anyone else. Determine which problems you can eliminate or solve for your prospects. Plan and ask questions, to uncover and draw attention to those problems.

- **Skill #3: Selling to people outside your comfort zone.** Most salespeople who are "people persons" already think they are good at this. Let me ask you a question. The last time you lost a sale, how was your rapport with the key person who decided against you? You can't afford to look away and ignore people with whom you do not have natural rapport. The good news is people like people like themselves. To gain rapport, all you have to do is to stretch your behavior outside your comfort zone, until you become like the other person. Match speech patterns with people, to gain rapport outside of your typical sports or weather conversation.

- **Skill #4: Reaching decision-makers through voicemail.** There are two ways to make more sales. One is to close more of the prospects you contact. The other is to get more prospects into the pipeline. When prospecting, you can see voicemail either as your friend, or your enemy. With 70% of your prospecting calls going to voicemail, it's time to make friends with it. Although you will never come close to getting every voicemail message returned, you can get a significant number of messages returned when you treat them as one-on-one commercials.

Prepare three to five separate benefit-focused voicemail messages that you can leave over a period of days or weeks for a single decision-maker, before giving up on him. Each message should focus on one unique, customer-focused benefit.

- **Skill #5: Delivering "I gotta have that" presentations.** Let's face it: a lot of business presentations are really boring. Salespeople talk about why their product is great, why their company is great, and the history of their company. Prospects do not relate to this, which is why they look so bored. Great presentations engage the prospect's imagination; the best way to achieve that is through storytelling. Stories rich in descriptive detail get the prospect to picture himself using your product, and evoke an "I gotta have that" reaction. Study one to three of your best customers, and develop detailed customer success stories that will inject emotional power into your presentations.

- **Skill #6: Gaining commitments instead of closing.** Eliminate "Closing Cheese" from your vocabulary. You know what I'm talking about: "Would you like that in gray or in black?", or, "If I can show you how this will help you, will you buy it today?" Lines like these are why salespeople inhabit the bottom of society's respect list - somewhere near lawyers. Instead, learn the power of asking for incremental commitments from the beginning of your sales cycle. First, get your prospect to show you what he most wants (hint: see skill #2 above.) Then you can negotiate incremental commitments in return for more of your time, information, or resources. Practice asking for simple commitments once someone has expressed a clear want, pain, or desire.

- **Skill #7: Having fun.** Selling is fun when you're in control, and closing deals. It can be miserable when you're under pressure to close business. Take the pressure to close off yourself, and focus instead on qualifying and motivating your prospects. Shift the responsibility back to the prospect to solve his own problems, and the pressure to make the sale will be gone. Focus on selling only to qualified prospects, and you will close more of them, and have fun doing it.

- **Bonus sales tip.** When giving a presentation, selling on the phone, or pitching one-on-one in your prospect's office, picture your prospect with the words SO WHAT? stamped on his forehead.

Imagine that to everything you say, the prospect is asking, "So what, why should I care?" Remember: prospects only care about how what you are selling can eliminate a problem they have, or help make their business or life better. The answer to this question is always what your product *does* for them (benefits), not what your product *is* (features).

Success doesn't come overnight, but it doesn't have to take a lifetime either. Work on these skills a little bit each day, and before too long you will be closing more sales, and making more money than ever. ∎

Shamus Brown is CEO of Industrial EGO Sales. For biographical and business information, see page 265.

Editor's Note: Rick Phillips has spent the past 20 years training and speaking for clients like IBM, DuPont, Monsanto, and State Farm Insurance. This renowned sales expert has taught at major universities like Tulane and Duke University. Here Rick explains how you can improve on an essential sales skill.

Listen Your Way to More Sales
by Rick Phillips

Someone once said, "A diplomat is a fellow who lets you do all the talking while he gets what he wants." Professional salespeople would do well to take heed. Good listening skills are critical to the success of a professional salesperson. In fact, a good listener will listen his way into more sales than a good talker will ever talk his way into. To some, listening for more sales may seem odd, because those who've been in sales for any length of time primarily have been taught techniques for talking people into sales. Moreover, most salespeople were taught to control the sales call, to dominate and take charge of the interview from start to finish.

However, when you're talking, you're not learning anything about the prospect. Constant talking does little to build rapport with and gain trust from the prospect. Most importantly, when you fail to gather enough information about the prospect's real needs (because you're talking nonstop), rarely can you recommend the right solution. Ask the right questions, however, and you can easily direct the flow of the sales conversation.

Most salespeople readily admit they are better talkers than listeners. The problem is, we seldom recognize how that impacts the prospect; nor do we realize how poor our listening skills really are. To evaluate your listening habits, take this little test.

- Do you ever catch yourself looking at your watch while listening?
- Do you ever finish other people's sentences?
- Do you ever find yourself patiently waiting for your turn to talk?
- Is it hard for you to maintain eye contact with people who are talking to you?
- Do you really give the other person a chance to talk?

- Do you ever interrupt while someone is trying to make a point?
- Do you ever think to yourself, "I've heard all this before?"
- Do you sometimes anticipate what the other person is going to say?
- Do you find yourself occasionally distracted while the other person is speaking?
- Do you ever find yourself wondering what the other person has just said?
- Do you ever mentally begin structuring your remarks while the other person is talking?
- Could you encourage the other person to continue their remarks more often?

If you answered "yes" to more than half of the above questions, you're about normal. Not right, but normal. Most salespeople are guilty of poor listening habits. However, most of us are not excellent sales professionals either. Listening is often the one trait that separates the best from all the rest.

The Importance of Listening

Why is listening so important? Because the customer holds all the information you need to know in order to sell to him, or address his needs. Remember: you can't learn anything about the customer while you're talking. If you want to discover how to sell the prospect, you must be open to his comments. Listening also helps you gain rapport, because listening to someone is the ultimate compliment. Listening says, "I believe you, and your comments are important." Everyone likes to feel important. As my old friend Cavett Robert is fond of saying, "If you don't think your customer is important, try doing business without him."

To improve your listening habits, practice the following skills:

- **Develop questions that stimulate listening.** Develop a list of open-ended questions that will get your prospect talking and you listening. Open-ended questions stimulate conversation by requiring more than a one- or two-word response like "yes" or "no." In general, open-ended questions start with words or phrases like, "What," "Tell me about," "How," and "Why." Questions like, "What do you like about your present vendor?" or "Why is that important to you?" will prompt your prospect to give you valuable information. And having a list of questions, even if you never get through a third of the list, will give you a sense of direction and confidence for each sales call.

- **Encourage the other person to talk.** Many salespeople think that when the customer is not talking, they should be. However, often the prospect pauses to think of a particular point, only to have his thought interrupted by a salesperson.

I once met a truly remarkable gentleman, Dr. Kenneth MacFarland, who had a real knack for making the other person feel important. First, he was sincerely interested in finding out about you. Second, he asked open-ended questions, and listened with empathy. When you responded, Dr. MacFarland encouraged you to speak more, and elaborate on your answers. We can all learn from Dr. MacFarland's listening skills, and look for ways to encourage our prospects to talk. Try phrases like, "Go on," "Tell me more," "I see," and "Then what happens?" These conversation-extenders show the prospect that you are listening, and give him the opportunity to talk about his needs in more depth. The more the prospect speaks about his needs, the more you will understand those needs, and their value to the prospect and his organization. Like Dr. MacFarland, you will build an incredible rapport with people, because people like people who listen to them.

- **Give them feedback.** Be an active listener. Concentrate on listening with your mind and body as well as your ears. Make eye contact, and show with your facial expressions and physical manner that you are listening. When you do this, your body language reassures prospects that you are truly interested in their needs and concerns. Prospects may easily interpret passive listening as indifference. The more feedback they hear, the more information they will share, better equipping you to find solutions to their problems.

Giving feedback includes letting the prospect know that you understand his comments. You can do this by asking confirming questions such as, "To ensure that I understand your concerns, let me review... ." This reassures the prospect that you have listened well. Also, if you have missed the intent or meaning of a comment, the prospect will correct you immediately, which saves time and prevents lost sales.

So the next time you catch yourself talking away at a prospect or customer, stop and shift into listening mode. To paraphrase Yogi Berra, "You can learn a lot just by listening." ∎

Rick Phillips is founder of Phillips Sales and Staff Development. For biographical and business information, see page 272.

Tim ConnorEditor's Note: At the tender age of 24, Garrison Wynn started his career in sales and marketing in a branch office of a Fortune 500 company. Three years later, he was a department head at corporate headquarters. He researched and designed processes for 38 company locations nationwide, and developed and marketed products still being sold in 30 countries. A rising star in the corporate world, Garrison says he got tired of making others rich, and struck out on his own. Today he combines business savvy with his experience as an actor and standup comic to train sales professionals.

What to Do When You Don't Get the Sale
by Garrison Wynn

"After careful consideration, we have chosen our vendor—and it's not you." These are hard words to hear. That big deal, the account you've been courting for months, has fallen to someone else. To make matters worse, these words are often followed by, "We appreciate all the time and effort you put into your bid. It was quite professional." Yeah, *right!* They may appreciate your months of grueling work, but not enough to actually write you a check. You feel like you've just been elected mayor of Loserville.

So what do you do now? At this crucial point, many salespeople make one of two mistakes. They either forget about this big potential customer (and all the time invested) forever or they make a desperate move that further cements their fate as "The Company That Couldn't." For example, "Hey, wait a second, Mr. Prospect. Are you really mentally prepared to give me a final no? Hello? Hello?"

One thing that separates a good salesperson from a great salesperson is the ability to become a backup vendor. Positioning yourself as the secondary supplier for the account sets you up to continue building a relationship with the client, and to someday win that business. Most companies want to have depth in their supply chain, and everybody likes to have options. Few clients will deny your last request. When you ask for the opportunity to become the backup vendor, the reply may be less than enthusiastic. In fact, it often sounds something like, "Sure, whatever." But

even if the customer doesn't sound sincere, he has still given you an invitation to keep the relationship alive. Now you can go to work showing
him what a great vendor you can be.

- **Be a good loser.** Never criticize the company that won the business. If you talk badly about the winning competitor, you are crit-
  icizing the customer's recent decision. Calling your potential
  customer stupid is never an effective sales tactic.

- **Find out exactly why you lost the deal.** People typically do not have
  much trouble telling you where you went wrong. If they balk, explain
  that to be an effective backup vendor, you need to know more about
  their specific needs. Before long you will find out what you did wrong,
  and what you need to do right to eventually secure the business.

- **Look in the mirror.** Look for the role you played in the failed deal.
  Every bit of detail you discover will help win the account one day.

- **Continue to build the relationship.** Do all the things you would
  do if you were the primary vendor. Put regular ticklers for the
  client in your contact system, and touch base with him. Develop
  an email relationship, and let him know occasionally—not every
  two days—how you are helping your other happy customers.
  Stock the products he uses, and send updated product information. Offer solutions to any problems he may tell you about. Refer
  him to other companies which provide products or services you do
  not provide. Most of all, keep reminding him that you will be
  ready when he needs backup. These types of activities will ensure
  that you stay on his vendor list, and will build your reputation as
  a problem-solver.

- **Ask for referrals.** You will be amazed at how easy it is to get leads
  from a company that just told you it has chosen another vendor. Sell
  to those other leads and get testimonial letters from them, then send
  copies and a thank you note to the company for giving the referral.

- **Be nice to everyone in the company.** Someone who is not making
  the final decision now might be in the future. As a matter of fact, I
  have seen situations where the low person on the ladder became a

decision-maker. I was able to get the business because I treated him with respect when he was Mr. Nobody. In another case, I discovered that the purchasing agent had been replaced, and that the new one could not stand the current vendor. I have also built strong relationships with want-to-be decision-makers who moved to other companies to become real buyers. Guess who got their business?

- **Invite the client to company events and parties.** A company I worked for had a Skybox at the Astrodome. On one occasion, I hosted some folks from a company that had never bought anything from us. They hung out, and watched the game with all our happy customers. At the end of the day, the CEO walked up to me with a plate of barbecue in his hand and said, "How come we're not buying from you?" I said, "I have no idea!" I signed them the next day.

- **Practice poised, consistent persistence.** All the while, continue to document what did not work the first time with this client, and make sure to cover all your bases for the future. If your product and service are superior to the competition, hang in there. Your potential customer will be replacing parts, or suffering inferior service, while you start to emerge as the low-risk provider.

- **Never give up!** A company once told me I would "never, ever" get its business; never turned out to be exactly 18 months.

Treat lost customers well enough, and they will start to imagine how well you would treat them if you really had their business. The company that keeps up the communication longest will eventually get the business. Treat them just like a customer—and sooner or later, they will be. ■

Garrison Wynn is president and founder of Wynn Solutions. For biographical and business information, see page 277.

Editor's Note: Tim Connor has been teaching sales skills since before many of you were born. He still exudes intense passion for, and commitment to, his work. This isn't mere chest-thumping. When you talk to Tim, you can't help being impressed with his deep-rooted belief in what he does. Tim believes that people buy from people they trust, not people they like. Tim's clients may not all like him (he tells them some hard truths), but they trust him enough to bring him back: each year, 85% of his programs are return engagements. Learn from this selling master.

Selling is *Not* a Numbers Game
by Tim Connor

It's interesting how one little word can make a *big* difference. For years, sales managers and trainers have been saying that selling is a numbers game. In fact, I can still recall my first sales manager telling me over 35 years ago, "If you see enough people, you will make enough sales." I realize now that he left out one very important word. He should have said, "If you see enough *qualified* people, you will make enough sales."

Over the years, I've learned that it's not just the numbers, folks; it's about focusing on prospects who qualify for your product or service. I'm not suggesting that you see fewer prospects. What I am suggesting is that sooner or later, focusing on numbers alone guarantees failure. Why? Because the more people you see, the more poor prospects you see, creating more rejection. The average salesperson cannot handle the amount of rejection that results from using this approach, which is why so many salespeople become discouraged, and fail—or quit.

Think about it. Suppose you see or call 25 prospects a week. You close one out of five, which means you wasted most of your time on 20 poor prospects. If you took the time spent with those 20 poor prospects and invested it in more qualified prospects, or in cultivating the five sales you made into repeat or referral business, imagine what this would do for your career. By focusing on the right prospects, you could potentially improve your closing ratio to one-third, or even one-half! Sadly, many managers and trainers still push the notion that you can't identify poor prospects until you see or spend time with them. I don't know why they still teach this nonsense; my guess it is that they don't know how to teach more effective prospecting, so they ask you to make up for it with more sales calls.

Here's a real recipe for success: do both! See or call more prospects *and* make sure they are qualified before giving them too much of your time and energy. This philosophy won't win me any popularity contests with some of my fellow sales trainers, nor with a few of my clients. But it works for me, and I'm suggesting it can work for you as well.

There are plenty of sales myths out there that simply don't cut it anymore. Actually, they never did—but who was going to question them? A new sales rep? A failing sales rep? I think not! Either way, here are a few myths to ponder:

> Myth: People buy from people they like.
> Truth: People buy from people they *trust*.
>
> Myth: People buy because of your enthusiasm.
> Truth: People buy because of *their* enthusiasm.
>
> Myth: People buy what they need.
> Truth: People buy what they *want*.

As you can see, a lot of misinformation is still being perpetuated by sales trainers and managers: outdated ideas that no longer make sense in the real world of selling. But few are more damaging than the notion that you should see as many people as possible in order to make your sales numbers. Instead, focus your time and energy on getting in front of qualified prospects. Then, and only then, will your closing ratio climb to where it needs to be. ■

Tim Connor is CEO of SalesClubsofAmerica.com. For biographical and business information, see page 266.

Editor's Note: Despite increasing challenges getting past voicemail to reach decision-makers, Art Sobczak believes the biggest challenge facing salespeople today is internal: their unwillingness to put in the work. While others tout systems to avoid cold calling, Art notes that the wealthiest salespeople are the best at calling people they don't know. So why is all that cold-call avoidance advice so popular? Because it preys on your greatest fear, instead of telling you how to move past it, as Art does here.

Fear of Phoning
by Art Sobczak

Ever have one of those days when your phone weighs 2,000 pounds? You know what I'm talking about. You've got your list, you've set aside some quality time for cold calling, and you *know* you need to get your pipeline flowing again. But for some reason, you just can't bring yourself to pick up the phone and make those calls. Maybe you're in a bit of a slump, and you feel like nothing is working. Maybe the last few prospects were rude to you on the phone. Or perhaps the fear of rejection has reared its ugly head, and drained you of all motivation. Whatever the reason, you find all kinds of excuses for doing anything except the one thing you need to be doing: making the cold calls that are essential to an ongoing flow of business.

Don't feel badly. At some point in their careers, even the best sales reps experience "phone phobia," the sudden and inexplicable inability to pick up the phone and engage in cold calling. It's nothing to be worried about; it only becomes a problem if it starts to happen on a regular basis. The real issue, then, is not so much that we occasionally fear picking up the phone. It's what we do to rectify the situation when it occurs. Here are some good strategies I've learned for overcoming occasional "fear of the phone", and jumping back into the fray with energy and enthusiasm.

- **Do things differently.** Food doesn't taste good when it's stale. Walking down the same grassy path over and over will kill the grass and create a rut. The same holds true for sales. Approach each and every sale in the same manner, and after a while things begin to go stale, to die. To recharge your batteries, make a list of all the ways you do your job, then write down how you could improve your work. It's amazing how changing your perspective freshens things up, and helps you dig out of a rut.

- **Trade tapes of your sales calls with other reps and managers.** The best sales reps are never satisfied with their level of expertise; they're always working to improve themselves. One way they improve is by taping themselves in action. Listening to your own tapes is a great way to improve your phone skills. To get the most leverage out of this technique, open yourself to being evaluated by others. A lot of salespeople will dismiss this idea. But they're the ones who aren't even close to reaching their full earning potential.

- **Refuse to be rejected.** Eleanor Roosevelt said, "No one can make you feel inferior without your consent." Likewise, no one can reject you without your consent. When you approach every call with the minimal objective of learning something from the call, you will accomplish at least one important goal, regardless of the outcome. Keep in mind that if you did not have a "yes" going into the call, you will not lose anything if you get a "no."

- **Don't make it hard on yourself.** It never ceases to amaze me how many salespeople create prospect resistance every time they pick up the phone. If you continue to mutter the same guaranteed resistance-inducing openings and go-nowhere questions, you'll keep getting the same results, and will find it harder and harder to pick up the phone to make the next call. Stop saying the wrong things, and repeating unproductive behaviors. Even lab rats quit pressing the buzzer when they get zapped repeatedly.

- **Think larger.** The biggest obstacles to sales success are the limitations we put on ourselves. In reality, there is very little you are not capable of, as long as you really try. Set a larger target for yourself and say, "Why not?" You'll realize what you've been missing, and be more motivated to pursue your goal.

- **Feed your mind.** When reps feel depressed, they can be especially reluctant to place sales calls. What causes the depression? The same old negative thoughts running through your mind, like a tape loop. Breaking out is not that hard to do. You need to put yourself in a more positive mood. Buy some self-improvement books, take them home, and get to work on your attitude. After reading a few pages, start creating an action plan. When you focus on positive action, it's impossible to stay preoccupied with negative thoughts.

- **Hang with achievers.** You've probably heard the quote, "It's tough to soar with eagles when you hang around with turkeys." Think of some of the most successful people you know, whom you really admire, and model your behavior after them. High achievers do not blame others or circumstances for things that go wrong. Instead, they exude a positive attitude, which is highly infectious. Go catch it!

- **Do your very best!** To paraphrase Brian Tracy, "If you're going to do something anyway, why not commit to doing it the best way you possibly can?" I was astounded by the stories of people spending 14 hours or more staking out McDonald's the day Teeny Beanie Babies became available. Some of these people worked in teams using cell phones, and created sophisticated trading networks to collect complete sets. Think about what you could accomplish if you applied a fraction of that same passion and energy to your career!

If your phone suddenly weighs 2,000 pounds, and you can't pick it up no matter how hard you try, don't despair. Grab hold of these proven techniques—and in no time at all you'll be calling on clients again, with a smile on your face and a renewed zest for selling. ■

Art Sobczak is president of Business By Phone Inc. For biographical and business information, see page 274.

Editor's Note: Telesales expert Jim Domanski has heard his share of brush-offs as a rep and trainer. Here he shares some powerful techniques for dealing with a familiar one.

"Let Me Think About It"
by Jim Domanski

What would selling be like without a daily dose of "Let me think about it?" Probably a lot easier and much less frustrating. It's unlikely this objection will disappear any time soon, so let's look at some ways to tackle it.

Is It Real?

When prospects say, "Let me think about it," are they telling the truth? Let's face it, some prospects toss out this gem simply to get rid of you. They say it, not because they mean it, but because it's a polite way of getting you off the line. If you're not savvy to this brush-off, you could waste a lot of time and energy following up with futile e-mails and phone calls.

On the other hand, some prospects really do need time to think about it. Some need time to ponder their options while others like to digest the information to ensure that they're not making a snap decision. If you are a cynical sales rep who has heard this objection time and time again, you may not take the prospect seriously and thereby fail to follow up, losing the opportunity.

How do you tackle this nasty objection? Here are three approaches.

Say Nothing

I love this technique, particularly for dealing with a prospect over the phone. Here's how it works: when the prospect tells you he wants to think about it, say nothing. That's all there is to it. Just wait patiently.

Silence over the telephone creates a vacuum. Most people become uncomfortable with the silence. After two, three or four seconds, most people feel compelled to fill the void with words. You will be amazed how well this technique works. The trick is to discipline yourself to hold your tongue for a few seconds.

Typically, the client will elaborate on the "let me think about it" objection which often uncovers the situation. For example, he may explain that he has to speak to his boss or partner. Suddenly you discover another player in the game. He may reveal that he is looking at other proposals; now you know you are in a competitive situation. Or, he may not be interested. In any event, you now have more information upon which to base your next move.

Grant the Time But Get a Commitment

Another approach is to give the prospect the time needed. Be sure to place a time limit on her pondering. The exchange looks something like this:

Prospect: "Well, let me think about it."

Rep: "I understand completely, Ms. Thomas. A decision like this needs some time. And what I would like to recommend is that I give you a call next week to get your thoughts and to determine the next steps. How does Wednesday at 8:45 look on your calendar?"

If the prospect accepts the recommendation, the objection is probably legitimate. The client needs time for whatever reason. You know this because she has agreed to a specific time and date. It shows commitment. Again, the key is to not only get a follow-up date, but also a specific time.

This approach is non-threatening and ideal for prospects who legitimately want more time. They will appreciate your courtesy and understanding. That's why you deliberately empathize by saying you "understand." These prospects don't like being cajoled or pressured. If you push too hard, they will say no to your offer because they don't like you and your "aggressive" approach. Your offer could be extremely valuable and well priced but these prospects value trust and relationships more.

If the prospect balks at your first suggestion, try another date and time. If she balks again, ask when would be a good time and date. If she cannot make a commitment, chances are she is brushing you off and your time is better spent elsewhere.

Probe for Legitimacy

I borrowed this approach from sales trainer Brian Jeffrey. His approach is to first empathize with the prospect and then question to determine if the objection is legitimate or a smokescreen.

Prospect: "Hmmmm. Let me think about it."

Rep: "I understand completely. If I were in your shoes I'd want to think about it as well. (Now ask one of the following questions):
"May I ask what concerns you still have?
"May I ask what's causing you to hesitate?"
"May I ask what questions I've left unanswered?"
"May I ask what your final decision will be based on?"

Needless to say, this type of probing gets the prospect to open up and helps you determine if the objection is real or not.

The next time a prospect says he would like to think about it, think about one of these three approaches. Give it a try and tell me what you think. ∎

Jim Domanski is president of Teleconcepts Consulting. For biographical and business information, see page 267.

Editor's Note: John Boe is an expert at reading people from their body language and facial structure to their speech patterns. He uses this knowledge to teach sales-people how to be more persuasive. Here he shows you how to establish rapport and read your prospect's buying signals.

Read Your Prospect Like a Book!
by John Boe

Top sales professionals recognize the importance of nonverbal communication in the selling process and have learned to "listen with their eyes." They understand that one of the easiest and most effective ways to close sales is to be aware of prospect's "buy signals."

Are you aware that your body language reveals your deepest feelings and hidden thoughts to total strangers? Body language is a mixture of movement, posture and tone of voice. It might surprise you to know that research indicates over 70 percent of our communication is done nonverbally. In fact, studies show that nonverbal communication has a much greater impact and reliability than the spoken word. Therefore, if your prospect's words are incongruent with his or her body language, you would be wise to rely on body language as a more accurate reflection of true feelings.

Gain the Competitive Edge
There is absolutely no substitute for a positive first impression. Research shows that we decide in the first few moments whether we like someone or not. You can create a favorable first impression and build rapport quickly by using open body language. Here's how:
- In addition to smiling and making good eye contact, show the palms of your hands, keep your arms unfolded and your legs uncrossed.
- Create harmony by matching and mirroring your prospect's body language gestures. *Matching* and *mirroring* is unconscious mimicry. It subconsciously tells prospects that you like them and agree with them.

The next time you are at a social event, observe how many people are subconsciously matching one another. Likewise, when people disagree, you'll notice they subconsciously mismatch each other's body language gestures.

You can build trust and rapport by deliberately, but subtly, matching your prospect's body language in the first ten to fifteen minutes of the appointment. For example, if you notice that your prospect has crossed his arms, subtly cross your arms to match. After you believe you have developed trust and rapport, verify it by uncrossing your arms and see if your prospect will match and mirror you as you move into a more open posture.

If you notice your prospect subconsciously matching your body language gestures, congratulations, because this indicates you have developed trust and rapport. Conversely, if you notice your prospect mismatching your body language gestures, you know trust and rapport has not been established and you need to continue matching and mirroring.

Body Language Basics

Be mindful to evaluate the flow of gesture clusters rather than isolated gestures taken out of context. Here are some important body language gestures that will help you close more sales in less time.

There are two categories of body postures: *open/closed* and *forward/back*. In an open and receptive body posture, arms are unfolded, legs uncrossed and palms are exposed. In a closed body posture, arms are folded, legs are crossed and the entire body is usually turned away.

Here's a quick body language reference guide:

Posture
- Leaning back and closed = Lack of interest
- Leaning back and open = Contemplation and cautious interest
- Leaning forward and closed = Potential aggressive behavior
- Leaning forward and open = Interest and agreement

Head gestures
- Head neutral = Neutral and open attitude
- Tilted back = Superior attitude

- Tilted down = Negative and judgmental attitude
- Tilted to one side = Interest

Facial gestures
- Eye rub = Deceit, "see no evil"
- Eye roll = Dismissive gesture that indicates superiority
- Looking over top of glasses = Scrutiny and a critical attitude
- Nose rub = Dislike of the subject
- Hand or fingers blocking mouth = Deceit, "speak no evil"
- Chin stroking = Making a decision
- Thumb under chin with index finger pointing vertically along the cheek = Negative attitude and critical judgment

As a professional salesperson you must continuously monitor your prospect's body language and adjust your presentation accordingly. By knowing your prospect's body language gestures you will minimize perceived sales pressure and know when it's appropriate to close the sale!

Action Plan

Keep this lesson handy and read it again just before your next client appointment. Before you begin matching and mirroring the body language gestures of your prospects, first practice by matching and mirroring family members, friends or associates. During your appointment, make a mental note of your client's three most frequently used gestures. Identify your three most frequently used gestures and work on eliminating any negative or intimidating gestures. Practice these techniques and you'll soon be closing more deals with ease.

John Boe is president of John Boe International. For biographical and business information, see page 264.

Editor's Note: Author of How Winners Sell, *Dave Stein is a recognized business expert featured in* Fast Company, The New York Times, Business Week, Inc., Fortune, *and* Forbes. *He explains how to outmaneuver buyers using tactics like blind RPFs and price quoting.*

How to Avoid RFPs and Price Quoting
by Dave Stein

As you are reading this, you can be reasonably sure that someone in one of your customers' organizations is reading about how to get the most out of you. Buyers, whether budget holders, economical buyers, or purchasing agents, have more power and leverage than ever before. And, they are getting better at buying every day.

You know the reasons: oversupply, commoditization, corporate buying processes. There are more fatal traps to fall into than ever before. Here are some strategies and suggestions for avoiding the three most deadly traps: telephone price quotes, blind RFPs (Requests for Proposals), and price-driven deals.

Premature Telephone Price Quotes

"Ring, ring…"

"Sales Training Company, Dave speaking. How may I help you?"

"Hi Dave. Can you quote me your best price on a customized training program for 450 sales reps, 62 telesales people, and a separate one for our European sales managers?"

Now I realize I've stretched reality a bit, specifying what would be a snap price quote for a very customized solution. But you get the idea. What are your choices? Give the quote? Refuse to provide it? Get his number so you can think about it and call him back? Once you quote a price, you're locked in. You can only go lower from there. You're trapped. So, how do you avoid this situation?

Try this strategy: Use the request to gather information about the opportunity. If he won't divulge, then you know you are considered just a commodity or you have already lost. If the deal is not winnable or worth winning, you can focus on higher quality opportunities. Here is what you might say to the caller:

> "I'd be delighted to provide you with some sense of what you might expect your investment to be, however, there is a bit of information I need first..."

Here are some suggestions for gathering the specific information you need:

- To find out his reason for buying, ask: "What is your business objective?"
- To determine the scope of the purchase (if he hasn't already mentioned it), ask about how many, how much, etc.
- To uncover time frames, drivers, and events, ask: "By when do you need this?" Then, "What happens if you don't buy by then?"
- To learn about his buying process, ask: "What are the steps you'll follow for you to make a decision?"
- To find out who the real buyer or decision-maker is, ask: "Who owns the budget for this purchase?"

After you have gathered this information, proceed like this:

> "In situations such as yours, we've been able to provide products/services such as ours in the range of $X to $Y and even higher. The actual price is determined by a number of variables, including product options, installation services, post-sales service options, and quantity."

> "If you'd like us to provide you with a more precise quote, let's schedule a time where I can meet you and the other people involved in this decision."

Remember that quoting a low to medium price and the higher end will give you the opportunity to further qualify the prospect.

The Blind Request for Proposal

"Oh, a FedEx for me? Let's see… Wow. An RFP. I wonder how long I have to respond…" What are your choices? Answer it. Don't answer it. Think about it. Let's delve a little deeper here. Consider the possibilities that the company who sent the RFP is:

- Looking for a solution, wrote their own requirements
- Looking for a solution, your competitor wrote the requirements
- Looking for a solution, consultant wrote the requirements
- Kicking tires, project/initiative not funded
- Keeping existing supplier, just looking for leverage
- Needs to have three responses, but they intend to keep their current supplier

It's not unusual for an RFP to come from an existing customer. This may be the first tangible indication that you're on the way out. Here is a real-life example: I received a call from George, an experienced sales professional who inherited the "WonderCo" account from another rep in a territory reassignment.

Shortly after making contact with the company, George got a spreadsheet-based RFP from their CIO requesting information: How did George's company propose to meet WonderCo's enterprise software requirements for three additional sites?

George immediately became suspicious. "I didn't write the RFP," he thought. "The rep I succeeded didn't write the RFP. He obviously didn't do a good job with WonderCo; otherwise, I wouldn't be in this situation."

"The 480 questions in the RFP look just like features of a product that generally does what mine does, but it is clearly not mine. One of my competitors wrote this. That competitor has an ally in WonderCo, and he's going to use my answers as justification for not choosing my product."

George is a top performer, and he had other, more promising leads to pursue and accounts to manage. His instincts told him not to waste valuable time on this bid. But he had a hunch--one that would cost him and his tech expert only a few minutes to check out. They opened the RFP spreadsheet, went directly to File>Properties>Summary, and found the originator of the requirement list. It was the product marketing department of a competitor's company.

George went straight over the CIO's head to WonderCo's CFO. The CFO said he found it difficult to believe the evaluation was rigged. Several calls and heated discussions later, George decided to withdraw from the competition--one he knew he had little or no chance of winning.

This sort of thing happens every day. When a sales rep receives an RFP that he didn't write, it's a fair bet the competition wrote it, or at least heavily influenced it.

I suggest that you calculate how many deals you won last year from blind RFPs. Then determine how much time you will spend responding to them going forward. Leverage your willingness to respond to blind RFPs as barter to gain access and information. If the access and/or information isn't forthcoming, walk. (If you have an anemic pipeline, that's an entirely different issue. It is *not* a reason to pursue deals you cannot win.)

Try saying this: "I'd be delighted to respond to your RFP, however, for my company to allocate the appropriate resources, there is a bit of information I need first..." Then cycle back to the questions posed earlier:

- Reason for buying: "What is your objective?"
- Scope of purchase: "How many, how much, etc."
- Time frame, drivers, and events: "By when must you have this?" "What happens if you don't?"
- Buying process: "What are the steps?"
- Decision-maker: "Who owns the budget?"

Now, investigate how their requirements were determined. Here's an example:

Sales Rep: "I'll need to meet with the budget holder or decision-maker."

Prospect: "No." or 'Why is that?"

Sales Rep: "We've got 3,000 customers who use our product, everyone of them differently from how they thought they would when they began looking. We've learned that a brief discussion with the person who owns the budget for this initiative will save all of us some time and prevent mistakes from being made."

The Price-Driven Deal

Should you wind up in a price-driven deal, and you're not the lowest priced competitor, give some consideration to:

- Who else is in the deal. Are they a low-cost provider whose business model supports that competitive advantage?
- How they compete. Do they slash prices at the last minute to win the deal? If they are a commodity seller, they may very well be a commodity buyer.
- The prospect's company culture and history.

Now, get upstairs. Talk to the real decision-maker. Ask, "Will this be determined by price?" Try saying this, "We are not the least expensive solution. Will you still consider us?" Then ask: "If you are convinced that we provide a measurable difference from your other options, and we can justify the additional investment, are there any other reasons you wouldn't go with us?" Finally, ask: "Will you provide us the opportunity to prove our difference?" Remember: If you ask these questions of gatekeepers or lower-level staff, you will get a yes, but that doesn't mean yes.

When to Walk Away

I would decline to pursue an opportunity when the prospect:

- Will not allow you to qualify him or gather information.
- Will not provide access to the real buyer.
- Forces communication through a third party, i.e., a consultant, unless there is evidence that the consultant is unbiased and you will meet the prospect shortly.
- Produces an RFP that is substantially the same as your competitor's spec sheet.
- Is a commodity buyer in a situation where you can't meet your competitor's historically lowest price.

In today's tough selling world, you've got to be tough. Make sure you have plenty of leads. Seek the truth about your opportunities. Handle the truth. Deluding yourself won't pay you a commission and wastes precious time. Always practice what you are going to say. Don't wing it.

Remember: if you're in a bad deal, cut your losses and pursue something you can win. ■

Dave Stein is CEO of ES Research Group. For biographical and business information, see page 274.

Editor's Note: Bob Bly is an independent copywriter and consultant who has over 25 years' experience in business-to-business, high-tech, industrial, and direct marketing. Hailed by McGraw-Hill as "America's top copywriter," Bob authored what many consider to be the bible of copywriting, The Copywriter's Handbook. *Having run a highly successful business for the past 25 years, Bob knows a thing or two about surviving in good times and in bad. His strategies will help you thrive, whether you're selling your own services or someone else's widgets.*

Recession-Proof Business Strategies
by Bob Bly

The economy has a major impact on your ability to generate sales. In good times, it seems like customers line up at the door to buy your products or services. But when times are tough, landing new accounts requires considerably more time and effort. What can you do when customers cut back on their purchasing and deals get harder to come by? The following suggestions are especially useful for business owners, consultants, service providers, and others selling a product or service that might have a variable fee structure.

- **Give a superior level of service to your clients and customers.** When business is slow, do everything you can to hold onto your existing clients, your "bread-and-butter" accounts. The best way to hold onto clients is to please them. And the best way to please clients is to give them not their money's worth, but *more* than their money's worth. Now is the time to go the extra mile and give that bit of extra service that can mean the difference between dazzling the client and merely satisfying him. The best protection against a downturn in new business is an active list of happy, satisfied customers, who give you a steady stream of continuing sales that pay the rent and feed the family.

- **Quote reasonable, affordable fees and prices in bid situations.** If times are tough for you, they might be tough for others in your industry. Clients know this, and may seek to take advantage by sending jobs out for multiple bids, when previously they might have come only to you. And if there is a recession, the cost of services or products will become more of a factor than normal; customers and prospects will be unusually price-sensitive.

The solution is to bid competitively, but reasonably. If you are high-priced to begin with, and you insist on getting top dollar, be prepared to lose out in some bidding situations. How should you price your products or services during a slow period or a down economy? Do not instantly lower your prices to rock bottom, as you may never be able to raise them again. Also, you do not necessarily have to reduce your prices, especially if your rate card or fee schedule presents a range of fees. Instead, bid toward the middle or lower end of your published fee range, rather than at the maximum. For example, if you list $5,000 to $8,000 for a particular service, quote a price of $5,000 or $6,000, not $8,000, to make sure you are not charging much more than other firms bidding on the job. During a recession you probably want to adjust your bids to be 15%- 20% lower than what you would normally charge in a healthy economy. This gives your prospects the break they are looking for, shows fairness on your part, but doesn't cost you much in the long run.

Never tell customers that the fee is a special reduced fee. Simply present it as your bid on the project. If customers sense you are cutting fees because you are losing assignments, they will take advantage, and try to force your prices even lower.

- **Use low-cost "add-ons" to generate additional revenue.** One way to generate some extra profitable business is to encourage customers to add to, or expand, existing assignments or purchases. For instance, if one of my copywriting clients is doing an ad on a new product, chances are he needs a press release also. I can upgrade the total project fee by offering to do both jobs for a package price. If my fee for the ad is $1,500, I may tell the client, "You also should send out a press release to all the publications in the field. I can write a press release while I do the ad for you; the additional cost is only $500."

Frequently the client will accept such a recommendation, and I get an assignment that is $2,000 instead of $1,500. It's easy to do the small add-on project, since it uses the same basic background information provided for the main assignment. This is an easy income-booster. Using this technique, you can increase the average dollar value of each project 10%-40% or more with virtually no extra sales effort.

- **Avoid being a prima donna.** Face it: being busy, in demand, and having more work than you can handle is a great feeling. The tendency is to get a swelled head. My advice is: *don't!* When things are slow, it will come back to haunt you. Always, always act like a pro, like a helpful friend and consultant to your customers. Be useful, courteous, and accessible. If you give customers genuine reasons to like you and are always helpful to them, they will stick with you, and that can make a big difference when things get slow. Remember: in a depressed economy, continuous business from ongoing, current clients or customers is what keeps you afloat. Make sure you have that business when you need it tomorrow by acting professionally today.

- **Postpone any planned fee increases.** A soft economy is not the appropriate time to increase your fees or prices, even if you feel you deserve it and a raise is long overdue. Instead, defer any planned fee increase announcements until later, and keep your fees at current levels. Do not announce to your customers and prospects that you are "holding the line" on prices due to the recession and your desire to help them through it. Remember, even though you are feeling the effects of a soft economy, they may not be going through similar difficulties. Thus your announcement would clue them into the fact that you are in trouble, and some may take advantage of your perceived need for business by haggling with you on price.

- **Downgrade slightly your acceptable client or customer profile.** You have a set of written or mental guidelines that determine which clients are desirable to you, and which are not. During a business downturn, you may want to be more flexible in this area than usual. For instance, if you normally do business with Fortune 500 companies only, you may want to consider taking on assignments from smaller local firms, provided the pay is decent and their credit rating is good. Or, if you normally work only on large projects, you might consider knocking out some smaller ones to generate needed revenue.

This does not mean throwing your standards out the window and working for anyone who calls; far from it. Instead, simply readjust your acceptable client criteria during this temporary lull to accommodate a wider range of prospects and projects. How far should you take this? It's up to you. If, for example, you normally have a minimum project fee of $1,000, you might accept $500 assignments. But probably you should stick to your guns and not take on $100 assignments.

- **Plan an aggressive new-business marketing campaign.** When things are slow, increase the percentage of your time spent on marketing and prospecting for new business. For instance, if you normally devote 10% of your time and energy to marketing and sales, you might increase this to 25% during slow periods. Take advantage of a lull in business to make an extra effort to attract clients or customers, follow up on leads, and close sales. To prevent a lull from happening in the first place, market consistently and aggressively all year long, every week, not just when you need the business. Planning an ongoing marketing campaign ensures a steady stream of new business leads. Marketing done today begins a selling cycle that will result in new business when you need it six months from now.

- **Repackage your services to accommodate smaller clients and reduced budgets.** When you are busy, there is a whole group of prospects you probably turn away without a second thought. These companies are too small (read: too under-budgeted) to afford your product or service. But when things are slow, it pays to look for ways to generate revenue from this normally-overlooked market segment. This is best done by repackaging your service or product line to accommodate smaller clients and reduced budgets. For instance, the client who cannot afford to pay you $5,000 to write his direct mail package can afford to pay you $400 to critique a package he writes himself. He can also afford to pay you $100 an hour for your consultation services, take your full-day direct mail seminar for $200, or buy your book for $25.

Freelancers, consultants, and other service providers can repackage their expertise and services in a variety of formats, including hourly consultations, critiques, telephone consultations, newsletters, special reports, booklets, audio tapes, instruction manuals, books, seminars, and more. Manufacturers and other product sellers can offer compact models, economy sizes, no-frills versions, special discounts, payment plans and smaller minimum orders. These alternatives may not provide as complete a solution as the deluxe package, but they give the smaller client the help he needs at the price he can afford.

- **Add value to your existing service.** In a recession, customers in all areas are more concerned with price than ever before. However, their real concern is making sure they get the best value for their dollar. You can win new accounts and retain existing clients by enhancing your service and providing your clients with more value for their dollar. For instance, if you are selling a commodity item, you can add value by offering faster delivery than your competitors, or a larger selection, more colors, more options, easier payment terms, or a better guarantee. There is no need to give away the store by promising an excessive amount of extra service. However, a little extra effort or service on your part will be perceived by the client or customer as a significant increase in value.

- **Keep busy with ancillary assignments or accounts.** A slow period in your business is a good time to busy yourself with other projects, such as cleaning out your files, developing a new marketing strategy, making technical improvements to an existing product or service, auditing your customer support procedures, revising your standard proposal or sales letter, redesigning your slide presentation, or any of the hundred things that need doing, but never get done. Now you have the time, so do them! Do not waste the extra time moping. Instead, put it to good use by being productive.

- **Stay positive.** The most important thing about a slow period is not to be depressed by it. When you are depressed, prospects sense your desperation and fear, which has a negative effect on your dealings with them. Remember that everybody in business has slow times; those who say they never do are liars. You are talented and successful, and the lull is temporary. People will call you and hire you again. Above all, do not despair, and do not give up too soon. If you follow the strategies outlined here, you can turn things around, and become busy and profitable once again. ∎

Bob Bly is a freelance copywriter. For biographical and business information, see page 264.

If You're Not Selling . . .
by Michael Dalton Johnson

Are you working hard, but not getting the results you want? If you're a professional salesperson and you're not selling, it could be because:

- **You are boring.** Do customers cut you off in mid-sentence, or jump in when you pause for breath? Chances are, you're boring them. Paint a vivid picture and put them in it; use an example or interesting case history to illustrate your point. Whip out some visuals to show them how much they will save.

- **You insult their intelligence.** "Mr. Jones, would you like to save money on your long distance phone bill?" Polling prospects with lame questions in an attempt to get them to say yes is manipulative and insulting. Instead, ask open-ended questions to elicit their needs. Treat them with respect by tailoring your questions to their company, industry and circumstances.

- **You are uninformed.** Take time to visit the website of your prospect's company. Check out their competition, industry association and trade journals. Remember: the more you learn, the more you earn. If you do not understand what your prospects do, and what issues they face, how can you expect to determine how your product or service can best help them?

- **You are talking to the wrong person.** Oops! Once again, you have not done your homework, and end up pitching someone who has no decision-making authority. This hurts, because it's usually hard to get a second bite of the apple.

- **You do not listen.** Pay attention to what your customers are saying and how they are saying it, including their non-verbal communication. Effective listening will provide you with most of the answers to your qualifying questions without even asking them. You will learn about your customers' needs, what their hot buttons are, and how to convince them. Simply put: when your customer talks, you sell; when you talk, you lose.

- **You talk about features, not benefits.** You are crazy about all those neat bells and whistles your product offers, but you do not let the buyer know how they will directly benefit him.
- **You do not understand their needs.** In the world of sales, one size rarely fits all. Find out your prospect's special needs and concerns, and show how your product or service can help. Again: listen and he will tell you.
- **Buyers do not like you.** You have heard it a million times: people buy from people they like. If your prospect doesn't like you, he's not going to spend time getting to know your product or service. Investing some time in your rapport-building skills will pay big dividends.
- **They do not know you, and have never heard of your company.** All things being equal, who do you think your prospect is going to buy from: the company he has known for years, or you, the new kid on the block? Allay his fears by providing him with current customer lists (including contact names and numbers for some of your accounts), testimonial letters on your customers' letterhead, documented case histories, and press coverage. A referral from someone he knows and respects will swing doors wide open.
- **Make your buyers heroes.** Even in a business-to-business sale, you need to show your prospects what's in it for them *personally*. How do they personally gain? Will they look good to their boss? Will they save time and effort? Will they make their customers or employees happy? There's an important difference between, "Your company will save over $50,000 a year with our product" and "*You* will save *your* company over $50,000 a year with our product." People want to be heroes. Make it so.

It's the little things that make a difference in the sale. Pay attention to these ten factors, and make more sales. ∎

Michael Dalton Johnson is founder and president of SalesDog.com. For biographical and business information, see page 269.

Tony Alessandra

Tony Alessandra, PhD helps companies outmarket, outsell and outservice the competition. He is a keynote speaker and former graduate professor of marketing, earning his PhD in Marketing in 1976. He is president of AssessmentBusinessCenter.com, Chairman of BrainX.com and author of 14 books in 17 languages. Recognized by *Meetings & Conventions Magazine* as "one of America's most electrifying speakers," Tony Alessandra was inducted into the Speaker Hall of Fame in 1985. Call 702-567-9965 or visit www.alessandra.com/products/index.asp.

Bob Bly

Bob Bly is a freelance copywriter and the author of more than 60 books including *Secrets of Successful Telephone Selling, Selling Your Services, Magnetic Selling,* and *The Copywriter's Handbook.* He can be reached by email at rwbly@bly.com or on the Web at www.bly.com.

John Boe

John Boe presents a wide variety of motivational and sales-oriented keynotes, breakout sessions and seminar programs for sales meetings and conventions. An entertaining speaker who can keep an audience riveted and motivated, John is a nationally recognized author, sales trainer and business motivational speaker with an impeccable track record in the meeting industry. For more information, visit www.johnboe.com.

Dianna Booher

Author of 42 books (Simon & Schuster, Warner, and McGraw-Hill), Dianna Booher, CSP, CPAE, delivers keynotes and training on communication (sales presentations, proposal development, sales writing, technical writing, interpersonal skills, listening skills, customer service, and effective meetings) and life-balance issues. Her latest books: *Speak with Confidence, E-Writing, Communicate with Confidence, From Contact to Contract, Great Personal Letters for Busy People, Your Signature Work.* For more information, visit www.booher.com or contact Booher Consultants at 800-342-6621.

Ed Brodow

Ed Brodow (www.brodow.com) has been called the "King of Negotiators." Bestselling author of *Negotiation Boot Camp* and *Beating the Success Trap*, he has appeared as negotiation guru on PBS, Fox News, and Inside Edition. His ideas have been showcased in the *Washington Post, Wall Street Journal, Entrepreneur, Smart Money,* and *Selling Power.* As a speaker, his impressive client list includes Microsoft, Goldman Sachs, The Hartford, Philip Morris, Starbucks, Hyatt Hotels, Revlon, Learjet, and the Pentagon.

Bill Brooks

Bill Brooks, CSP, CPAE, CMC, CPCM former CEO of a $300,000,000 corporation and two-time sales award winner from an international force of 8,000, has real-world expertise. He has spoken or consulted in over 300 industries; been engaged by over 150 clients an astonishing six times each; and authored 17 books, including bestsellers: *High Impact Selling, The New Science of Selling and Persuasion,* and *How to Sell at Margins Higher Than Your Competitors.* www.brooksgroup.com. Email: sales@thebrooksgroup.com.

Jon Brooks

Brooks Dreyfus Consulting is a specialized sales consulting firm working with companies to improve the results of their telesales efforts. Whether creating an in-house telesales team or improving an existing unit, Brooks Dreyfus Consulting can help. Their results oriented approach assists clients across a broad range of telesales needs. From strategic vision to tactical execution, they focus on applying proven techniques to achieve their clients' goals. Email jbrooks@brooksdreyfus.com or visit: www.brooksdreyfus.com.

Shamus Brown

Shamus Brown is a Professional Sales Coach and former high-tech sales pro who began his career selling for IBM. Shamus has written more than 100 articles on selling and is the creator of the popular *Persuasive Selling Skills* audio program. Get free audio sales training MP3s from Shamus Brown and read more of Shamus's sales tips at www.IndustrialEGO.com.

Bill Caskey

With over 19 years as a leader and coach for hundreds of business-to-business sales teams, Bill Caskey is a sales development leader and experimenter. His ideas about selling are convictions about life, money, and meaning. Author of *Same Game, New Rules,* he has presented over 3,000 workshops in 100 business-to-business industries and invested over 14,000 hours training these companies. Learn Bill's new rules of high-income sellers at www.theelitesellerblog.com or email bcaskey@caskey-training.com.

Tim Connor

Tim is CEO of SalesClubsofAmerica.com, Connor Resource Group and Peak Performance Institute. A world renowned speaker, trainer and best-selling author, Tim has presented over 4,000 presentations in 21 countries. A results oriented business coach and consultant, he helps clients improve their individual and organization performance. He has authored over 60 books including international bestsellers *Soft Sell, Your First Year in Sales* and *91 Mistakes Smart Salespeople Make.* Visit www.SalesClubsofAmerica.com, www.timconnor.com, email: tim@timconnor.com or call 704-895-1230.

Kevin Davis

Kevin Davis is the president of TopLine Leadership Inc., a company that provides in-depth training workshops including the *Getting Into Your Customer's Head* consultative sales seminar and *Sales Management Leadership in the 21st Century.* Kevin has over 25 years of sales, sales management and training experience. He has negotiated million dollar sales and, he says, been swiftly escorted out of many office buildings for making cold calls. Phone: 888-545-7355; Web: www.toplineleadership.com.

Roger Dawson

Roger Dawson is one of the top experts in the art of negotiating. *Success Magazine* calls him "America's premier business negotiator." Four of his nine books have been main selections of major book clubs. A full-time speaker since 1982 he has trained managers and salespeople at top companies throughout the U.S., Canada and Australia. He holds the National Speakers Association "Certified Speaking Professional" designation. He was inducted into the Speaker Hall of Fame in 1991.

Jim Domanski

President of Teleconcepts Consulting, Jim Domanski works with businesses and individuals who are frustrated with the results they are getting when using the telephone to generate leads and sell products. For more information, visit www.teleconceptsconsulting.com or call 613-591-1998 or email jdomanski@igs.net.

Colleen Francis

Sales and Marketing Magazine has ranked Colleen Francis, president of Engage Selling Solutions, one of the "5 most effective sales trainers in the market today." Ask Colleen's clients why they call on her services—again and again—and you'll hear a common refrain: she gets results! Her refreshing candor, genuine, sincere message, and personal experiences she relates as a top-ranked sales executive motivate sales professionals to get to the top ... and stay there. colleen@engageselling.com, www.engageselling.com, 877-364-2438.

Tom Freese

With over 17 years' experience in the sales and sales management trenches, Tom Freese packaged his unique approach into a proven sales methodology called Question Based Selling. As founder and president of QBS Research, Inc., Tom has published three books on selling, and is recognized as one of the foremost authorities on sales effectiveness, buyer motivation, and business development strategies. QBS Research can be reached at 770-840-7640 or by visiting www.QBSresearch.com.

Patricia Fripp

Patricia Fripp is a sales presentation skills trainer, executive speech coach, and award-winning professional speaker. *Meetings and Conventions* magazine calls Patricia "one of the country's most electrifying speakers." *Kiplinger's Personal Finance* says, "Attending Patricia Fripp's speaking school is the sixth best way to invest in your career." Author of *Get What You Want!, Make It, So You Don't Have to Fake It!,* and Past-President of the National Speakers Association. Contact: PFripp@Fripp.com, 800-634-3035, www.fripp.com.

Ari Galper

Ari Galper is the creator of Unlock The Game™, a new sales mindset that overturns traditional sales thinking. With a Masters Degree in Instructional Design and over a decade of experience creating breakthrough sales strategies for companies such as UPS and QUALCOMM, Ari is considered the world's leading authority on building trust in selling. You can take a free test drive of his program at www.UnlockTheGame.com.

Joe Guertin

One of America's hottest sales trainers, Joe Guertin specializes in new business and selling value versus price. As a sought-after speaker and consultant, Joe has worked with thousands of salespeople, managers and business principals to measurably boost internal sales systems, customer development and team skill-building. His firm also features a state-of-the-art online training system. Visit The Guertin Group at www.guertingroup.com to receive his monthly e-zine newsletter. Joe can be reached at 414-762-2450, or joe@guertingroup.com.

Joe Heller

Joe Heller is one of the most influential sales consultants in the world, leveraging his sales expertise to secure geometric sales growth for his clients. Joe's unique selling model gives his worldwide clients an "unfair competitive advantage" in their relentless pursuit of geometrically increasing revenues, market penetration, and profitability. Joe frequently speaks to CEO groups, leadership forums, marketing symposiums and leading industry associations throughout the U.S. and abroad. Contact Joe at 713-927-4494; joe@joeheller.com; or www.joeheller.com.

Craig James

Sales Solutions Founder and President Craig James has over 12 years' experience in sales and sales management, primarily in technology and software. He may be reached at 877-862-8631, by email at craig@sales-solutions.biz or on the web at www.sales-solutions.biz.

Brian Jeffrey

Brian Jeffrey, CSP (Certified Sales Professional) and president of Salesforce Assessments Ltd, is a sales management consultant, columnist, author, and former sales trainer with over 40 years' experience. His company provides hiring tools and other resources to help sales managers and others make even better hiring decisions. To learn how he can help you avoid hiring duds, visit www.SalesforceAssessments.com.

Michael Dalton Johnson

Michael is a successful entrepreneur with over 30 years of business leadership. Among his many business activities, he is publisher of SalesDog.com, a website for sales professionals. Among his accomplishments, he has taken a small publishing company from three employees and two products to a multinational corporation with hundreds of employees and over 100 products. He has founded several successful businesses and published hundreds of magazine and newspaper articles. You may email him at Michael@SalesDog.com.

Dave Kahle

Dave Kahle is a consultant and trainer who helps his clients increase sales and improve productivity. Dave has trained thousands of salespeople to be more successful in the Information Age economy. He is the author of over 500 articles, a monthly e-zine, and six books. *Ten Secrets of Time Management for Salespeople* was recently released by Career Press. Join Dave's *Thinking About Sales Ezine* online at www.davekahle.com/mailinglist.htm. Email: cheryl@davekahle.com. Visit: www.davekahle.com. Phone: 800-331-1287.

Ron Karr

Ron Karr is a professional speaker, consultant, trainer and author who specializes in helping organizations build and maintain high performing sales cultures. He is the author of *The Titan Principle®: The #1 Key to Sales Success* and co-author of *The Complete Idiot's Guide to Great Customer Service*. Visit him at www.ronkarr.com and sign up for his free *Titan Sales E-Report*.

Jill Konrath

Jill Konrath, author of *Selling to Big Companies*, is a recognized expert on selling to large corporations. She helps her clients crack into corporate accounts, speed up sales cycles, and create demand in the highly competitive business-to-business market. Her website, SellingToBigCompanies.com, is full of resources to help salespeople win more sales. Get a *Sales Call Planning Guide* ($19.95 value) when you sign up for her free e-newsletter. Contact info: 651-429-1922 or jill@sellingtobigcompanies.com.

Dan Kosch

Dan Kosch is co-president, with Mark Shonka, of IMPAX, a sales training and consulting firm that has helped thousands of sales professionals improve sales, account management, channel management and leadership efforts. Clients include IBM, DuPont, Eli Lilly, D&B and AT&T. Their expertise is compiled in bestseller *Beyond Selling Value*. They have over 45 years' experience in sales leadership, sales consulting and training, and are sought-after authorities on sales performance improvement. Visit www.impaxcorp.com or call 800-457-4727.

Tina LoSasso

Tina has over 20 years' experience in publishing, marketing and business development. As managing editor for SalesDog.com, she is responsible for their weekly e-newsletter to sales professionals, website content and affiliate relations. Tina is an expert at finding the top sales specialists, selecting the best of their advice and serving it up each week. For a free subscription to SalesDog.com's weekly enewsletter, visit www.SalesDog.com or email Tina at editor@salesdog.com.

James Maduk

James is a Black Belt Martial Artist and Black Belt Web Marketer. He is the creator of the "Hub and Spoke Marketing" System and author of the international bestselling e-book *52 Secrets My Mom Never Told Me About Internet Marketing*. James' Online Selling University www.onlinesellinguniversity.com provides online sales professionals with all the tools, techniques, tips and training they need to sell online.

Jim Meisenheimer

Jim Meisenheimer publishes the *Knockout Selling Tips Newsletter*, a fresh and high content newsletter dedicated to helping sales professionals increase their sales and personal income. To subscribe to Jim's free *Knockout Selling Tips Newsletter* and receive a copy of his special report, *The 12 Dumbest Things Salespeople Do*, visit www.meisenheimer.com. Jim can be reached at 800-266-1268 or via email at jim@meisenheimer.com.

Michelle Nichols

Michelle Nichols is a professional sales speaker, trainer, and consultant based in Reno, NV. She is the *Savvy Selling* columnist for *BusinessWeek Online*, with readers in every industry. If you need to grow your sales and profits, contact her toll-free at 877-352-9684 or 775-303-8201 direct. Visit her website at www.savvyselling.com for more sales resources and tools, like *Savvy Selling 101* CD and *Overcoming the Price Objection* CD or email her at michelle.nichols@savvyselling.com.

Rick Phillips

Rick Phillips is a sales and sales management trainer and consultant based in New Orleans. He is the founder of Phillips Sales and Staff Development (PSSD), a nationally recognized training firm he founded in 1984. Should you have any questions about his training programs, please contact him at 504-905-3465 or via email at pssd@earthlink.net. Visit his website at www.rickphillips.com.

Tom Reilly

Tom Reilly is president of Tom Reilly Training, a St. Louis-based company specializing in training salespeople and sales managers. Celebrating 25 years as a professional speaker, he delivers about 100 presentations annually and has authored 12 books, over 40 audiocassettes and CDs, and a video series. His sales articles have appeared in business publications nationwide. His motto is simple: "Add value . . . not cost! Sell value . . . not price!" Visit www.TomReillyTraining.com.

Tom Richard

Tom Richard, a Toledo-based sales trainer, gives seminars, runs sales meetings, and provides coaching for salespeople nationwide. Tom is also the author of *Smart Salespeople Don't Advertise: 10 Ways to Outsmart Your Competition With Guerilla Marketing*, and publishes a free weekly e-zine on selling skills titled *Sales Muscle*. For more information, visit www.TomRichard.com, or email info@tomrichard.com.

Linda Richardson

Linda Richardson is president and founder of Richardson (www.richardson.com), a leading sales training and consulting firm. A recognized leader in the sales training industry, she is credited with the movement to consultative selling. She has written nine books on selling including *The Sales Success Handbook*. She has been published in industry and training journals and featured in numerous publications including *Forbes, Nation's Business, Selling, Selling Power, Success, The Conference Board Magazine,* and *The Philadelphia Inquirer.*

Keith Rosen

An engaging speaker, Master Coach and bestselling author, Keith Rosen is one of the foremost, respected authorities on coaching top executives and sales professionals to achieve positive change. He is the author of *Time Management for Sales Professionals, The Complete Idiot's Guide to Cold Calling, The Complete Idiot's Guide to Closing the Sale and Coaching Salespeople into Sales Champions*. To contact Keith or receive his free resources, call 888-262-2450, email info@ProfitBuilders.com or visit www.ProfitBuilders.com.

Mike Schultz

Mike Schultz is principal of the Wellesley Hills Group, a consulting and marketing firm that helps professional services companies to grow, and Publisher of RainToday.com, the premier content site for research and tools for growing a service business. Visit www.WHillsGroup.com for selling resources, including articles on selling services, How To Sell Professional Services 2-day Seminar, and *The Benchmark Report on Professional Services Marketing and Selling*. Contact Mike at mschultz@whillsgroup.com.

Mark Shonka

Mark Shonka is co-president, with Dan Kosch, of IMPAX, a sales training and consulting firm that has helped thousands of sales professionals improve sales, account management, channel management and leadership efforts. Clients include IBM, DuPont, Eli Lilly, D&B and AT&T. Their expertise is compiled in bestseller *Beyond Selling Value*. They have over 45 years' experience in sales leadership, sales consulting and training, and are sought-after authorities on sales performance improvement. Visit www.impaxcorp.com or call 800-457-4727.

Anita Sirianni

Anita Sirianni, The Professional Sales Coach is a recognized sales strategist and trainer. The Coach speaks from experience. For over two decades, Anita dominated the sales charts achieving the top 5% for every company she represented. Today, she is one of the industry's most popular consultants and sales trainers, providing customized programs for leading corporations worldwide. Anita designs and delivers custom sales and sales management training programs. For more information call 800-471-2619 or visit www.anitasirianni.com.

Mark S.A. Smith

After 22 years of working in high-tech sales and marketing channels, Mark S.A. Smith identified that success depended on building value, driving demand, forming a powerful network, and protecting profits. He founded Outsource Channel Executives Inc. to help sales channels sell more by focusing on the business issues, not just the technical product. A recognized business expert, Mark co-authored *Guerrilla Negotiating, Guerrilla TeleSelling,* and *Guerrilla Trade Show Selling.* Visit www.OCEinc.com or email Mark at mark.smith@oceinc.com.

Art Sobczak

Art Sobczak helps sales pros use the phone to prospect, service and sell more effectively, while eliminating "rejection." He presents public seminars and customizes programs for companies. See free articles and back issues of his weekly emailed sales tips at www.BusinessByPhone.com. Also ask for a free copy of his monthly *Telephone Prospecting and Selling Report* newsletter, and the new *Telesales Success* tips and resources magazine by emailing ArtS@BusinessByPhone.com, or calling 402-895-9399.

Dave Stein

Beginning in 1993, after a career in sales and sales management, Dave focused his unique skills in competitive sales strategies training and coaching. In 2004 he authored the business bestseller *How Winners Sell.* Dave is a regular contributor to leading journals, and the featured monthly columnist for *Sales & Marketing Management* magazine. Dave is CEO of ES Research Group, which advises companies on how to get the highest return on sales effectiveness training. Website: www.esresearch.com.

Bill Stinnett

Bill Stinnett is the president of Sales Excellence, Inc. and is a highly sought after speaker appearing at sales meetings, conferences, conventions and annual sales kickoffs worldwide. He is the bestselling author of *Think Like Your Customer* (McGraw-Hill 2005), and his new *Selling Results!* (McGraw-Hill 2007). His clients include GE, IBM, Microsoft, Verizon, and American Express. Bill can be reached at 800-524-1994 or by visiting www.salesexcellence.com.

Joel Sussman

Joel Sussman is a business writer and Internet marketer with over 23 years' experience in journalism, public relations, and marketing communications. In 2000, he created an online resource for small business owners called Marketing Survival Kit.com. It features a diverse array of small business marketing articles, downloadable books, templates, software, home study courses, and free newsletters. For more information or to inquire about freelance writing services, visit www.MarketingSurvivalKit.com or email jsussma1@nycap.rr.com.

Julie Thomas

Julie Thomas is president and CEO of ValueVision Associates, a worldwide leader in competency and process-based sales training offering proven strategies for seasoned sales executives and those just starting out through its proprietary ValueSelling Framework™ and Victory!® online training. Julie has been in sales and sales management for over 19 years. A noted public speaker, author and consultant, Julie published her latest book, *ValueSelling*, in 2006. She can be reached at 800-559-6419 or julie.thomas@valueselling.com.

Will Turner

After a twenty year career in sales and sales management, Will founded Dancing Elephants Achievement Group, an international sales training and consulting company. Will and his partner, Laura Posey, created the Sales Magnetism program and co-authored *Six Secrets of Sales Magnets* which highlights how to be among the top five percent of all salespeople without reverting to typical sales practices. Visit www.DancingElephants.net to subscribe to his free monthly e-zine, Impact! or email will@dancingelephants.net.

Al Uszynski

Al Uszynski is a results-focused sales trainer and professional speaker. His proven, quick-start sales training program, "15 Ways to Grow Your Sales Tomorrow" helps sales professionals ignite immediate sales growth. If you want to grow your sales—immediately—visit www.GrowYourSalesTomorrow.com. To learn how Al's professional sales presentations can supercharge your next sales meeting, visit www.Uszynski.com.

Steve Waterhouse

Steve Waterhouse and Waterhouse Group help companies increase their sales with consulting, training and coaching. Their powerful "Total Customer Selling" process guides sales professionals through the process of dramatically increasing their sales. Mr. Waterhouse is the author of many books including *The Team Selling Solution* (McGraw-Hill), *The Ultimate Prospecting Manual* and *How to Leave a Voice Mail Message that Gets Results*. For more information, visit www.waterhousegroup.com, call 800-575-3276 or email info@waterhousegroup.com.

Wendy Weiss

Wendy Weiss, "The Queen of Cold Calling," is a sales trainer, coach and author. To order her book, *Cold Calling for Women*, or any sales-enhancing Weiss Communications product, or to subscribe to the free email newsletter, *Opening Doors & Closing Sales*, visit www.queenofcoldcalling.com. For information about *Cold Calling College*, the intensive coaching program that helps entrepreneurs and sales professionals set more new business appointments in less time visit www.queenofcoldcalling.com. Contact Wendy directly at wendy@wendyweiss.com.

Jacques Werth

Jacques Werth, president and founder of High Probability Selling, discovered his passion for selling early in life. After over four decades in sales, sales management and training he continues to conduct research into the sales processes of top salespeople in twenty-three industries. His mission is to improve the lives of salespeople by showing them how top salespeople utilize mutual trust and respect as their guiding principle. Learn more at www.highprobsell.com.

Garrison Wynn

Garrison Wynn is a nationally known speaker, trainer, and consultant. He is president and founder of Wynn Solutions, specializing in turning talent into performance. His website can be found at www.wynnsolutions.com and you can contact his office at 888-833-2902.

Presented by SalesDog.com

2701 Loker Avenue West, Suite 148
Carlsbad, California 92010
760-476-3700
www.salesdog.com

This book is available at quantity discounts.
For information, call 760-476-3700.